Transformation
An Angel Walk-In Path
Angelica Rose

Copyright © 2017, by Angelica Rose, *All Rights Reserved.*
No part of *this* work may be reproduced or transmitted in any form, or by any means, electronic or mechanical, including photocopying, recording or by any information storage and retrieval system, without the prior written permission from the author, except for the inclusion of brief quotations in a review. For information, contact Angelica Rose.

Email: angelheartofmotivation@gmail.com
Website: angelroselove.wix.com/love

Printed and bound in the United States of America
Library of Congress Control Number: 2017901586
ISBN 97809639304-9-1

Acknowledgment
I am eternally grateful to my connection to the Universal Pure Love Beings and Universal Love

Table of Contents

Chapter 1: My Angel Walk-In Experience..1
Chapter 2: Having A Human Experience..6
Chapter 3: Moving Into The Angelic Expression..26
Chapter 4: Graduating To An Arcl Angel..47
Chapter 5: Closing Out The Second Leg Of My Life..54
Chapter 6: Univestations..89
Chapter 7: Oneness Vs. Duality Living..105
Chapter 8: Journey From Human Consciousness to Oneness..132
Chapter 9: Transformation..148
Chapter 10: Living the Angelic Purpose..219

Chapter 1

My Walk-In Experience

This book is about my journey as an Angelic walk-in, incarnating for the 1st time on Earth. By Incarnating on Earth, I discovered true spiritual and emotional freedom. The book starts off with me having a human experience as part of my purpose to elevate the vibration frequency from a fear and insecurity vibration to that of love so I can fulfill my Angelic purpose. The journey brings me to having an Angelic experience in the human form. I am grateful to share this journey. All please enjoy including other walk-ins and the crystal children who have healing abilities and are telepathic. The crystal children can heal people of physical ailments with their energy or touch and through their high vibrations of love, help those feel nurtured. Please enjoy with love and appreciation.

What would happen if instead of the human form dying, your spirit continued the journey as a spiritual being having a spiritual experience in human form? Usually, when a human is complete with what he or she came to learn on Earth their human form dies. They finished what they came to learn on Earth in that expression form they are in and they move on to the next experience of their evolution. Their spiritual journey helps with deciding whether that entails incarnating on Earth as someone different or moving on. When one chooses to evolve spiritually, some come to a point in their life where they wake up and realize they are a spiritual being having a human experience. Imagine incarnating as an Angelic walk-in discovering a human incarnation for the first time.

I am often asked what does a walk-in mean and what happened to the other soul that left. A walk-in experience is when two individual soul expressions switch places. The first soul has gone as far as he or she can in their evolutionary development and is ready to move on. The soul that has taken their place will serve in a different capacity than before. The Universe grants permission in order for this to take place. Another way to call the experience is soul transference. The other soul continues on their journey, either to reunite with a loved one and/or continues to another place to continue learning without returning to Earth.

With a walk-in, a more evolved spirit comes into the human body and continues the journey. Imagine dying with the knowledge you have and then you incarnate again on Earth as a baby. You come in wiser because you learned from your previous incarnation. For me, instead of coming in at birth, I dropped into a body at the age of 37 and continued the journey where the other expression left off. The other expression that was complete moved on by leaving the body as a spirit form. This is where the body normally dies. Instead, I dropped into the body, a spiritually more evolved expression incarnated than that of which was originally residing in the body, to continue the journey of awakening the human ego and serving my purpose as an Angelic. In the first 17 years, I experienced a braiding with the other expression. This meant she would periodically come into the body when self-defeating beliefs were getting transformed to help with the human expression's evolution. She would come in to learn what the self-defeating beliefs were teaching to bring it into full completion which evolved the human expression. It was awkward. I felt her at the same time I was in the body. It was like two people in the body.

The other expression had to learn more about maturing and strengthening the emotions and evolving them to a place of forgiveness and love. Through awareness of the self-defeating beliefs and emotions that were sabotaging self-confidence and self-love, she was able to transform the beliefs to healthier ones. She became wiser intellectually and emotionally purer in unconditional love. The family she was born into was abusive emotionally and had negative behaviors. The father witnessed his parents murdered in a concentration camp. Only he and his brother survived. The mother became emotionally ill after her mother died, leaving her feeling emotionally weak. She died of kidney problems when the other expression was 9 years of age. She was present when the mother died and one of the sisters ignorantly blamed her for the death. 20 years later she apologized, yet the feeling of being responsible for the mom's death had massive scars ingrained. Upon her death and moving into the light, the mother came into the physical realm wanting to take the other expression with her when she was 9 years old. This meant the other expression had to die. The other expression said she had lessons to learn to become emotionally stronger and refused to die. She had shut off part of her emotions to protect herself from emotional abuse and the heavy negativity to protect herself from the family.

Throughout her life, she received guided messages from the other side from the spirit of the deceased mother and she protected her through warning messages. The mother told her to forgive the family so she could live in a more peaceful way and release the past. It took her 35 years to move through and heal all the pain and on some level abandonment with the mother dying. She completed this and then was given a guided message to mature and strengthen the emotions to a more confident place. At some point in her life, she was complete enough to get ready to leave the body. Around this time, I was coming in and out of the body, without fully incarnating yet. We both experienced confusion during that time, like a split personality. I was going in and out of the body, without staying long only to get ready to incarnate. When I temporarily came into the body I was unaware I was getting ready to incarnate. The human mind was not recognizing my energy and became confused when I came into the body.

I am an Angelic Walk-in. A Fairy Angel that incarnated on Earth in 1997. My incarnation occurred at a meditation event with the other expression's boyfriend and his friends in Montana. It started when the other expression said out loud that she wanted to experience the highest vibration of a spiritual experience in human form. I said I will go and the Angels said, "are you sure? you can help us." All the house windows were left closed and they all sat in a circle. The wind started blowing and the other expression was pulled into an energy frequency field that was moving forward through some type of time warp. She collapsed, left the body and I literally fell into the body. We both were unaware of what was going on as this experience occurred, only that she left and I came in. I saw her above my head and she saw me in the body. We experienced confusion since the human mind was unaware as yet to me dropping in. I knew instructions before I dropped in, and when I initially dropped in the memory of the human mind did not know. I felt confined and uncomfortable. It was like wearing very tight clothes that were so uncomfortable and you could not take them off. The people put quartz crystals around the body out of fear. Quartz crystals provide power and protection. They were energy readers and felt my energy as being different. They asked where I was from. I told them I came from the Angelic Realm. I was having difficulty breathing and started to hyperventilate due to being dropped into more confined and denser energies in the human form. They had to give me a paper bag to blow into to calm down. I had to sit in a tub of water for hours to acclimate to Earth's density. Sounds funny to look back and see me in a tub of water. I guess that was similar to a baby in a mom's womb.

The relationships with her friends and family all abruptly ended out of fear and noticing I was different. I received guided messages by the Angelic Realm to break up with the boyfriend knowing he and I were different. I felt alone on this planet in the human form and did not know what to do. I yelled out loud," did you forget the book of rules and regulations about this planet?" I felt them smiling at me. That night I had a dream telling me what was going on. The Angels informed me that I was a chosen one to incarnate and help with the planetary evolution and everyone on the planet, by channeling higher frequencies of love. They showed me a vision at the birth of the other expression, where I was to drop in and fulfill my Angelic purpose. The Angels in the dream shared that I am to stay connected to the ethereal realm. I initially was mostly isolated from others because that would be a distraction. They shared that I would be guided and instructed and to stay present each day and listen. They told me in the dream that I would have helpers in nonphysical form to assist with the expansiveness of the human consciousness.

These nonphysical beings initially included the Angelic Realm and Christ. Starting in 2012, these Expansive Pure Love Beings came to assist. Christ was familiar with the Earth and helped me understand how to live here on Earth. He would talk to me through the human filters to help me navigate the energy to a different frequency making it easier to release the emotional control. Christ also sent nurturing love when I was around dense energies to help me feel loved and protected in that love. The Angels explained that they would be downloading energy to start the process of activating the Angelic frequency. The energy transmutes the denser energy, such as fears, insecurities, negativity, and limitations and replaces it with a higher love frequency energy that creates healthier belief systems. The downloads would transform the human body's DNA to a light body and clear the human mind and emotions of any remaining self-defeating energies. The Angels and Christ helped me evolve the human belief programs by transmuting dense energy patterns, such as limitations, insecurities, fears, judgments, and negativity. There were times during this expansiveness that the other expression's spirit would come in to the physical realm to learn what was necessary so the human expression would evolve. The Angels would download higher vibrations of love in the body, mind, and emotions.

They shared that part of my purpose was to continue to evolve the emotions where the other expression left off so that the energy of the human emotions can shift to more of an Angelic frequency. I would then be assisting with awakening human consciousness through channeling higher frequencies of love.

My Angelic Walk-in Journey begins.

Having A Human Experience

It is my first time incarnating as an Angelic walk-in in a human form. I felt like I did not belong here on Earth. I had difficulty due to the human form's dense frequency. Incarnating on Earth for the first time and having to deal with the collective consciousness was difficult. The human emotions was operating from a denser vibration than that of the Angelic Realm and was causing conflicts. My path started with transforming the self-defeating belief systems. They were coming from remaining ancestral family beliefs from the other expression. There are many self-inflicted beliefs that were self-sabotaging. I saw so much emotional energy turmoil which started at body's birth. This led to low self-worth. I knew the only way to help it expand into higher frequencies was to nurture the human emotions as often as I could. It was necessary to transform the belief systems to healthier beliefs in order to expand the human consciousness to a higher love frequency. This took lots of energy and time. Earth has lots of planetary aspects that did not resonate so I had to learn how to work with that energy. I felt like I was living in two worlds. The Angelic Realm had a pure love energy and Earth had a denser vibration. My connection to the Angelic Realm made it easier to deal with the dense vibrations I experienced on Earth.

The Angelic Realm has pure loving energy frequencies. It was challenging adapting to the density. The dense vibrations of fears, limitations, negativity, and insecurity was confusing. I was learning how to adapt to the denser energies on Earth while keeping my connection to the Angelic Realm. It was important to remember to be in this world without forgetting where I am from. In the midst of transforming the self-defeating beliefs, I was able to get clarity on what I was learning and evolving. There were lots of insecurities and fears due to the other expression experiencing the world with so much negativity. Knowing pure love and experiencing some people who had anger, judgment, coupled with fear and insecurity, made it uncomfortable to live on Earth. That only triggered more of the same energy inside which made it difficult to clear. There was so much negativity that it was challenging to raise the vibrations to a higher love frequency. I felt like I dropped into a mess of emotional unfinished energy that the other expression never fully completed.

When I incarnated in the human form many of the friends and family that associated with the other human expression said I was not the same person. They were familiar with the other expression's way of relating. All the family and friends that were present stopped contacting me, leaving me in human form with no one to turn to. I had no one to talk to or share with which was a difficult thing for me. I kept asking for more Angels to incarnate so I would have friends. I had the dream informing me of the reason I was isolated, I still had challenges dealing with it. Being so sensitive to energies and taking in other people's energies, made it challenging to associate with others on an intimate level. I wanted to be around higher frequency of love with others and instead I was around those who had fears, negativity, insecurities, and limitations. I was dealing with expanding the vibrations of the human expression while simultaneously staying focused on who I am as an Angelic. This made it easier to release the self-defeating energies and prepare for my Angelic purpose of being on Earth.

At times I saw lost energy souls caught in energy grids on Earth. I energetically showed them how to go into the light. Some people would call them ghosts. I prefer to call them lost souls that had required some support. There are ghosts that never resolved issues while on Earth as a living person. They may choose to live in the house they had lived in as spirits to finish unfinished business and then move on into the light with greater peace. The guidance I received from the Angels was so nurturing. I often missed "my" family of Angels. Being on the planet with the contrasting energy at first was unbearable. I had no idea what I was doing. Learning to live in human form was so foreign to me and to share my experience made it even harder. I had to learn to adapt quickly to the shifts of the energy, which took 2 years. The amazing support I got on the ethereal realm helped me go through the process. I was mastering shifting my focus and alignment more on Universal

Love and less on the collective consciousness. The more I had this oneness connection with the Angels and support from Christ, the easier it was to live on Earth.

I discovered the way the human ego operates. It has a belief system of ideas and concepts adopted during life. It uses duality as a comparison based on a human's belief system. The human ego identifies with the belief system and uses comparisons to associate how it feels and thinks. The human ego using duality words such as, good and bad, right and wrong, happy and sad, are ways the human ego compares and analyzes an experience or person based on another person's belief system. A positive response occurs when the human ego associated the belief system with the condition or person as a favorable outcome. A negative reaction occurred when the human ego associated the belief system with the condition or person as unfavorable. The human ego going into a control mode was so efficient in attempting to fix, correct, teach. or judge.

The human emotions experienced so much emotional abuse. I chose to love and nurture the human emotions to help rebuild the self-value. I asked the Angels and Christ to help me with this, making it easier to transmute the energies that were in conflict. The emotional energies were operating more from density due to the remaining belief patterns that required evolving. They had insecure signature patterns that were attracting unworthy energies attempting to sabotage the positive energy downloads. The Angels instructed me to strengthen the inner human emotions so that it stayed connected to Universal Love. I experienced many challenges while attempting to shift my focus off the denser energy vibes. When I focused on these denser energies, I experienced more fears, negativity, and limitations leaving me feeling insecure.

I became discouraged and insecure, thinking I did something wrong to experience negativity, judgmental people, and sometimes angry people. It did not make any sense to me at all on why people behaved the way they were. I knew of joy and playing and what I experienced was drama and complaining. The Insecurity I was experiencing had taken me into lower vibrations. Nurturing the human emotions amplified self-love. I would silence the human mind chatter and come into the present moment as quickly as I could by focusing on gratitude. This helped increase the vibration. I also did meditations on a daily basis and sometimes 2 times a day. The Angels helped by shifting the dense energy to a more expansive love frequency.

I put more attention on what was going on inside the human expression vs. giving my power away to the outside world influences. This included people I interacted with, the collective consciousness, and lost non-physical energy souls. Focusing on the energy of what people represented vs. each person helped me respond more from compassion instead of judging. I had a greater understanding of what I was to learn. The lineage from the other expression's family heritage was mostly cleared with forgiveness. I experienced a greater sense of inner peace and acceptance with where they were at and living my life without entertaining in theirs. I did not hear from them and I was freeing the inner energy around them. It was healthier to let go and enjoy my life and accept our different life styles. With that knowing, it was easier to move forward with inner love and peace. I had fewer mind stories about them and blaming them was no longer an issue.

From 1997-2007, I did temporary work. I did secretarial work, was a mystery shopper for Safeway, and organized shelves in grocery stores. I enjoyed the simplicity the work provided. The temporary work lasted 2 years. I developed attitude and communication training programs. I transitioned to freelancing in after school programs with children which I enjoyed. In 2005, I was feeling pulled to move to California. I took a temporary job with a bank that lasted 6 months. I met what I call a light being in human form who also worked there which was fun. Our eyes shot a light of love to each other recognizing each other's signatures. I was not able to tune in and get confirmation as to where his energy as a nonphysical form was from. There were lots of people in the bank which made it difficult to tune in. I was guided to work with the kids again for 2 years. In 2005, I got certified as a hypnotist. In July of 2007, I was felt guided to go to Portland to finish transforming the ancestral lineage energy. I was not aware that I was to not move there. I thought I was being guided to move there and to channel love there. I learned when the emotions were at a denser frequency, the choices I made resonated with that.

I would live in areas that were heavy in negative drama. I learned after moving 7 times in a year and 3 strangers in a week came and said, "do you get that you do not belong in Portland?" I had replied to them saying, "I do now." Living in denser areas were not nurturing me in a positive way. The dense energies were actually a huge distraction. If I gave my power to them, the human ego would go into a control mode. I became insecure, confused, and fearful. That pattern was something I had to break. I kept wanting to move to find a nurturing and positive place to live. I discovered taking care of myself was more of an inside job vs. searching outside. I heard messages about going inside. I kept wondering why I was not feeling my Angelic energy in the heart instead of the emotional turmoil. I packed my things and headed to Corvallis, Oregon. I stayed with this couple temporarily. I was guided to move to Lebanon Oregon temporarily as a resting place.

I became aware of a wounded inner child that never got loved properly. I experienced life through those eyes of feeling wounded, I experienced life and people from a more protective fear-based place until I transformed enough of the self-inflicting beliefs into love. Some of the deeper insecurities and self-doubts stemmed from this. The choices I was making in life stemmed from that as well. I felt held back and regretted things in life that I did not get to experience because I was focusing on building self-worth, self-confidence, and self-value. Parts of my personal life got sabotaged because the inner wounded child was dominating my life. By releasing the energy around the wounded child, I experienced nurturing and freedom to live life peacefully. This is when the protected barriers around the heart shifted. The more I embraced and transformed the self-defeating beliefs, the greater my confidence became. The more the self-defeating beliefs got transformed, the easier it became for my Angelic expression to become more active and the connection to Universal Love became even stronger. Any choices in life thereby became more aligned with love instead of the wounded child.

Over the Holiday Season in December of 2008, I saw the other expression go into the light, saying she loves me. She was with her husband of many lifetimes. She told me she cannot assist with finding my beloved partner and that the Angels will help. She did not stay fully in the light until the human expression was complete enough for me to come into my purpose. She would come into the physical realm in spirit form, to experience what I was learning in the areas she needed to complete. Mostly when I was completing the unfinished ancestral family lineage. She said she would watch over me to make sure I was ok. I saw energies from her family heritage also go into the light. I still had some cleaning up to do with regard to the emotional energies for 7 more years. A challenging task I did not enjoy. I experienced both healthy and self-defeating beliefs. The human ego is the central core of the human mind which has a subconscious and a conscious. The subconscious has beliefs that we are not aware of and the conscious has beliefs we are aware of. Self-defeating beliefs trigger insecurity and fear if fed. The healthy beliefs are empowering. Human ego's natural instinct is self-preservation.

The human ego has a protection mechanism that gets activated when the personality feels threatened. As you become aware of a self-inflicting belief, you handle conditions and people based on your level of spiritual maturity. Lessons help you become smarter, "spiritually." The human ego control becomes active If you allow the self-defeating beliefs to run your life. You go into a flight, fight, or protect mode. The human ego wants to either fight back with reactive words, flight by running away or avoiding the situation out of a discomfort of confrontation or protect with teaching, correcting, or fixing. Through these self-defeating beliefs, we incur challenges to learn and evolve the beliefs to become smarter, "spiritually." Some people struggle because they put more focus on the limitations around the beliefs instead of what the beliefs are teaching us. Beliefs initially come in as energy before they turn into a denser form.

When the self-defeating beliefs are dominating, the human ego is overly active and controls situations and people through the filters of the self-defeating beliefs. Judgment, fear, insecurity, negativity, sadness, anger, limitation, and jealousy are examples of denser vibration energies that can play out in our beliefs if allowed. The human mind has familiar programs in the form of beliefs that get entertained by participating in the mental stories and emotions. These stories create an outcome on the physical realm that mirrors those stories and emotions. These mental stories come from our belief systems. Some serve our highest good and other beliefs no longer serve our overall well-being. If we play out the same self-defeating beliefs repeatedly, we get stuck in it because we never let them go. We can become so addicted to the story and emotions around that story. Until one day, some quit cold turkey, realizing this was not healthy. We become enlightened and move forward in a positive way in life.

We do not have to hit rock bottom to get there. Staying on the higher energy vibrations is more enjoyable instead of going down in the scale to denser energy vibrations leading to more problems. When we choose happiness, then we don't entertain mind chattered stories, unpleasant emotions, experiences or people who are not aligned with that. We don't allow our self to get stuck in something that does not feel good. We stop and shift our attention to Universal Love. We are not ignoring life's challenges rather choosing not to feed the drama. Life is about loving and enjoying life vs. struggling, problem solving, and just living. We attract abundances in our life when we focus, allow, and know we are worthy of this abundance. We let go of identifying with the limitations as who we are. By committing to living life in love, joy, and peace, the contradicting energy no longer can survive. It eventually transforms into higher frequencies of love. Earth is like a school, learning lessons and achieving wisdom. You can either go into the lessons with a fear mentality, being overly cautious and closed off to new paradigms or learn through an adventure oriented route. The adventure is getting the human ego control to relax so you shift from the familiar human beliefs dictating your life to innovative new ways which show up as inspired insights.

From 2008 to 2009, I learned about detachment from physical items and inner beliefs that were no longer aligned with my Angelic expression. The physical attachments to things like clothes, furniture, pictures, journals were easier to release. Detaching from core beliefs by disconnecting identifications with the stories and emotions that got triggered was more challenging. I was able to see how these energies were coming from inside energy grids and reflected in the outer world. These energy grids stores the beliefs in the form of energy in the subconscious. I saw how the human ego controls out of fear, insecurity, limitations, and negativity. When I fed it with my attention, it would control my life since I identified with it as the truth of who I was. Through the identification, I became attached which created more struggles. I attached to the lesson that a person or situation was showing me which triggered emotional drama and mental stories. The more we resist the lesson, the greater the level of struggle, creating more struggles and negative influences.

The more I fed the self-defeating beliefs, the denser the vibrations became emotionally, mentally, and in the body. Self-defeating beliefs get fed through complaining, judging, blaming, unpleasant emotional attachments, and resistance. For me two things happened when I allowed the human emotions to control, I either created behavioral patterns in the form of addictions or I surrendered and put my attention on Universal Love. As I connected to Universal Love, I was able to calm the human emotions so it would not run my life. Connecting to Universal Love helped break the addictive pattern, and I experienced inner peace. I was letting go of attachments in all forms, both internal self-sabotaging beliefs, and tangible physical items. It became even easier to let go of physical items. The internal self-sabotaging beliefs were still challenging to detach and release. I started this by focusing on self-nurturing and being open to the Angels downloading a higher vibration of love. In the earlier chapter, I shared how I became so confused with processing what I experienced from the human conditions. I honestly did not know what I was doing. I kept asking for a manual on how to live in human form thinking they forgot to give that to me when I incarnated. I said, "Others on the planet seemed to get it, why not me?" I felt the Angels smiling and sending love.

I found it easier to release the hold on the emotional discomfort and mind chatter by talking it through and getting encouragement. I would call strangers at churches and spiritual practitioners to help me with the processing and understanding. I was not comfortable sharing I was a walk-in so I shared the human part of what I was experiencing to help to get the clarity and nurturing that at that time I felt I needed. I felt the emotions required human comfort from other humans to help let go of the attachments to the mental stories and emotional discomfort. This was how the needy energy became stronger. The part that was challenging was that I did not feel I was able to nurture the emotional part enough. I experienced deep sadness, loneliness, and a sense of being lost. Nothing I did seemed enough. At times, I allowed the human emotions to suck me into that sad energy only to feel confused. It was important to stay alert, so I stayed confident. The mental stories would start and the human emotions became reactive and defensive. Before I knew it, I was experiencing what felt like being human from a negative, fearful, limited place. Initially, I had no idea how to get out of it. I kept asking for the manual from the Universe. The Angels kept saying, "take care of yourself." I would shout out loud, "I AM!" I kept allowing myself to get sucked into the denser vibration, where I identified with the human emotions and then react with judging and complaining, only to keep me stuck in that vibration. I'd quickly clear my energy so I did not get sucked into the human personalizing.

After many times of exhaustion and emotional tiredness, I would surrender and the human ego was ready for the Universe to help. I learned to surrender the emotional and mental attachments and become more of an observer vs. participate in the mind stories or emotional discomfort. When I was attached to the outer world, I was needier and wanted them to assist me with the discomforting emotions. This only made it difficult to stay open to receiving love from the Angels, Christ, and Universal Love. Looking back on that, it made no sense at all to why I would focus my attention on receiving love from others vs. the Angels, Christ, and Universal Love. The only thing I knew was I had a hunger for that experience from humans which only kept me stuck in the needy energy. The human emotions were dominating my life wanting human love to be fulfilled from the outside world. Through consistent awareness, I was able to shift from the outer world fulfilling emotional love that was desperately needed to that of receiving it from the Angels, Christ, and Universal Love.

Before I knew what human ego control was, I felt like I was living inside with another person. I became self-empowered in my relationship with the human ego by not giving my power away to it. Some people told me I had too much human ego control when I was persistent with sharing the services and products I created. I had no idea what they were talking about. I felt rejection that was shooting at me like bullets. All I could do was bow my head and leave since reacting only made it worse. I asked what they were talking about, to help me understand. I heard, "trying too hard, a pushing feeling, and asking too soon." I replied, "is asking if my products and services is of interest to you, pushing too hard? Is introducing myself trying to hard? Is waiting two or more weeks to call back asking too soon?" I would get this look like I was crazy. At times, I wanted to quit. The conflicts between the emotions wanting acceptance and my Angelic expression was overwhelming. I discovered the human emotions they were picking up on was a reflection for each other. The insecurity was coming from both them and the human emotions were feeding off each other. I personalized what they said, feeling rejected and unworthy. Going through that experience helped me see how fear and insecurity are the biggest triggers to human ego control.

The human emotions controlled my life whenever I judged them. When I nurtured them with love, the human emotions became confident. When I experienced fear, negativity, limitations, and insecurity, the human emotions got stuck in these denser energies creating turmoil. The human ego control became active with this turmoil by going into a protective, flight, or fear mode. Its natural instinct is to protect when it feels threatened. Resistance only makes it more challenging. The challenges came from more of fear, negativity, and insecurity. What you fear or become insecure of, you attract more in different forms to develop inner love and confidence. I had to detach from identifying with the self-defeating beliefs, quiet the mind chatter, and calm the emotions. I quieted the mind chatter by moving my focus off the story and calmed the emotions by nurturing them. As I raised my energy, the dense energy vibrations got transformed to a higher vibration of pure love. Embracing and surrendering any discomfort helps to calm down any resistance with any fear or insecurity. By not participating in the mental stories or emotional discomfort, it was easier to raise my energy to a higher frequency.

Breathing, self-nurturing, and silencing the thoughts calms the human ego down. Meditation, exercise, high vibration music, laughing, and nature are tools to help to calm the human ego from going into a control mode. The Angels downloading energy helped to amplify the energy even more. The more love the human emotions felt, the calmer it became. It was one of the hardest lessons to shift the attachment to expecting the outer world to feed the emotions with love to that of the Angels, Christ, and Universal Love feeding it. As the bond became stronger, I started to experience more inner peace. It is much easier to connect to Universal Love and the Angels when the human ego is calm. When the mind chatter is silent, the emotions feel nurtured, and the body relaxes, the frequency is higher. It was easier to connect to Universal Love, feeling peaceful. I did not feel alone when I felt my Angelic family and Universal Love. Having a connection to the Pure Love Beings and the Angels, felt comforting and safe. The Pure Love Beings helped me feel loved and cared for. I could not imagine my life without them and the Angels by my side. Earth is a vibrational planet that responds to frequencies. Love being the highest frequency is the best way to stay connected to Universal Love.

On January 1, 2009 at 1:11 AM, I married Universal Love in a wedding dress, ring and read a wedding vow. I had a private ceremony to confirm my love and commitment to Universal Love and my purpose on Earth. I saw lots of Angels and heard, "I am so proud of you." Number 1 symbolizes individuality and new beginnings. Number 11 is a master number which amplifies the number 1 to a higher vibration of love. I was mastering standing strong in my Angelic expression of love instead of giving my power to people who judged and complained a lot.

It is easier to transform self-defeating beliefs as energy vs. transform the belief system. In energy, there is no resistance and attachments to the familiar beliefs. The self-defeating beliefs got transmuted as energy and downloads of expansive higher frequency vibration of love energy replaced it. The downloads were making the body's energy frequency lighter. I would raise the body's energy to a higher vibration to make it easier to feel the pure loving energy. This is what the Angels meant by shifting the DNA of the body from carbon to that of a light body frequency. I was learning how to strengthen the bond I had with the Angels and Universal Love vs. the human ego control and looking <u>outside</u> for the higher love vibration. I was learning how to master this while simultaneously releasing the denser beliefs systems that were creating this vicious cycle of losing connection. The human ego control taking over and attempting to control the outcome made it challenging. I knew this intellectually yet had to release enough of the human emotional blocks in the form of programs before I could experience the lighter love vibrations. The Angels, Christ and Universal Love became more comforting. The more I was open to receiving unconditional, pure love deeply inside, the easier the solidification became. My commitment to being happy and living in peace was greater than entertaining drama.

I received a channeled message about the <u>connection to Universal Love.</u> Energy is pure love, joy, and peace. It then manifests into form our belief system.. When these beliefs align with Universal Love, we are at the highest frequency. When the energies of pure love, joy, and peace are tainted with judgment or fear, the vibrations of the human expression becomes dense, This creates feelings of. separation from Universal Love. A disconnection to this pure love, joy, abundance, and peace. Experiencing discomfort, insecurity, limitation, and mind chatter attempting to figure out or understand. Any resistance to the uncomfortable feelings only causes more struggle. I define judgment as perceiving experiences, situations, and people as being right or wrong and good or bad based on ones' belief systems. If we partake in judgmental thoughts, we identify the negativity, fears, insecurities, and limitations as who we are.

We create a type of checklist that either resonates with our beliefs or doesn't. When they don't, judgment can occur, because the human ego is attempting to protect that belief system. If we feed the judgment, we start to experience discomfort. That triggers behaviors that are self-focused, insecure, fear-driven, and needy. Judgment creates attachments and you continue to experience the area being judged until you learn what it is teaching you and come to peace with it. Same with fear. Being fearful creates lower frequency energies that attract more of that fear energy. When a condition or person aligns with that belief, there is an acceptance and a feeling of joy and peace. When a condition or person is not aligned with a belief, judgment occurs, creating conflict. Judgment is like a bunch of knots that sits in one's energy field. The greater the judgment around something or someone, the stronger the knots become and the more it appears in your life in different forms. Beliefs come from the past, not the present. That is great news. You can transform them since you created your own beliefs. you transform them through embrace them knowing these beliefs are temporary and there to learn and evolves. It then becomes easier to connect to Universal Love.

We have to let go of the control around the beliefs to move out of judgment to love,. That includes letting go of righteousness, over analyzing, opinions, fears, living in the past with beliefs that do not serve us, and the future attempting to force an outcome. Being mindful in the present moment and choosing love is the strongest way to experience authentic love, joy, and peace. It helps to quiet the mind chatter and calm the emotions. As we shift the beliefs that aren't aligned with love, We expand consciousness. Judging incurs struggles because we are letting the problem run our life, leading to greater discomfort and pain. This only leads to more problems that destroy our confidence and can trigger fears and insecurity. Forgiveness and compassion helps us move out of judgment. It doesn't mean you condone the behavior rather free yourself from the attachments to the mental stories and emotional discomfort Sometimes apologizing to the person directly cuts the energy cord with that experience, creating inner peace.

Negativity is another dense energy that keeps us feeling disconnected from Universal Love and puts the human ego into protective mode. When we give our power away to negativity, we get caught up in the denser energies in our thoughts and emotions. When I first incarnated, one of the biggest challenges I faced was dealing with negativity. I felt like I was trapped in a coffin. It felt confined since I had no idea what to do. I was still learning how to live in a body which also felt confined. I was experiencing two confined conditions. That triggered the human ego to become so active which made it even more difficult. I was so grateful I was getting instructions in my sleep through the dreams. I was able to understand how to process all this energy that was in conflict with the expansive, loving, and free-flowing energy I knew as my truth. To experience a contrast was overwhelming in the body circuitry since my Angelic frequency was conflicting with the denser energy. I left the body often to bring love from above down into the body in place of escaping energetically from the body. Experiencing being a human was no picnic for me. I had lots of challenges. I had to learn to keep the thoughts in gratitude and emotions in appreciation to move out of the dense vibrations.

As an Angelic, I choose love. This made it easier to build self-love, self-awareness, and self-confidence. Self-love is important so we are whole and available to share love with another. Instead, we have what I call conditional love based on identifying with the beliefs as being truthful and potentially project them on to another. When we live in the vibration of self-love, we take responsibility. We are able to transmute self-defeating beliefs through awareness and evolve them into more loving belief forms. We are not concerned about others' negative opinions nor do we personalize them. We know our own inner truth. We become aware of being an individual expression of Universal Love. When we have a direct connection to Universal Love inside, we are whole and complete. We know the human personality is not who we are. We know there are lessons and experiences we came here to learn and evolve. We choose to "be" love instead of playing the teacher role by attempting to fix, correct, and/or judge. It is freeing to live in the world and get along with others through compassion, acceptance, and unconditional love. It is not necessary to attempt to focus on understanding before accepting others. That is coming from the human belief system structure. Acceptance brings higher levels of wisdom which eventually explains the reasons.

Sometimes we can give our power away by focusing on that which is not feeling like Universal Love and judge it, allowing it to suck us down into negativity or prejudice. There is a tendency to want to fix, correct, blame, protect, and potentially react. That never solves anything. It only creates more of that of which is not coming from the power of love. When we choose the power of love and stand committed to it, the focus becomes more about love. The more committed we are to the power of love and come from compassion and forgiveness, the softer our heart becomes. We are no longer hardened by hurt and pain from past or present experiences. The focus is on the moment and choosing love over past pains and mental stories. Forgiveness allows us to completely let go of any unpleasant memories and feelings. Emotional freedom started when I embraced all emotional and mental discomfort around any contrasted area. I embraced the insecurity and fear instead of complaining, resisting, or judging it. I became an observer of the human thoughts instead of participating in the chattered story, or any unpleasant situations. I was more effective in diffusing its power over me, feeling inner calmness.

I chose love over reacting in anger with any unjust condition or person involved. I surrendered the resistance and anything that was becoming overwhelming to Universal Love for support. I chose to be humble and receptive to Universal Love's help with gratitude and appreciation. Compassion and love helps reconnect to Universal Love. Chattered thoughts takes up so much time and energy because the human mind wants to figure out what is going. on. Letting go and allowing, provides for greater clarity and wisdom. I shifted my focus more on the Angels and Universal Love. The Angels told me to feel appreciation and gratitude. I put all my attention on what I enjoyed in the outer world, such as nature, birds, swimming, and children playing. I appreciated the Angels loving energy downloads for the human emotions.

4 years later, is when my Angelic expression started to become more active in the human expression. Enough of the self-defeating beliefs got transformed to healthier beliefs. The human expression had to function at a high enough frequency to get ready for expansiveness. I was getting the body, mind, and emotions ready for energy downloads from these Pure Love Beings that arrived in 2010. They assisted with elevating the body's energy frequency so that I was able to both hold and experience the Angelic frequency in the mind, body, and emotions. I did not experience them as often in 2010 and 2011. Starting in 2012, the Pure Love Beings were with me more often because my Angelic expression was more active with the energy frequencies being higher in the body. In the early part of the year 2010, the Pure Love Beings first arrived in my dream.

One of the Pure Love Beings came to me with a smile on his face. He first came as a young male and then turned into an elder. He told me I am here to help elevate human consciousness. He shot energy in my head. I felt some dense energy leaving. I noticed made my thoughts more positive. In November 2010, I had another dream where the Pure Love Beings came as an African-American female with gorgeous clear eyes. She worked on my body saying positive stuff is coming and will be starting in March 2011. They'd come into my dreams because the emotions, body, and mind are more receptive to receiving energy downloads. While sleeping, the human mind is not rationalizing or resisting the energy downloads. The more I let go of the human ego control running my life, the calmer I felt. I instead focused on the connection to Universal Love. The connection to Universal Love created more of a oneness connection. Through this oneness, there were no comparisons and fewer reactions to conditions in the outside world since the beliefs were not triggered. I chose to make the human ego my friend instead of attempting to kill it off or hate it. The human ego keeps the body alive. It is like a computer that provides communication feedback based on the stored programs. By making it my friend, I was able to retrain it to not go into control mode.

I observed others talking about the human ego control being bad and wanting to kill it off. I knew in my heart that the human ego is not bad rather doing its job. What it knows best. You could not kill it off anyway unless you died. You live in the body and that operates the human ego. Trying to kill it off, hate it, or get angry with the human ego is not the answer. See what triggers the human ego control and calm it down before it becomes reactive. Making friends with the human ego and calming it down helped me to lessen the control it had over me. This helped me to train it to connect more to the Angelic Energy and feel the aliveness of love, joy, and peace in a heightened way. I had a huge awakening when I mastered aligning more to Universal Love. Universal Love fed the emotions in a heightened way which relaxed the human ego control. I was then able to raise and expand into the higher vibration frequencies where I was able to use the intellectual mind and Angelic Love energy more effectively in the human form. It became easier to focus on evolving the human soul.

When I was processing lessons, I enjoyed experiencing the human ego staying calm vs. immediately go into a control mode wanting to take action. The lack of action stopped the triggering of mind chatter and emotional discomfort. There was this awareness of knowing better. The human ego became aware that if it fed the mental chatter and emotional discomfort, then the control would kick in and I as an Angelic would become a victim to it. That would only lead to a sense of feeling weak and helpless and the fight, flight, protect mode would then become dominant. Participating in this was not an option. I was able to become the observer of rather than a participant. I knew I was not the body, mind, or emotions rather experiencing them as an Angelic being in human form. From that awareness, I was able to experience the human ego from a positive perspective. This awareness was a starting point that shifted the way I process lessons. I was able to breathe and calm the body down, then the mind chatter, and finally calm the emotions by feeding it with lots of love. I would call in the Pure Love Beings, Universal Love and Angels for more nurturing love. I put a class together to teach this. I was retraining the human emotions to go inside more for connections to inner love instead of looking outside. I looked at the human ego as if it was a student that required love and attention.

I imagined life as a playground to help make life more fun and playful. It got easier to let go of the control the human emotions had on me by focusing on Universal Love. Life started to become more enjoyable. By nurturing the human emotions it became easier to avoid giving my power to outer world conditions. I started to feel the Pure Love Being's expansive love in the body, mind, and emotions. I was building a stronger connection with the Pure Love Beings. The Angels told me to keep focusing on joy to bring higher levels of joy within. The more I did this, eventually, I felt a partnering between the spirit mind and the human mind. Anytime I had emotional discomfort and allowed it to play out, I would experience a longing for a personal life, including a life partner and friendships. The more I allowed that habit to take over, the greater the fear and insecurity. Stopping the mind chatter and focusing on gratitude and love brought me into higher frequencies of love. The higher frequencies of love helped calm and break the addictive pattern. This habit lasted many years as I unraveled the core areas that triggered this habitual habit.

Hating the emotional discomfort or chattered thoughts was not the answer. Attachments to emotional discomfort only creates more intensity. It also triggers the human ego to go into a fight, flight. protect mode. Anytime I had emotional discomfort, and I gave it my attention, my energy vibrations dropped. This led to judgment, fear, insecurity, or negativity. By embracing and loving the experience, the vibrations escalated and the condition no longer had a pull on the emotions. Thereby, the human ego control was not active allowing for a stronger connection to Universal Love. More enjoyment occurred with feeling heightened joy, peace, and \love. I started to experience more freedom from the denser energies running my life. Freeing the emotional neediness allowed me to live life more peacefully. I did not allow the emotions to get into judging, fear, insecurity, or negativity since I was no longer entertaining that. I chose to raise the emotions to feelings of appreciation, love, compassion, acceptance, and joy. It took many years to shift this. The loving energy downloads from the Pure Love Beings helped me transform the human thoughts to gratitude thoughts and feel greater self-love. I enjoyed life more by learning to live in the moment vs. the past with analyzing or the future with too much focus on wanting an outcome.

In 1997, I had a future vision that I was going to Europe in the year 2010. The vision was so strong that I thought I was moving there.. For 10 years, I was accumulating miles for a free ticket by using my Visa card. As 2010 approached I needed 10,000 more miles to get the free ticket. In January, I got a promotional email from American Airlines. It said, "sign up for a Citi-Credit Card with no yearly dues, spend $200 within 3 months and earn 10,000 miles." I started to laugh. I knew the Universe orchestrated that. I got the card and filling up the car gasoline and food, I spent the $200 in 2 months. I had my free ticket. I thought at first I was going to Italy, Greece, and Paris. As I started to research where to stay and what to do, my heart was not feeling pulled to go. I explored the Norwegian Countries and still I did not feel pulled to go there. Finally, I asked out loud, where can I go? Out of nowhere I felt pulled to go to Ireland. I felt that would be the perfect place. It had a history of Irish Leprechauns and Fairies plus the beauty of nature. I also planned on traveling to Iceland and nurturing myself with their mud baths.

As I planned the Ireland trip, it flowed smoothly with the exact date that I wanted to go, April 14, 2010. Iceland was not flowing at all. I kept getting date conflicts with traveling there. I chose to accept. I even attempted to go to Switzerland, and that did not flow. I got real clear that Ireland was the only place I was to go.

As I flew into Ireland, I noticed a volcanic erupting in Iceland. I saw Volcanic ash. Right after I landed, all airlines canceled flights due to the volcanic eruption. That explained why I couldn't go to the other countries. My flight out to the other countries would have been postponed, leaving me stuck for weeks without being able to leave Ireland. I had a tour planned, and that got changed to a more elaborate one due to people not being able to fly in.

Many people were stressed out with their flights being postponed where they could not leave. I prayed for everyone. They resumed flights at the exact day and time of my scheduled flight I was to leave. I experienced deep love and gratitude. While I was there, I got to experience the beauty of the land.. I also experienced many unsettled ghosts at the castles I toured. I sensed they did not die a natural death. Many died at war. I told them I was an Angelic walk-in. They felt it and left me alone in peace. I met many people and asked about the Irish Leprechauns and Fairies. Many forgot about their spiritual heritage around this. I asked them to remember this and to share this. The people I asked agreed with a smile and I felt their heart become more alive. I channeled energy that created grids and vortexes on Earth to raise the energy frequency. I became a conduit for the Pure Love Beings to channel through me to create a grid in Ireland. After the grid was created, I read that Ireland was bailed out of bankruptcy.

The part-time work with the after school programs started to taper off. I felt guided to do Angel messages. chakra alignments and activating the inner spirit by channeling the Pure Love Beings into people's energy fields. This started my Angelic purpose of helping to awaken human consciousness. I translated messages from the Pure Love Beings. The chakra alignments entailed reading the energies in 8 areas of the emotional, mental and physical body. Seeing where there were energies that looked stagnant. Using colors and higher frequency sounds to help the energies flow. An Analogy of this would be a rock in a stream being removed so the water flows more. The activation sessions entailed guiding the Universal Pure Love Beings to download energy to activate the Inner Spirit while participants were in deep state of relaxation.

Moving Into the Angelic Expression

Each morning, I would first meditate and fill up the emotions with lots of love. This helped to strengthen the human emotions. Then I would call in the Pure Love Beings and they would download heightened frequencies of loving energy. When that was intact, the human emotions felt nurtured and calm. When I was assisting others, I would move out of the human filters and call in the Pure Love Beings. They would download pure loving energy to clear and activate their Inner Spirit. If I did not set healthy boundaries, I would absorb their energy and become protective. There were so many times I wanted to quit doing the energy work with others so I could focus on evolving the emotional energy within in a more nurturing way. When I dropped in, my Angelic Guides told I was here to help with the awakening of the human consciousness, so I was never able to walk away from it.

I surrendered the resistance and graciously accepted what felt like an assignment. The more I embraced it the more I enjoyed it. It was assisting me with my connection to the Pure Love Beings. It seemed every time my energy was high and playful, I would be surrounded by those in drama. I would lose my focus, becoming distracted in their energy and become disconnected. The next thing I knew was I felt lost, insecure and confused. I had to find peaceful places and activities to get my energy back up like swimming, going into nature, meditating, and talking about it with others to process and release the mental story and emotional attachments. I would leave intense situations and people before it became too much of a distraction. Emotional nurturing and connecting to the Angelic consciousness gave me greater strength to hold my connection to Universal Love. This helped me solidify any new energy downloads in a stronger way.

I learned that I had a habit of care-taking. I did not like others suffering so I would do what I could do help them feel better. What I realized was that was hurting me in the process. Taking on this only enabled dependent relationships. I chose to stop care-taking and playing the savior. I was not responsible for other people's lessons. I chose to take care of myself and be supportive vs. care-take others. Care-taking attracted people who wanted saving. It felt like they were using me more for my spiritual gifts. In care-taking or playing the teacher role, I felt my feelings discounted, and I allowed others to dampen my inner joy, peace, and well-being by giving them power. Embracing the past pain and sorrow I had gone through in life, made it easier to take gentle care of myself. The human ego can become so protective when it senses pain or suffering. Forgiveness and peace was my key to freedom. Allowing the pain only kept me stuck in that energy until I made peace with it. When I let go of care-taking and chose to take care of myself, I didn't feel like they were taking advantage. It became so much more enjoyable to BE love and allow others to learn their own lessons.

Breaking the pattern of teaching was one of the hardest lessons to learn. Replacing teaching or a social worker with that of sharing through channeling released this burden I placed on myself. It freed any dependency. It allowed those I use to teach be more self-directed with their life. That freed me to enjoy my life more. I accepted others with where they were at and used discernment, blessing them to help release any form of attachment. I chose to enjoy life more. Participating in others' complaining and negative behaviors only put me in a saddened state and that did not serve either one of us. As I became more aware of focusing my energy on taking better care of myself, I was able to break fully and completely from participating in any form of fixing, care-taking, correcting, teaching, and judging. The more I focused on my connection to the Pure Love Beings and choosing joy, the less I got involved in others' stories and drama. Eventually, many stopped coming to me to express their problems. I was supportive, accepting, and allowed others to learn without discounting my own well-being in the process. I noticed they were able to learn and evolve without me enabling them to become dependent on me. As I embraced, accepted, and blessed the experience it became easier to not get sucked into others people's energy.

I started to feel more connected to the Pure Love Beings and nature. I was finally getting it. This is what inner peace, inner joy, and inner love felt like in the physical form. With this heightened level of love, you have desires to share it with others instead of looking to get or give it to others. You enjoy sharing from a "we" focus. You flow with life in a calm, peaceful, humble, happy and positive way. You may attract those that want what you are experiencing. As you stand strong in love, you become a beacon of light reminding others of their own Inner Spirit. You do not have to play the teacher role. "Being" love is a teacher in itself. Depending on where they are in their own evolution, they will either express love back to you or run like the dickens out of fear because they are not ready. Some live life in negativity, fears, insecurity, and limitations which come from their beliefs and they react out of protection. They don't recognize anything but that, so they are not able to stand in that which contrasts what they are familiar with for very long. When negative human emotions are active that is a sign that the human ego control became active. That is its job when it is not taught how to connect to Universal Love for positive support and nurturing. The Human Ego creates a defense mechanism going into a fight, flight, protect mode. ▫ You can strengthen your connection to Universal Love by doing the following:

Step 1: Take a step away from the situation or person to break the energy connection.
Step 2: Breathe.
Step 3: Quiet the mind chatter.
Step 4: Surrender the challenge to Universal Love.
Step 5: Embrace and nurture the human emotions until it calms down and you start to feel more love inside.
Step 6: Imagine your Inner Spirit nurturing you.
Step 7: Trust and Listen for clarity from Universal Love
which will help you stay calm and positive.

There are beliefs embedded in the form of energy, stored in the emotional, mental, and physical plane. They have their own meaning relating to love, communication, confidence, creativity, finances, peace, and health. There's a high vibration of energy, which comes from love or a lower vibration of energy which stems out of fear and insecurity. These beliefs can either be for your greatest good or hinder and limit you from experiencing a deeper connection to inner peace, love, joy and overall well-being. Depending on how we feed the energy, it can either come in the form of unconditional love fed by joy, and peace or conditional love fed by fear and insecurity. Unconditional love does not attach to unpleasant conditions and people and lives in the present moment instead of the past or future. We live life with heightened levels of love, joy, prosperity, and peace as we connect to Universal Love. Alternatively, conditional love has attachments to beliefs that come from the past and present.

When self-defeating beliefs dominate your life and you let them run your life, you experience fear and insecurity. The more these self-defeating beliefs control, the stronger they become and turn into habitual habits. The great news is that energy is easy to transmute before it comes into form so that you do not feel stuck in self-inflicted beliefs. Self-defeating beliefs are teachers to help you learn lessons and become smarter, "spiritually." If you perceive these lessons as a problem-oriented focus, you will have a tendency to complain, blame, and judge them experiencing more struggles and suffering. As these beliefs, in the form of energies get transmuted, more of your Inner Spirit becomes "activated" and can express in a fuller way. Eventually, you experience Spiritual Freedom, a heightened frequency level of inner peace, greater joy, and pure love in human form. You become more of an observer of any thoughts and emotions that may stand in the way of your happiness and quickly bless and release them. You let go of the attachments to the past beliefs to measure up to what you are currently experiencing or expectations of future outcomes You are not basing your experiences on past beliefs and either judging or accepting them based on whether they are aligned with what you want to experience. The more you unravel the outdated beliefs, the more active you Inner Spirit and freedom begins. You enjoy the now moments in life.

For example, Imagine the body, mind, and heart covered with layers of clothing representing beliefs. These beliefs consist of ones that serve you and ones that do not. Every day you meet others who wear similar clothes. Some clothes you resonate with and others irritate you. The ones that irritate you bring up memories. If you focus on these thoughts, they create stories from the past. As you continue to focus on these stories, emotional discomfort comes up, bringing on drama resulting in your body feeling heavy and tired. You want to get rid of these clothes, yet the memories keep you attached to them. You decide to peel off that layer of clothes (the memory) with love and peace vs. judging them. Your thoughts are peaceful, you feel joy, and your body feels lighter with greater vitality. You become aware of these layers and peel off the layers that are not serving you. You get rid of the clothes that no longer fit or are not bringing joy or peace in your life. You are now wearing undergarments which represent your core beliefs. If you take them off, you are nude. That represents your Inner Spirit. Pure and Loving.

As you release enough of the denser energies from the self-defeating beliefs, the DNA of the physical body becomes expansive in love frequencies. The Inner Spirit starts to become more active. Now you are experiencing this purer form of love with the connection to the Inner Spirit and Universal Love. This is a pure divine love of oneness, inner peace, abundance, and joy. You become aware that the humanness is the body, thoughts, and emotions with the familiar patterns. You are aware that you are not the body, thoughts, and feelings rather you express thoughts in the mind, feelings in the heart, and actions in the body. When you go into a deeper understanding of this, you start to relate more to formlessness vs. attachments to form.

When you are aware you are a spiritual being and live life from that place, you relate more to energy. Spiritual based love energy is pure love and positive where the humanness accepts and embraces life, living from gratitude and appreciation. Love focus increases vibration, creating more loving beliefs that serve your overall well-being. You start to relate more to the pure energy vs.

just the form. This is where you begin to have a relationship with energies and become more sensitive to them. Sometimes people get caught up in fear around the different vibrations of energies. Feeling invaded or taken over by them. Giving your power to them is a way of feeling invaded or taken over by them, thereby feeling depleted by those denser energies. These denser energies are fear based vs. love based. I discovered shining loving pink energy light in the human expression releases the hold and attachment to any dense energies.

You can raise your energy vibrations by keeping the thoughts on silence or imagining something you are grateful for. Focus your emotions on appreciation. Be grateful for all situations to present the perfect opportunity to express love. Embrace and accept, bless it, and know Universal Love is always in you and everywhere. Life is not about solving problems or suffering. If we embrace the discomfort, we do not amplify the energy of suffering. This can include how you perceive people's behaviors or situations. Focusing on both inner love strengthens the truth of love, joy, peace, etc. Universal Love is omnipresent and omnipotent. Connecting to Universal Love allows for greater love, joy, and peace at higher vibrations. There is nothing to fix. You are not broken. Choose to celebrate life and the love it has to offer.

You can shift a fear-based mentality, by seeing people and outer world conditions as temporary energies instead of attaching to the form they are in. Focus on heightened love and appreciation vs. judging it, so you don't get stuck in that energy. Judgment sucks you into the experience out of insecurity or fear. Love it all using discernment with that which is not serving you and your chosen lifestyle. If you see a repeated pattern in your life with people and situations, become the observer to see what beliefs are dominant. I call that being mindful. Focus on appreciation, love, gratitude, to keep your energy frequency high. This will prevent you from taking in the dense energy. Choose forgiveness and peace. It is not about being right rather having freedom from that which keeps you stuck. If you feel turmoil or discomfort, there is something for you to learn from that situation. Move any potential thoughts out of judgment and into the heart feeling love with situations that could potentially annoy you or surrender it to the Universe if it becomes easier to do that instead. Stay present without comparing beliefs about the past or future. Connect to Universal Love for unconditional love.

Sometimes we get caught up in prayer with the uncertainty we experience. The prayer is either coming from fear, limitations, or insecurity or from love, abundance, and confidence. Prayers come from a lack focus when you feel something is missing. Prayers come from an abundance focus when you have a knowing the Universe supplies all. I call that intention setting in place of prayer because there is more of a belief it is already done. This allows you to flow with life and trust. Human ego controls when you put too much effort in attempting to force an outcome. This creates undue stress where you over think and over analyze. Lessons occur for spiritual evolutions, suffering is optional. Freedom reigns when you let go of past regrets. Focus on now, not tomorrow or yesterday. Clarity comes at a heightened level and better than the human thoughts can conceive. Focusing on the now makes life more adventurous. As we let go of any resistance to life lessons, we are choosing to *align to Universal Love..*

In the latter part of March in the year 2011, I had a dream where I saw this alien ship spin fast. I saw a male, and he said that I was far enough away from the 1st leg I completed where the energy was really dense. That it would be easier to attract more loving relationships. He said there are 3 legs broken into years. I am completing the 2nd leg. He told me about meeting a relationship in the 3rd leg of my life, which is the last leg, at some work project. He will recognize me. His heart is pure and will share a pure love. He is 3 years older than me. I felt excited since I have been single since I dropped in. My heart wanted to experience a loving relationship with a mate. Each morning, I brought expansive energy into the human mind and poured pure love into the human heart. The Pure Love Beings were there every day since I relied on them now. I continued to work with the human ego releasing any control triggers around challenges. Instead, I shifted my focus to acceptance. In the summer of this year is when I felt the split between the human ego control starting to lose its control and moving into my Angelic expression. As I continued to master the art of allowing with trust and faith, the human emotions became more relaxed and I was able to connect with the Pure Love Beings easier. I trained the human emotions to stop most of the forcing and attempting to control desired outcomes which when fed created pain, struggle, and sadness.

I knew I was taking the human expression into unknown unchartered territories. I decided to make it more of an adventure by living in the now with the unknown and listening for guidance along the way. I remembered to not associate myself with being the body, human thoughts, and emotions as me rather a vehicle used to support my purpose as an Angelic Being. I was able to do this by allowing things to happen vs. using the human mind to analyze, question, or force. By not identifying with the human thoughts, I was able to relax the mental chatter with love and listen for inner guidance from the Pure Love Beings. I discovered the human mind and emotions got stuck in a negative realm, dropping my vibrations. This was making it harder for me to hear the Pure Love Beings. I would still get messages in my dreams, billboards, from people, and through nature. Quieting the mind and calming the emotions, made it easier to raise the vibrations so I could hear them.

On Oct 25, 2011, I experienced a deep knowing that I was going through training to become an Arc Angel. I felt this barrier that felt like a huge block on the 3rd chakra fall away as I put all attention on the Pure Love Beings. The year was teaching me about building the inner confidence in the world and not allow myself to get sucked into the denser energies. I felt like this sponge, being sucked into negative energies, becoming insecure. It was challenging for me to connect with people for long periods of time. I was still attracting people with heavy dense energy due to them focusing on their pain and struggles and complaining about them. Healers suggested shielding myself, using colors, expanding the aura and creating mirrors. Nothing seemed to work.

I kept requesting guidance from the Pure Love Beings. Part of what became clearer in my guidance was that I had a lesson of strengthening the human core which was a 4-year cycle of learning and experiencing. This made sense as to the reason the shields, colors, and expanding the aura did not seem effective. I discovered that embracing it with love and raising my energy above it helped more than shields, colors, and expanding the aura. Shields, colors, and expanding the aura comes from a protective focus which comes out a fear. I created a loop of repeated patterns in different forms to see the addictive pattern. I created more lack, fear, and negativity from not knowing what to do and from focusing on what I didn't want to experience. It was not that the shielding, colors, and expanding the aura were non-effective tools. It was the reasoning behind doing it that was not effective. Fear attracts more fear when empowered. Love transmutes the fear, providing a greater connection to the Pure Love Beings.

I kept seeing signs with the word "LOVE" or heart shapes. Flower heart shapes, leaves, rocks, in the clouds, even in writing when I did nature walks or on billboards when driving. I saw hearts all over the rocks, on the ground, and on a mountain top. I would get messages on Facebook, see messages on billboards, people would say something to trigger love. The Universe was sending me signs to put all my focus on love and to "be" love. The initial challenge was when I experienced temporarily going into a human identification, which felt like an extreme dense energy in the human form. This occurred when human lessons required maturing and evolving, and the emotions hooked in with that lesson. I would get sucked into that vibration and become disoriented. If I resisted or judged what was necessary to evolve or release, the energy became more intense. The lesson behind the experience would continue with others or with the same person until a peaceful closure came about. I learned resistance is futile. I started to understand that judging and fear are like the glue that sticks to what we are judging since it is a human-based reaction. Forgiveness is the first step to un-gluing. One of the biggest challenges I also was mastering was not to personalize or identify with other people's behaviors. If I did, I started to have more of a human experience instead of expressing Angelic love.

The human emotions had so many self-inflicting beliefs that required transforming. Transforming them required strengthening my inner confidence and enhancing self-love. Empowerment strengthens the mind and heart to greater levels of self-love, self-worth, and self-value. These self-defeating emotions were so ingrained, that I had to dive deeper within to experience them to free their hold on me. When I gave those self-defeating emotions power, I became sucked into that vibration. It was like I got mesmerized by them and fell asleep in those energies. When I identified with the self-defeating emotional beliefs, my awareness of being an Angelic spirit having a spiritual experience went into a sleep mode. The human ego would become active and the self-defeating beliefs would play out where my self-worth and confidence would start diminishing. The more the self-defeating beliefs got fed the greater the negative influences.

It became much more difficult to detach from the experience. until I surrendered the hold and shifted the vibration into love. The attachments to the familiar seemed more comfortable than the unknown. The human ego enjoys instant gratification. When the human ego starts to feel contrasts to that, it goes into a protective mode. I learned how the human emotions operated during these emotional energy shifts. I became aware how whatever we put our attention on long enough we attract more of that. Focusing on lower emotional frequencies such as, anger, sadness, jealousy, and fear all deplete people's energy. When I identified with any of the lower emotional frequencies, It was like I was living in two worlds. One world being the Angelic Realm of pure love and the other being the human emotions experiencing neediness. They seemed to conflict with each other since the human emotions were craving love from other people and it showed up as neediness.

When I gave my power to the human emotions, I would entertain the experience and join into the vibration without even knowing I was doing it. It felt like I was in sleep mode have one nightmare after another and giving it my power. I got sucked into this dense energy and allowed it, making it more difficult to get out. I would leave feeling exhausted and lost. It took sometimes up to 2 days to get the energy back up to a more positive loving energy. Eventually, the 2 days turned into hours, where I was able to process and raise the vibrations sooner and reconnect to a higher expansive vibration of love quicker and easier. I was always aware of being an Angelic Being. I was not experienced with handling dense energy inside. Sometimes I became insecure due to becoming attached to the energy around the self-defeating beliefs which triggered the mental stories and emotional discomfort. I quieted the mind and embraced the emotions. What would normally take someone days or weeks to process, I was able to release the outdated beliefs quicker due to the awareness of not being the body, mind, or emotions. I had a deeper love connection to the Pure Love Beings.

When I identified with the human needy emotions and got sucked into them, I experienced so many lessons that seemed like negative influences. I kept going outside to find positive nurturing influences, only to experience the negative in the form of drama instead. I learned so much about detachment, acceptance, patience, and compassion. Instead of looking at the lessons as problems that required fixing and correcting, which would only lead to blame, I shifted the perspective. Detachment from the emotions was one way I was able to shift the emotional control. Accepting the current negative conditions was the next step to moving my attention from giving my power to the outside world. I kept giving the unpleasant conditions power so, I got stuck in the trap of identifying with the human negative emotions letting them control me. With patience and lots of nurturing, I was able to start taking better care of myself. I chose to have compassion with what I saw in the outer world so I did not get sucked in with judging, care-taking, or playing the teacher role. I fully understood what the Angelic guidance meant when they said to "take care of myself." One day I sat down and asked, Why would we waste so much energy focusing on forgiving someone? How about not judging them and then moving on and living our life with greater joy? We waste so much time getting upset with others about what they are doing either because they can or they do not know any better.

A challenge perception turns lessons into growth. It is defined as serendipity living where you turn lessons into wisdom and greater opportunities.. Challenges teach us lessons to learn, where we acquire emotional growth and wisdom. The focus is more on the unseen positive opportunities. Trusting and allowing for direction on bringing what one would like to experience in life. We have more fun because we have a positive attitude with the lessons. Life is more enjoyable. A problem-oriented focus turns lessons into struggles and pain. It is defined as Murphy Law Syndrome where you turn lessons into failures and complain about them. The focus and attention is more on what you don't want resulting in fear, insecurity and drama-based living. Fearing only kept us stuck in insecurity and the negative influences. This pattern continues with more of the same life experiences until a choice is made to quit focusing on what is wrong and complaining about it. Then, there is an opportunity to make a commitment to focus on appreciation and gratitude. To take steps to choosing to be happy.

Embracing the challenge provides greater insights and growth on what the challenge is teaching us. Once we are complete with what the challenge is teaching us, we receive clarity and insights from the learning. We move into inspired action where we can take proactive steps to create favorable results. My Angelic Guides instructed me to raise my vibrations and transmute the self-defeating energy. This is one of my gifts to shift energy from a dense vibration to an expansive frequency through love. By raising my energy above to a higher frequency level, I was able to shift the self-defeating beliefs to an energy and transmute them. The human ego was not able to attach to them since they were now in an energy format so it was easy to transmute them. After the energy around a particular self-defeating belief got transmuted, the Pure Love Beings would download a higher loving frequency energy into the emotional energy field. That turned into new healthier beliefs and emotions. The pure loving energy downloads made it easier for me to connect to Universal Love since the frequencies were higher. I would get clarity on what I was learning after these downloads. The more I rose the emotional vibrations, the more I freed myself from allowing negative influences to control my life.

Since I did not feed the human ego by reacting, I felt calmer. Then I would quiet the mind by allowing the thoughts to float on imaginary clouds and nurture the emotions by imagining love soothing the heart. With practice, I was able to shift the focus away from the mental stories and instead put the focus on love. Fears and insecurities eventually weakened its pull on my attention. I was able to move the energy from a dense place to that of a higher vibration since my attention was on love. This provided greater wisdom and strengthened inner love and confidence. In order to have a healthy and strong emotional foundation, I chose to stop participating in any form of drama based or story based chatter. By not participating or giving any power to the drama or story based chatter, I was able to keep a stronger connection to Universal Love. We all know that Love is the highest vibration and the Inner Spirit and Universal Love comes from a place of pureness and unconditional love. Gratitude, appreciation and positive focus thoughts are of a more expansive vibration of Love. This keeps us connected to the higher vibration of Love which enhances greater levels of joy, inner peace, and playfulness. Alternatively, fear, insecurity, negativity, and limitation moves one into a lower vibration, thereby experiencing judgment, conditional love, struggle, pain, and conflicts.

In the earlier years, I was mostly supported by the Angelic Realm. In the year 2010, I got more support with pure loving energy downloads from These Ascended Pure Love Beings and the Angelic Realm. Christ would also appear sending love in my heart. I knew as I focused on love, I would not get caught up in the lower emotional frequencies. I was still getting reminders in a variety of heart forms to keep my energy expressing love. I was seeing leaves fall off the tree in the form of a heart, heart-shaped rocks, hearts ingrained in cement, in the soil, and in the clouds. I remember seeing hearts on top of trees and the word love all around the floor one time. I was getting messages on billboards, Facebook from strangers and from people reminding me of love. It helped me remember to focus on love and stand strong in the energy of love. Sometimes I would actually leave the body, pull the energy that was not serving out to get transmuted. The Angelic Realm and the Pure Love Beings would download pure loving energy. The body felt lighter as I came back into the body.

Strengthening the partnering bond with Universal Love, allowed me to flow more with life and see the world with a different set of eyes, my Angelic eyes. When others received the energy downloads and their self-defeating beliefs got transformed, I saw how they became aware and their energy in the body got lighter in energy frequency. Their Inner Spirit's mind became more awakened where they experienced a heightened level of freedom from limitations, fears, and insecurities. Prior to that, they experienced feeling stuck in a lower vibration which created struggles and confusion. Freeing yourself from these dense vibrations consists of having a committed relationship with Universal Love. People can help. It is still up to you to commit to this freedom. Excuses with regard to limitations, whether it be money, past relationships, or age, is the human ego controlling and this will only keep you stuck in what you are judging, complaining about, or disliking. I learned that the human ego attaches to beliefs vs. energy behind the belief. The mind sees the belief, and either enjoys or judges it.

I focus on energy which is formless until it is "grounded" in the human ego's mind, emotions and body. The human mind becomes educated through an Intellectual mind, the Inner Spirit. The Inner Spirit for me is the Angelic expression. The intellectual mind is innovative, unlimited and free-flowing. The intellectual mind is completely free of any familiar stories that the human mind has stored. Human emotions are condition based that associate with their belief systems. The human emotions develop greater levels of unconditional love as the emotions become more evolved spiritually. Universal Love provides greater frequency levels of pure love. When inner love is solid enough, confidence increases and outside influences have less impact.

My quantum leap into my Angelic expression occurred one day when I started to experience out of nowhere this longing and a very deep feeling of emotional discomfort. My commitment to connect more within to Universal Love to feed the emotions. The human ego wanted to act on the desire for human love, bringing up desired memories about wanting to experience a relationship and get married. The human mind attempted to create some meaning and wanted to figure out the reason I was not married. I was experiencing a habitual mental story that kept focusing on what was wrong and missing. This only led to insecurities, fears, and limitations which attracted experiences that mirrored those fears, insecurities. and limitations. I chose to transform the addictive pattern. The pattern continued on and off until 2015.

The more I focused on Universal Love, the less the emotions pulled on me for their attention. It was like a child that finally felt love and relaxed in that deeper love. I kept going deeper within strengthening self-love and enhanced feelings of worthiness. This also shifted my perception to compassion vs. personalizing other people's behaviors. I let go of thinking something was wrong or I was missing out. No more wanting to fix, correct, and judge those parts that got perceived as insufficiencies. I knew I was Universal Love's reflection of pure love, joy, peace, prosperity, and health. Whatever you focus on long enough keeps you stuck in that vibration. By staying connected to Universal Love, I was able to break the attachment around being married.

The more I chose to know the truth of Oneness with the pureness of Universal Love, the higher my energy of love became. I had learned to shut off the energy of duality and turn on the energy of expansive vibration of inner love, inner joy, and inner peace. Feeding this solidified a stronger connected bond to Universal Love. Feeding the duality only kept me stuck in fear and insecurity. It kept me trapped in an illusion that felt separate from feeling love and I experienced emotional turmoil. This turmoil only made me feel needy and lost where I wanted to be married and loved. I continued to dive deep into some core self-defeating beliefs in November and December of the year 2011. The Angelic Realm, Christ Love, and the Pure Love Being which I now called, the Universal Pure Love Beings assisted by transforming the beliefs into healthier beliefs. Below are important dates of the interactions I had with the Universal Pure Love Beings.

November 15th, 2011, I experienced a deep awareness of how my confidence was getting stronger and not taking in others' beliefs and energies as much. I came into a realization that I no longer chose to fix, correct, blame, teach or judge, where people are at in their own evolution. Acceptance and using loving discernment vs. protective energy made it easier to be around denser energies. I had reached a plateau of experiencing longer time frames of strength in the new energies that continuously got downloaded. Much of the programs from the other expression's family heritage got transmuted. It became easier to hold the higher frequency of love vibrations without getting sucked down into the denser energies. I still had to empower the emotional belief system making it easier to express my Angelic purpose more effectively.

November 16th, 2011, I imagined putting thoughts on clouds to float without putting attention on them. I became an observer of the thoughts and if it started to move toward a story chatter, I would visualize it sitting on the clouds and put my attention on the heart and breath. I would open the energy field and ask the Universal Pure Love Beings to download love to help the human mind experience the expansive energy of unlimited abundance.

November 24th, 2011, I experienced a deep realization that I no longer had to experience the material "limitations" in life from all the programs that were continuously being played out. I had so many programs about survival and saving. It took energy and time to diffuse the reactive energies surrounding the beliefs when they got challenged. I had some limiting beliefs around money. The beliefs around spirituality and the relationship with money were one of them. I kept getting spiritual people do not like money.

Materialism and spiritualism seemed to clash. The other expression's ancestral family beliefs around saving got triggered often. Unraveling the self-defeating beliefs was a chore yet well worth it. As the energy got transmuted through observing, neutralizing the hoarding through embracing, transforming the dense energies around money, and then downloading a higher vibration, I started to experience the energy of prosperity.

Materialism turned into prosperity consciousness, which had a different vibration and meaning behind it. Witnessing others with a materialism mentality I saw more of a "me" focus. To me, spiritualism has a "we" focus. This includes the Universe, the well-being of the Earth, and all that resides. Prosperity is much more than money. The more I aligned with the abundance energy, the easier it became to release the outdated beliefs of limitations and new beliefs around it got formatted. It took 3 years to clear and transform the limitation energy into healthier beliefs. Universal timing also played a key role.

November 28th, 2011, I consciously chose to close my relationship to drama energy. I no longer chose to associate with people who told drama stories and complained. I did not participate in their stories. Instead, I would bless them with love. I was aware of how drama depleted my energy when I gave it power and I felt disconnected from the Universal Pure Love Beings. I would feel deep sadness and insecurity. I also experienced confusion since the energy didn't resonate with the connection I had to the Universal Pure Love Beings. I did not relate to the drama even though the human expression did since it experienced it throughout this lifetime. I set boundaries and even verbally expressed that I no longer allow drama in my life and choose joyful living. I heard angels clapping at the choice I made.

December 12th, 2011, I had a dream where I received lots of messages about connecting stronger to Universal Love and less to the outside world so I was less affected by the outside negative influences. I knew my connection to love would strengthen as I kept my focus on the Universal Pure Love Beings and raising my energy to connect stronger to them. Strengthening the inside leaves less room for outside appearances having a negative impact. When I focused on the outside world and fed it with mental stories, I would get sad and physically tired. This would leave me in a place of frustration. I would take the time and ask for forgiveness with the situation and people involved. The struggle was not worth it. I would often go into hiding and isolate myself so I could get my energy back up. I enjoyed my company so much that I went into a monk phase. At times, I felt lonely only creating addictive patterns around searching for the mate. That led to me finding incompatible relationships.

I knew it was necessary for me to break that pattern quickly since it got fed often when I went into isolation. This only triggered the human emotions to become dominant again this hunger for love. That only created needy relationships wanting me to help them where I would go into a protected mode. This became too much of a distraction for me where I was not able to connect to the Universal Pure Love Beings. I went deeper inside and allowed the vibrations of love in. This helped relax the human emotions. Once I became more aware of how to do this, I started to feel freer from the human emotions controlling. I became more supportive, accepting, and compassionate with others without getting caught up in their stories and emotional drama.

December 18th, 2011, I felt the human mind expanding more into the intellectual mind. I was able to have a deeper connection to the Universal Pure Love Beings. I experienced abundance which I felt was different from what I experienced with the human ego desires. It was at a heightened energy level.

December 19, 2011, I started to feel a deep releasing of the other expression that resided in the body with regard to relationships. I recognized that this form of releasing was coming from the emotional and mental plane in the physical realm. After the energies got released, I experienced energies from the Angelic realm coming into the human expression. I saw how the physical realm is denser when it turns into form and how the energy can either get stagnant like sitting water and become more "polluted." That causes emotional discomforts, physical ailments, and mental stories which would trigger the human ego control to become active with a fight, flight, protect mode. When energy comes into the physical realm at a higher frequency and solidifies, you experience more gratitude, appreciation, vitality and health.

I did 12 days of silence, not talking to anyone. I decided to train the mind what it feels like in silence and chatter less with gaps of silence. When chattered thoughts occurred, I was able to move it into silence quicker since I chose to stay in silence. This created more of a self-reliance instead of emotional neediness. I was so aware of how the emotional discomfort got triggered. If played out, it would create an anxious feeling, and a scattered energy wanting to have comfort and support. My decision at that moment was to break this pattern of neediness. It took 8 months to shift from feeding the denser energy of negativity mirrored from the beliefs, fed by the fears, insecurities, and limitations to that of a higher vibration of love, confidence, and abundance. I practiced taking deep breaths, nurturing myself, surrendering the story and emotional discomfort to the Universal Pure Love Beings, and then rose my energy to a higher love vibration. The Universal Pure Love Beings continuously download pure love energies in the body, mind, and emotions. These energies supported the calming effect. My commitment to being happy and having inner peace helped make the process easier. By strengthening the connection and focus to self-love, the human emotions became more relaxed instead of making life more of a struggle.

December 31, I continued the silence without talking to anyone where I experience practicing going inside. I was so used to processing lessons by talking to others and getting caught up at times in the energy. I became so aware of how I quickly wanted to call someone when the lessons became too much for me. Seeing how the human emotions would amplify where I wanted to share to get internal support. I was not able to pick up the phone since I was in silence. I was so taken by how I was able to stop myself and just be in the present moment with this energy that I was processing. My commitment to silence was greater than breaking it to talk to someone. In meditation, I experienced a deep and profound connection quicker to The Universal Pure Love Beings. The energy was so expansive and playful. There was no fear, negativity, or judging coming from the thoughts or emotions. It felt so freeing and alive. I experienced deep emotional joy.

I saw how I became so caught up in the form of this body that I got stuck in the control of the human emotions. I chose to break the pattern that was created when I allowed the human emotions to control. The strength of the Universal Pure Love Beings was so amazing that it amplified the energy of love. This felt so nurturing and peaceful. My confidence grew with this awareness. My choice was to break the pattern of immediately going to the phone when I was processing and instead go into meditation. It was not an easy pattern to break, and I committed to doing it anyway. The human emotions were so used to panicking when it went into the fight, flight, protect mode. Not having enough human nurturing in this lifetime was part of the issue. Connecting to the Universal Pure Love Beings helped, yet there was this longing for human connection. I was learning to *not feel* I had to have it with others and instead get it from the Universal Pure Love Beings.

I decided to train the mind to go from silence to gratitude and then into silence and the emotions to feel self-love and appreciation. I knew I wasn't the body, mind, and emotions. I experienced life through the human expression. This made it easier to go into silence and feel love. I surrendered outdated beliefs to Universal Love so that the mental story was not getting fed. Feeding the mental story would have caused the emotions to react. I focused on love and then I would call in more nurturing love from The Universal Pure Love Beings so that I would feel it more in the body, mind, and emotions. I meditated, swam, and enjoyed nature to regain my inner connection. I committed to strengthening my inner confidence. The more I was able to raise the vibration the less affected I felt by those in fear and insecurity.. I knew I had a lesson around empowerment so that I would live my life having a positive impact on others instead of giving others my power and losing my connection to love, peace, and inner joy.

As an ultra-sensitive, at times I would feel pulled into their intensity. When I was around denser energy, it was easy for the body to go into a protective mode to avoid getting sucked down by the heavy energy and becoming insecure and upset. The human emotions would take over and I would go into a panic mode. I felt like a victim losing my sense of inner peace. I had challenges holding on to the higher vibration in denser energy with those in judgment, negativity, or anger. The only relief was to get it to a high enough vibration to calm the human emotions down. Keeping my energy high was crucial to staying connected to Universal Love. Eating healthy, rest, exercise, meditation, walks in nature, baths, happy music, staying positive, and surrounding myself with other positive people are examples of how I kept my energy high. If I noticed my energy was low, I would become the observer. I focused on love, joy, and peace as I stayed present with what I was experiencing. This calmed the emotions. Instead of going into a protective mode, I embraced my feelings with greater love and focused on Universal Love.

When I was around others that were drama oriented, I was either changing the subject, accepting where their consciousness was and blessing them, or interjecting that I chose to stay positive and happy. We can get so concerned about hurting others' feelings that we listen and get discouraged when we give our power to the drama. For me it was about setting healthy boundaries and honoring the choice of how I would like to live my life. If something was not serving me or was making me unhappy, I would shift my attention to take better care of myself. Saying, "I chose happiness." I avoided giving opinions. I knew that would compare self-beliefs with what others were saying.

Chapter 4

Graduating to Arc Angel

Evolving the emotions allowed for an energy shift in the heart to that of an Angelic. Eventually, the frequency started to expand at an energy level that felt more comfortable living in the human expression. I started to channel energy grids for higher love frequency energy to come on Earth to support the awakening and activate the Inner Spirit of those in human form. In order to fulfill this mission, I had to go through rigorous experiences to graduate to an Arc Angel which completed in 2012. I learned to align and solidify the connection to the Universal Pure Love Beings so that I was a strong conduit for channeling the pure love frequencies.

The body was getting ready for 2016, where, my Angelic Being takes over and the human ego control no longer exists as it did in the past. In order to start the process, the body had to shift to a higher love frequency. With the support of the Universal Pure Love Beings, I started the commitment to this process. I committed to breaking the pattern of allowing negative influences to affect me. I was learning to become more aware of my focus on love vs. giving my attention and focus on the negative vibes from people or situation. Being an ultra sensitive, I first had to take a step away from that person or situation that felt negative.

I would move my focus and become the observer to see what lesson the experience or person was showing me. I would take a deep breath, laugh to break the pattern of the human mind focusing on the experience, and avoid any judgments. I would put all my attention on Universal Love and talk about this amazing love to keep me focused. If I noticed the human mind wanting to gather the meaning of the situation and the emotions playing out the discomfort, I would surrender that to Universal Love. If it was difficult to let go of the mental stories and the emotional discomfort, I would call a practitioner or minister to share and get nurturing support. After sharing, I was able to let go of the stories and nurture myself. Calling for support vs. going immediately into meditation was necessary during this lesson.

I was not aware of how I was allowing others to pull my energy down to a denser vibration until I felt disconnected. At times, I felt overwhelmed. It felt like people were attempting to sabotage my connection to Universal Love. It was like going into one room filled with happy people and leaving feeling pumped up and excited. Then going into a room filled with drama and leaving feeling exhausted I had to learn how to set healthier boundaries. Since I was not aware of how I was giving my power away energetically. I had to first learn how this was happening.

I started observing everything from an energy standpoint. This helped me see how energy works in the human form. The ability to have more space between myself and the people I was in contact with helped me to understand how energies work on the Earth. I quickly became aware when I judge or become uncomfortable, I immediately got pulled into the experience I was judging and became uncomfortable until I made peace with it. That seemed to break the energy cords. I created an energy grid around the body so that I can practice in a more peaceful way and learn how to master being "in" the world without being "of" the world. I started to focus on strengthening the inner world by going deeper within with my connection to the Universal Pure Love Beings. There were core beliefs that were conflicting. I paid attention to what I was experiencing with people from an observer standpoint. Feelings and thoughts of something not being right, not feeling enough love, or something was not aligned with my Angelic purpose kept getting triggered.

The more I fed the insecurity, limitations, and fears, the more I identified with the human expression and the frantic energy in the body, mind, and emotions became a hook. Continual doing of activities to keep busy-a form of avoidance, worrying, analyzing, attempting to figure out, fixing, complaining, judging, resisting, reacting avoiding, procrastinating, etc. only feeds it and creates more of it. I just became so aware of this pattern. When something triggers human insecurity, limitations, fears, I nurtured the human emotions and became present to see what was going on. I did not play out the mental stories or allow the emotions to take over. As a detached observer, I was able to see what the people were showing me without getting hooked into the story or emotions. This helped me relax, experiencing inner peace, joy, and love and free myself from identifying with any mental story or emotional discomfort. Quieting the mental chatter around any familiar belief patterns and self-nurturing supported a stronger connection to Universal Love.

The thoughts and emotions were weakening their control, and I created a oneness with the connection to the Universal Pure Love Beings. In the process of mastering this lesson and shifting it to a solid foundation, I experienced out of nowhere this deep longing and a deep feeling of pain like I never felt before. The human ego wanted to act on it and attempt to stop the pain. I called in the Angelic realm to help me, feeling a burning warmth in my heart. I was able to acknowledge I had an addictive pattern that was dying off. I took deep long breaths, staying present, feeling the energy around the emotions. I kept embracing all that was coming up. I would move into observation without attempting to get a meaning behind what I was experiencing. I knew that would only prolong the pain. Instead, I chose to love, accept, and embrace vs. judge or resist. I did not make any phone calls. I chose to relax and just be one with what I was experiencing. Within a short amount of time, the pain started to subside, and I started to feel relief. When I applied this with any self-defeating habits, they became weak and lost control over me. I chose not to blame the condition. I knew that as I stayed present to the experience that whatever was happening would eventually subside. I did not reject it or make it bad. I chose to continue to let go of any mental stories and nurture the emotions. I didn't take any action until I felt my connection to inner love, peace, and joy again.

Outer world conditions and people can attempt to get your attention and get you to entertain in the drama. Bless it with love saying no thank you and put your attention on self-love. Focus on gratitude, appreciation, affirmations, people, and places that are nurturing. Reacting to others' behaviors means then there is something within you that requires transformation. The area you are reacting to is the clue to a self-defeating belief that is active. Reacting to that behavior only gives your power to it and then you get hooked into it and start participating in it. Instead, you can become aware of that behavior and transform it by embracing it vs. becoming fearful or insecure. You do not have to react from the self-defeating beliefs others are showing you. Participating gets you sucked into the negativity, limitations, fear, and insecurity around the self-defeating beliefs. Instead, you can bless it all with love and stay in compassion. That is discernment.

Ideally by strengthening your inner sanctuary on some level you are not empowering the human self-defeating behaviors. Instead, you are strengthening unconditional self-love, joy, peace, health, vitality, and prosperity. The minute you give any self-defeating behavior power, it takes you away from your connection to joy and into sorrow. You can become frustrated, insecure, and fearful of that behavior and possibly that person. Your human ego control goes into the fight, flight, protect mode where it then attempts to rid, solve, fix, judge, or correct the self-defeating belief and the person. You will feel stuck in the limitations around the belief, continuing to attract more of that. Putting effort in by trying hard to shift, change, fix or correct that of which you do not like or want will keep you stuck in the struggles of that of which you don't want to experience. Lower frequency energies only keep your heart more on reactive mode, feeling insecure and fearful, and expressing negative and judgmental thoughts. Avoiding, resisting, judging, or attempting to get rid of these energies is counterproductive. Instead, you can embrace the self-defeating belief pattern and become non-attached. Then immediately focus on the opposite of what that self-defeating belief is showing you, amplifying what you choose to experience. Have courage. Relaxing, accepting and choosing joy, peace, gratitude, and appreciation is the way to unhook the attachment.

You are not the thoughts or emotions rather experience them. What you give power to in your attention or focus, only strengthens it. Almost like a bully energy where you become the victim to that of which you give power. The more you fear it.

reject it, attempt to run or push it away, the stronger it becomes. If you attempt to run away from some lesson to avoid it, it will only follow you to other places so that you can evolve the belief. You know that is an illusion to the real truth which is being happy, being peaceful, experiencing and sharing love, enjoying prosperity, and being healthy. By becoming non-attached to the contrasts, you avoid playing the teacher role by fixing, judging, correcting, solving, etc. Instead, you realize that is not who you are rather an illusion on the way you are behaving based on a belief program that you are playing out. You become aware that you are not those behaviors rather playing out a program that you attached to. Embracing and standing strong with conviction in letting it go brings inner peace. Embracing and choosing happiness, love, and peace helps you stay connected to the higher frequencies of love,

You choose happiness and peace so you decide to let go of the attachment. This keeps you from reacting and getting hooked into the story. Eventually, you transform the self-defeating belief to that of a healthier belief. By strengthening the new belief, the contrast no longer has your power. Self-defeating beliefs can keep you stuck in a life you do not want. You can become addicted to the pattern if you give it power. That is the reason I like working with the energy behind the belief. It is easier to transmute the energy because there are no attachments, fears, and insecurities when I bring the energy to a higher frequency. It is easier to transmute the energy by bringing it to a lighter love energy frequency. I discovered when the human ego is not controlling you have a greater flow and ease with life. It is easier to stay in the energy of love vs. resistance or judgment. When in judgment, the heart center closes feeling harsh energy. Love. acceptance, and discernment, opens the heart center where you feel happier and peaceful. It is more peaceful to stay loving without personalizing others' feelings even if they do it in a mean way. Potentially they could become calmer by not feeding the harsh energy. They may respond in a more loving way as well. Connecting to Universal Love brings more of that energy as you stay open to allowing it to come to you. Universal Love provides new beginnings as the new beliefs becomes stronger.

On February 1, 2012, I felt an official graduation to becoming an Arc Angel. After becoming an Arc Angel, the gifts expanded more into activating others' Inner Spirit and creating energy grids, and vortexes on Earth to support the process of downloading higher frequency love vibrations. I eventually committed to it full-time as my means of livelihood.

This year I learned more about the energy vibrations of joy and experiencing it more fully. The Angels reminded me to choose joy in my daily life/ They told me it would take time for the mirroring on the physical plane to catch up and to not personalize nor allow it to affect me. The Angels said to continue to focus on gratitude and appreciation to stay in the high vibrations of love, and to periodically go into gaps of silence/ They told me to continue to nurture the emotions to build self-empowerment. Being ultra sensitive, I experienced lots of challenges with not giving my power away. I experienced insecurity and struggled with staying connected to love. I kept bouncing back and forth between love and judgment. Whenever I experienced fear, I would either isolate myself or move into a protective mode.

I laughed often to keep me feeling joy, quieted any mental thoughts, and focused on love. I put my attention on thoughts of gratitude even if I had to pretend at first. I would focus on objects, such as the sunshine, the trees, and the birds singing, expressing gratitude and feeling appreciation. I felt emotional nurturing as I connected to nature and Universal Love. Because the human emotions felt nurturing, I felt the energy vibration of love increase. This broke the pattern of not relying on outer conditions to make me feel better. The more I fed nurturing internally the less I looked outside for it. I started to feel emotionally more whole and complete, and the more I felt this the more secure I felt inside. I focused more on the energy of love and become detached with identifying with any beliefs. I knew if I judged or feared any dense energy, I would get stuck in it.

I would experience what it was attempting to teach me, yet that was more of a struggle oriented process. If I blessed any unpleasant condition or person I encountered, I would become free of its attachment, feeling more confident. That was more playful. I already knew I was not the body, mind, or emotions rather experiencing the sensations, thoughts, and emotions. Through this realization, I was able to let go of any self-defeating beliefs. I stopped focusing on what I thought was wrong with the world. I brought the inner love, joy, and peace out into the world by playing and welcomed those that chose to join me. Those that did not, I quickly blessed and left. It became easier to align with Universal Love and nurture the human emotions. I would find objects to admire and be grateful for keeping the vibration intact as well and go into nature and swim to help increase the frequency of love. Everything seemed more mystical on Earth when I did this.

I was strengthening the partnership with the human expression and Angelic expression. As I was becoming more active in the human expression, I knew the partnership around love was pertinent. The more I more I nurtured the human expression, the more confident I became. The more connected I was to Universal Love, the higher my frequency in the human form. Both were serving the partnership. You do not ignore the human ego or discount it. You evolve the human ego and enhance self-empowerment. Solidifying the connection to Universal Love as an Angelic and nurturing the human expression made it easier to have a strong inner sanctuary foundation. I was mastering being "in" the world and not getting caught up in the "of-ness" of the world. I was "being" love from inside to the outer world instead of taking the outer world inside and becoming distraught by it.

Closing Out The Second Leg of My Life

Because the human emotions were still active on some level of control, I felt it was necessary to go slow with acting on decisions. Any decision that are made from a fearful and insecure place would only lead me more to what I did not want to experience. I didn't want to repeat experiences and run away from them. I would rather learn from the experience and walk away in peace. Then the decision I make are coming from new beginnings and happier experiences of what I would enjoy having. I made sure any decisions I made was not to run away from something. I was listening to my heart and following what I would enjoy. I chose to have clarity from Universal Love so any action I took was for my highest and greatest good. I was still closing out the 2nd leg of my life. I had some intense emotions coming up for me to transmute in a core belief system around self-love.

I knew it would not be wise to make any major life decisions. I would make sure the emotions felt nurtured and was at a more empowered secure place in my life. I would then make sure any decisions I was making was coming from my purpose as an Angelic vs. the human emotional desires. I learned not to act solely on human emotional desires in any decisions of my life. That included activities and events. If I did, it would put me in places that were not serving my overall well-being. I would leave discouraged because I would witness reflections of self-defeating beliefs or addictive patterns. I learned the hard way to nurture the human emotions, so I did not personalize any self-defeating beliefs or act on any addictive patterns. I would first meditate and make sure I felt confident and love inside. Then I would see how I felt about going to an event. If I felt happy that was a sign to go. If I felt any anxiety that was a warning not to go. Running late or not finding the vent was also a warning not to go. Universal Pure Love Beings assisted through guidance with any choices by confirming they were coming from the purest form of love.

I would ask what choice would I make if I was confident in this area and then see how I was feeling. I would check and see if I was feeling excited and ready or fearful and hesitant. If I was feeling excited and ready and felt this heightened level of love, then I knew that I was taking the right steps. If the latter, I would look inside to see what belief was not serving me. I didn't act on the choice as yet as I knew the consequences would be what I didn't want which would lead to pain and frustrations. I would check inside to see what was making the human emotions feel fearful and hesitant. I was checking to see if it was a legitimate warning or something standing in the way of my moving forward. I would write any thoughts and feelings around the experience to see if I could find a pattern. Writing helped me from staying stuck in the story or emotional discomfort.

I would write first with the dominant hand and then the non dominant. The right hand is the logical side, and the left is the feeling. By writing both using the dominant hand, and non-dominant hand, I was allowing myself to process, so I was able to let go of the attachment in the unconscious and bring it up to a conscious awareness to release. I would make it playful, so that I did not get sucked into the emotional discomfort or story and fall "asleep" in the illusion of that belief. That would only keep me stuck in a denser vibration. Keeping it playful allowed me to keep the vibration high, receiving insights at that level vs. the human mind playing out the familiar patterns and stories. The heightened awareness gave me the insights to know how to break the chains that were keeping the emotions stuck in repeated patterns.

It felt like the human emotions would share what was going on and by embracing that I was able to set what was in the way free. Other times I had no idea what was going on. I chose to accept and just let it be without pushing for clarity. I would run loving energies in the emotional, mental, and physical field to release any stagnated energies, creating more of a flow. I was more effective transmuting any stagnated energies in energy format vs. them in belief form. Energy transmutes easier to a higher vibration because the belief was not resisting or attaching to the mind chatter stories. Having awareness is great to solving and the commitment to move through and evolve it, freed me. Holding on to the self-defeating beliefs only creates mental stories and emotional discomfort. The stronger the attachment to the stories, the greater the discomfort because of giving power to it thereby it would dominate my life. I learned that loving everything was helping me to enjoy life more.

The teaching contracts with the children abruptly ended. I had about 10 contracts and all within 3 days came to an end. I was informed that it was due to budget constraints. I knew the Universe was moving me into something else. I felt sad to leave the work with the kids yet I knew there was a purpose so I trusted. More of my inborn gifts became obvious to me and I decided to use them as part of my livelihood since I work with energy and I became more confident on how to work with it on the Earth plane. Not everyone was ready for the Angelic vibration. I still experienced so much resistance to it. It did not make any sense to me. Angelic vibration is a love vibration that is pure and joyful. struggles, limitations, negativities, judgments, or fears do not exist. It is so pure and nurturing. The human mind could not understand it and yet the heart did. I realized some people were not ready and so I chose to show compassion.

When people are so used to living in a denser vibration that resonates with the limitations, negativity, judgment, or fears, they are identifying with that energy. Their mind stays stuck on the negative stories and their emotions on the discomfort. It is like being in a sleep mode without knowing how to wake up. Once awakened to this vibration of love, you will not want to go back into the denser vibration because the expansive higher frequency of love is so alive, vibrant, freeing, nurturing, pampering, and playful. The human ego control is not in the protective mode, flight mode, or fight mode. You have a sense of flowing with life in the process and enjoying the moment instead of getting to the destination and then enjoying. How exciting that is to enjoy life by living in a heightened energy of love.

The Angels shared the message again about the 3 leg phases while in meditation and in a dream while sleeping. They said the life I incarnated into had a total of what they called 3 legs. Each leg had a 27-year phase. I was completing the 2nd leg so that I can move into the expansiveness and my purpose on this planet in a greater way in the 3rd leg. I was starting to experience the UFO ships more often as the year unfolded. Below are dates that stood out in the year 2013 with my UFO contact.

January 2, 2013, I saw 3 UFO ships the size of stars. One UFO ship moved in a lower direction after I said, "if you can hear me come lower." I then felt it scan me. The other 2 UFO ships flew by it. It flicked its lights. I felt a huge surge of loving energy. I sensed that the flicked lights seemed to be their way of saying hi.

March 30, 2013, I dreamt an alien came to me and asked me a question. I don't remember the question and I answer yes. The alien stuck a needle in the lower back or butt area. I woke up.

September 10, 2013, at 1:46 AM, I felt this UFO ship scanning me. I was not sure if the UFO wanted something or was actually sharing love. I communicated telepathically, asking where they were from and to come closer. I saw them come closer seeing the light from the UFO in the apartment window They started to scan the left side of my head. It felt a little intense. I turned my body away from them. They said they were from Sirius and then left.

October 18, 2013, at 2:45 AM I saw 2 UFO ships. I heard a high pitch sound. I looked and saw one in front of me in the sky and one to its right. The moon was almost full, and the sky was clear and bright. I sent love to them. I then raised my energy into a higher vibration. I saw and felt a male energy come through the walls and turned into a man. He watched over me beaming love. I felt him make love to me and then left.

October 26, 2013, I had a dream where Sirius came to visit me in his ship spinning real close to me. I told him to come in human form. He then appeared in a human form, cute with dark hair. He told me he is here to bring light love energy on the planet. He does medical healing work with those in need.

October 28, 2013, at 1 AM I looked outside and saw a UFO ship and felt a huge surge of love energy coming from it.

October 29, 2013, at 12:19 PM, I felt the UFO ship scanning me. I again felt a surge of pure love.

November 24, 2013, I woke up and felt Sirius's loving energy. I saw human hands come down through this light from the other side for me to reach. I held onto the human hands and they started to lift up the human body. I was lifted up to a higher vibration and then I saw the Arc Angels lifting the angelic part of me up. I saw dense vibration energies inside the body getting pulled away from me. I asked if I can go a little higher and they lifted me up higher. I saw a light through this tunnel that looked like an energy portal. I started to feel more confident on Earth at this higher vibration.

November 27, 2013, I felt Sirius's loving energy. He told me telepathically that he is attempting to get to me sooner with the Universe's permission in human form. I did not know what that meant. I asked him, "Are you the relationship I am waiting for? I did not get an answer.

December 7, 2013, Sirius came to visit me. I recognized his energy signature.

December 8, 2013, I awakened feeling Sirius's loving energy. He then appeared again at 6:30 PM.

My connection with the UFO ships was coming more frequently in 2014. Below are the dates and connections that stood out the most in that year.

January 24, 2014, At 1:31 AM, I heard Sirius's high energy pitch. I felt Sirius's energy while I was in a phone conversation with this female from New Mexico. She was sharing how she thinks she is

Palladian. Her energy became heavy with drama. I felt drawn to look at the sky and out of nowhere, I saw Sirius's UFO and what seemed like 4 stars appeared to the right of Sirius's UFO. The phone conversation became static where she first could not hear me and then the phone disconnected. I knew they were protecting me from the dense energy. The phone disconnection seemed to happen every time I talked with someone who had dense energy and started to pull on my energy. I felt so relieved knowing they were watching over me and assisting by disconnecting the phone. I eventually knew that if I felt a dense energy to get off the phone quickly or they would disconnect it for me.

January 26 and 31, and February 19, 2014, I felt Sirius's energy real strong with the highest vibration of pure love. On February 19th, the energy surge of love was higher than I ever felt. Once I reached the vibration I was at, I was slowly getting the messages that I was ready to move from Lebanon, and allowing the clarity as to where. With all the traveling I was doing and exploring, I still was not getting clarity on where I was moving. I knew it was due to Universal timing. I accepted and embraced the present moment. making it easier with allowing all to unfold. The more I partnered with the Universal Pure Love Beings and let go of the human ego controlling my life, the more playful my life became. Each day I was focusing on amplifying love inside which increased self-confidence. I played the game of shutting off the outside world and tuning in and turning up the volume to the inside world. I was meditating 2 to 3 times a day. My Angelic expression in the human form was becoming more active which supported a higher vibration of love, joy, peace, and abundance. Universal energies were flowing through me making it easy to share unconditional love. I was experiencing heightened levels of abundance in a more joyful, peaceful, loving way.

As the summer of 2014 unfolded, the body had enough of the higher vibration for me to get clarity on where I was moving. I was moving rapidly into my Angelic purpose. It became clear when my Spirit Guides told me to move to Bend where I would experience the expansiveness. I received confirmation with this move when I went to visit Bend. The sky turned pink, doves flew over my head, and I felt ethereal hugs. It was magical. I moved to Bend in June and starting in July, the expansive energy started. This expansiveness felt like a balloon where my energies were continually being stretched. The energy inside the body, mind, and heart was experiencing heightened levels of loving frequencies. I received clarity from The Universal Pure Love Beings during these past 16 years. They told me I had to go through many lessons before this expansiveness could occur. I had went into nature often while waiting for clarity There was nothing I could do to speed it up. It was all Universal timing..

When I moved to Bend, the expansiveness was beyond anything I ever experienced. It was both exhilarating and exhausting. I went to the bank to deposit a check. The ATM was not working. As I left the bank, I met this lady asking her if there was another Wells Fargo close by. She offered to drive me, telling me it was close, and it was a nice walk. I laughed saying you do not know me and you are offering me a ride. How loving. She said she knows how loving I am by looking into my eyes. I told her I just moved here and was looking forward to making friends. I shared that I was having challenges finding compatible friends to play with. I chose to play anyway so I did many activities by myself. We hugged and she said to be patient living here in Bend it will take some time. I wish I had taken her phone number.

After I released enough self-defeating beliefs in a core belief system, I would experience an insightful revelation like movie clips of all the lessons I went through. I saw how the meaning behind the self-defeating beliefs that triggered all the lessons and the emotional turmoil I went through. The movie clips helped me to understand in a great way. I would feel inner peace and joy at the conclusion. The new energy downloads got expressed as new perceptions. The expansiveness felt like I was flying on high frequencies of inner joy, peace, and love. I was getting downloads of energy now 2 to 3 times a day. I had to rest often to acclimate to the new energy. Evolving and expanding became easier as I let go of the energy and focus on what was no longer serving me.

Everyone has a unique individualized spiritual path.

Meditation and affirmations are tools to help deepen the connection to self-love which is necessary for the expansiveness. Amplifying energies of self-love allows the human ego to feel heighten love and thereby relaxes its control. It becomes more receptive to these heighten levels of love which support the expansiveness. Commitment is necessary because sometimes the human ego gets impatient and wants instant gratification. In working with others with the Inner Spirit energy downloads, I noticed the roller coaster feelings and experiences subsiding to a place of inner love, joy, and peace when enough of the beliefs that were not aligned with their Inner Spirit got transformed. When you commit to self-love and being happy, life becomes more enjoyable. It is so important to put your attention on Universal Love, gratitude, and appreciation daily to strengthen the bond. With this strong bond, you are not distracted from your focus to Universal Love when you are transforming outdated beliefs.

Sometimes the human ego is too attached to a problem where you become caught up in the stories and emotional discomfort. This creates dense energy. These beliefs are self-defeating or outdated because they are not serving your highest good. The more you attach to them through fear, resistance, insecurity, analyzing, or avoidance, the denser the energy. Thereby making it difficult to let it go due to the belief programs that are active. By letting go of the meaning behind the story and the attachment to the belief, you are able to move your energy to a higher frequency of love. This will transmute the self-defeating belief easier because you are not hooked into the story or emotional discomfort at a denser vibration. It is not necessary to figure out what is causing the dense energy. The human mind learns and the Inner Spirit Mind and Universal Love teaches lessons you are going through in life.

The human mind attempts to figure out, solve, judge, over analyze and compare with a condition or person. The human mind triggers self-beliefs that either resonate with the condition or person or does not resonate. If the condition or person does not resonate with the familiar self-belief, you can go into a reactive mode. Reacting with your feelings and expressing judgments. The focus is more on self-absorption and if you continue to focus on what you don't want you get stuck in a rut. You thereby. experience fear, limitations, and insecurity. To skip this process, you can surrender to Universal Love and focus on love without using the human mind to analyze, figure out, judge, or compare. If you make decisions from a limiting, fear-based, insecure place, you will attract more of what you do not want. If the condition or person does resonate with the self-belief there is more of a sense of calmness and joy. The focus is more on a "we" mentality choosing to work favorable with the condition or person in a peaceful way. In both situations if the mind is aware of choosing peace, then there is a calmness and receptivity to acceptance and greater understanding. In time if it is necessary you will know in a more heightened way beyond the human mind patterns.

As you start to move your energy into a higher vibration of love, you may come across others who have negative, judgmental, or insecure behaviors. Choosing to accept others where they are at is more peaceful than attempting to fix or change them. Avoid personalizing their behaviors, knowing they are doing the best they can from where their consciousness is at. Personalizing will only suck your energy down and then you will behave in a similar way. If you come from compassion and love, you will be more of a role model for them to learn from without having to say anything. You can choose to either leave the situation if it is too challenging or strengthen your connection to Universal Love. As you strengthen your connection to Universal Love, you become a role model for others and hopefully they wake up to love. It is best not to have expectations that they will. That is playing the savior game only to create a pattern of attracting more of that. Blessing them with love and knowing you are not responsible for their life and choices they are making is the best thing you can do to take care of yourself. Put your focus more on sharing love with those who can share it back with joy, peace, and love.

Entertaining in others' negativity, judgments, stories, drama, complaining only keeps the human ego control active. Where the teacher, social worker, caretaker, mother, father come out to fix and correct. The focus is more on the condition or person than on taking care of yourself and choosing to be happy. It is not selfish to love and take care of yourself. You are no good to anyone else if you are not in an empowered and loving place within. Set healthy boundaries to take care of yourself. Turn your attention inside your sanctuary of love and strengthen that by focusing on Universal Love. This will prevent you from going into flight, fight, protect mode when challenged by another's behavior. This will also stop any story chattering or emotional discomfort to a point of becoming insecure, negative, or upset. Nature, meditation, listening to calm upbeat music, taking a bath, and lighting candles, are ways to keep your energy at a higher love frequency. When the human ego goes into a deeper state of relaxation, you can connect to Universal Love with greater ease.

Universal timing plays a role here as well. Linear time does not exist in the ethereal realm. It is all made up on Earth. The memories of what you learned and experienced, the present which is current reality, and the future with desired outcomes you would like to experience. It is made up time in the physical realm. We get to experience this so we learn, grow and become smarter. Once a lesson is learned, it is complete and you can move forward experiencing a new lesson. Universal timing still plays a role in one's spiritual evolution. Linear time on the physical plane can keep us feeling stuck with our focus on the past with regrets, resistance to present lessons, and wanting to have future desires materialize. We can choose to enjoy life by accepting the past with appreciation and gratitude for what was learned, the present with excitement and the future with anticipation.

Multidimensional time occurs at a faster frequency with nonlinear realities where multiple time-lines are operating simultaneously. The time polarity of past and future can keep us stuck in the present repeating unpleasant patterns we are not wanting to experience in our life. This can affect our life through fear and insecurity, thereby replaying the patterns over and over until we say enough or our connection to Universal Love stops it. The past can play out in stories from familiar patterns that keep us "asleep" in that story, dramatizing it from a thought to what can appear as a book or movie with many unpleasant thoughts. Some want so much attention as they tell their story, acting like they are receiving a nomination for best imaginary book and film that feels real in life. Some want to talk about it, fix it, correct it, ignore it, avoid it, or play the pity pot role in it wanting comfort. This keeps you stuck in lower vibrations of fear, lack, insecurity, and negativity-a lose-lose situation.

We can give our power away to past, present, or future time. We can worry about future outcomes through fear and insecurity because of the unknown of what the outcome is and we can regret past choices instead of looking at it as learning lessons to become a wiser person. Even the present can create feelings and thoughts that are not serving us keeping us stuck in an uncomfortable experience or situation. If we allow time to control our life, we will never feel the true freedom of enjoying life in the present moment. As we start to expand our consciousness and connect to Universal Love, we move out of the boundaries of linear time and the densities that keep us stuck in fear, insecurity, and limitations. When we allow time to constrain us, we stay stuck in a boxlike structure on Earth filled with duality and separation. multidimensional time has no post or future. Universal Love is unlimited abundance. Therefore, through this connection with Universal Love, our consciousness knows of oneness with love in place of a separation out of fear, insecurity, and limitations.

If you believe your identity is the human programs, you become one with it. If you believe your identity is Universal Love, you become one with that. Your choices come from either the human conditions that are in human ego control, a greater level of struggle or from your Inner Spirit, a more playful, loving, and peaceful expression. Duality living creates mirrors-reflections as to where your human mind is operating from. In multidimensional time you can envision an abundant positive outcome by pulling yourself out of the current condition, without the attachment on how the outcome will occur. Visualize yourself moving out of the linear time to that of multidimensional time by dropping into one of the imaginary timelines. Your perception is what shifts you from a polarity time-line to multidimensional time by fully being in that new time-line. Notice your feelings when you move into the new time-line. Your feelings are measuring device as you let go of attachments. Linking the patterns in your thoughts with past experiences and future outcomes. keeps you stuck in them. Allowing each experience on its own instead of linking the experiences frees you from hooking into the pattern and the time sequence. You can energetically free yourself using timeless reality. Think of it as simultaneous timelines.

In the linear timeline where density is found, you have a tendency to get caught up in it like quicksand. You become confused, insecure, and fearful not knowing how to get out. The denser energy plays the game of higher and lower energy with regard to energy frequencies. When you start to feel the expansive energy in the multidimensional timeline, you are better equipped to transmute the denser energy in your current experience. See yourself moving into a multidimensional energy with a totally different outcome. One that is favorable experiencing joy, appreciation, and gratitude. Let go of the attachments to making it happen and allow Universal Love to bring to you what is necessary for your spiritual evolution. It could be different from what you hoped for and even better. Envisioning is a process to help you move your attention from what the reality of don't wants to the unseen of amazing possibilities. The key than is to let go and allow Universal love to deliver according to Universal timing. Sometimes lessons occur before the desired outcome comes into fruition to get you ready.

You can experience this multidimensional energy in all life situations, work, relationships, self, and health by focusing on moving your focus off the timeline polarity where a situation is occurring that you do not like, without judging it and then focusing on expansiveness and what you would enjoy. You can rewrite a past program that is a repeated pattern being played out by altering the energy surrounding the timeline. Choosing to have a more favorable loving, joyful, and peaceful process. Even if you are not aware of what the pattern is, you can still shift the focus by choosing to put an energy of what you would like to have. If you are aware of the pattern, you can lovingly sever any cords, energies, attachments, etc with that pattern. You can shift to an observer of that pattern and see what it is teaching sending love and positive energy in that timeline. Again Notice your feelings when you move into the new timeline. That is your measuring device if you are free of what that experience was teaching you. Any fears, judgments, insecurities with this will keep you stuck in that timeline experience until you learned enough to free you from the unpleasantness.

I had many dreams within the last 2 years where aliens and spirit guides would consistently share that as I got close to the 3rd leg that I would not be affected by denser energies in a detrimental way. I will be able to hold the higher vibrations of love easier. During the second leg of learning, I discovered how I got pulled into the mental mind stories by correcting, fixing and complaining. Once I shifted out of that, it got easier to stay in gratitude and appreciation more. I had to experience shifting the human emotions from looking outside into the world for love and instead get it from the Universal Pure Love Beings. From this knowledge, I was able to get the clarity and wisdom necessary to see how the human ego functions and what the awakening felt like in the human mind, body, and heart. Some call that spiritual awakening. As I was going through lessons to expand the human emotions, I was aware of how the human ego was more active in my life. In order to stop the human ego from controlling my life, the self-defeating emotional patterns had to evolve to a higher frequency. The emotions became more empowered with the Universal Pure Love Beings energy downloads. This eventually allowed my Angelic expression to become more active.

What I experienced was the necessity for the human mind, emotions, and body to awaken, for a total alignment with

Universal Love. There was still some fears, limitations, judging, negativity, powerlessness feelings, and judging coming through from the programs in the mental realm yet I did not give my power to them. These denser energies were having less and less power over me. I was able to transmute them quicker through embracing them. The DNA of the body was shifting from a dense energy form to a more expansive love frequency form. I experienced a stronger partnering relationship between the human ego, my Angelic expression, and Universal Love. The Angels told me this is oneness. This is where the magic of abundances occurs organically because of the direct connection. When enough energies from the self-defeating beliefs are transformed, the process of awakening starts. There's nothing I had to do. My Angelic expression becomes active with Universal timing and I was feeling prosperous, loving, and happier.

As an Angelic walk-in, I became the observer of the human mind to learn more about how it operates. I became aware of the different vibrations it goes into when it feels challenged and reacts from those challenges if fed as problems. When the human ego reacts and goes into the fight, flight, protect mode, the energy becomes denser and cords start to get created. These cords store the energy. That is how the addictive patterns get played out until the cords that hold the energy are transmuted These energies play off each other and create a spider web of more dense energies that feed off each other. The energies create a pattern of beliefs that build into a cocoon. This cocoon continues to grow if it is not resolved peacefully. You literally fall "asleep" in it, creating a domino effect of problems relating to those beliefs. The human ego becomes active when you participate in the chattered stories or emotional discomfort. Fear, insecurity, and limitations occur and the human ego attracts experiences at that vibratory level.

Self-defeating beliefs, situations, and people at that energy level continue in your life until you choose to stop feeding it, make peace, and learn from what it is teaching you. When you start to feel emotional discomfort, where the mind wants to analyze, solve, fix, resist, or blame and start to chatter about it, embrace the discomfort and quiet the mind immediately. Don't complain about the experience and feed it with more dense energy. Embrace it, nurture it, and let it go. Some people feel better and can let go of what is bothering them by talking to someone. It helps them process and receive positive feedback on how to mature that area they are learning. Like a coach, providing wisdom. By becoming the observer vs. participating in the dense energy, you can see how the story gets created, without becoming attached to the outcome or triggered by the emotions and reacting.

Choosing peace and nurturing helps to stay connected to love instead of fear. Surrendering the experience to Universal Love helps to let go of the attachment with the mental story and attempting to get clarity. Sometime the desire for clarity pushes you to react and complain. When you surrender the experience, you literally are surrendering the focus around that experience and moving into trust and faith. You then shift into abundance energy through gratitude thinking and feeling appreciation. When you let go of the fears and insecurity, or judgment around the condition, you can connect to Universal Love. You eventually will experience freedom and higher frequencies of love, joy, peace, and prosperity. Ready to take the step?

The more you practice surrendering any mental chatter and discomfort, the easier it becomes to stay centered in love, joy, and peace inside. This calming experience helps the human ego to relax. From that place, life becomes more joyful during the learning phase instead of attempting to complete it as quickly as you can so that you do not have to experience the discomfort or any confusion. Once you get the hang of how to do this, you move through lessons with greater ease, inner peace, and greater joy. This keeps you in a higher level of love instead of frustrations. Imagine how much more enjoyable life would be if you were to go through life partnering with Universal Love in a deeper trusting way. As you go through challenges, instead of sitting in them and living in the pity pot phase, you let go, learn, and move forward. You get to ride the wave of life by flowing with it instead of against the currents and attempting to swim up the stream as it pushes you down and further down. You get to ride in this luxurious boat of life with ease and comfort because you chose to live life with greater ease and you mean it. That meant you did not pick fights, or kick in the righteousness, or resist the experience that it is teaching you. You embraced it all, chose to stay optimistic and receptive to listening for guidance.

The lessons and the process toward the outcomes are both enjoyable. The emotions are calm instead of experiencing the roller coasters. You live in the present moment instead of being stuck in the past with the belief and the familiar patterns around those beliefs. You experience expansive learning because you are more aware of letting go of the human ego control and listening for inner guidance. No matter how long it takes, you know that answers will come and thereby you take it one day at a time. When you notice others who choose to stay in their stories and/or an emotional discomfort from a complaining drama oriented place, you choose to not have this type of dialogue. You realize that it is not healthy for either. People are responsible for their spiritual evolution. If they are not committed and would rather entertain the drama in life, you bless them and move away without choosing to judge or entertain them in it. As you become stronger emotionally, you vibrations increases where you don't resonate exude any fears, insecurities, negativity, or limitations.

There is this awareness that life is not about struggles, attempting to solve or fix them, only to discover another one to solve or fix. You know that focusing on struggles only attracts more problems. Instead, your attention is now on joyful living and anything that contradicts that you continually release the attention of and put it more on that of which you are in gratitude for and appreciating. You put your attention on raising the frequency to a higher vibration of love in any challenges, limitations, and discomforts that you are experiencing. You commit to shifting the focus from limitations to that of abundance. Your attention moves away from the challenge and you place it on Universal Love. Observe, embrace, surrender, release, love, and evolve, are the key words to remember. You do not ignore or resist the challenge. Your face it head on or surrender it to Universal Love. You look at the challenge as if you are staying temporarily at a hotel, experiencing something from it. You know you don't live there, just visiting so you can detach from owning the challenge as if it is permanent. You are not those lessons, rather experiencing them to evolve. Your attention if off any limitations, fear, negativity, insecurity, or judging with regard to self-defeating beliefs because you know it would keep you stuck in them. You put all your attention on gratitude, appreciation and Universal Love.

Choices we make are based on the most dominant belief system-Transform the belief system-Transform Your Life.

Bring your connection to Universal Love wherever you go, whoever you are with, whatever you are doing and when you are in your own space. Stop giving your power away to experiences or people. Everyone came to Earth to learn their own lessons and to live life. The human expression is imperfect because it came to learn and get smarter. The Inner Spirit is perfect and therefore you can trust the Inner Spirit will guide you to what you need to learn and if choose enjoy in life. Empowerment and self-love will support you to making healthier choices. Focusing on love vs. the chattering thoughts and unpleasant feelings will help to strengthen your connection. It is not about ignoring the feelings or thoughts just not feeding them with more complaints and judgments. I have an altar I created where I go to meditate and connect to the Universal Pure Love Beings. I open my heart and receive loving energy. I remember a time when I would go out and experience too much chaos, then run to the altar to recover from the experience. At that time in my life, the Angels told me to bring love into every experience instead of running to my altar. The life lessons made me emotionally empowered.

Think of it as taking your inner world of love and the connection you have to Universal Love wherever you go, with whom you are with, where you are, and with everything you are doing. The more you focus and strengthen this bond the greater inner peace, love, and joy you have. When in the midst of anything that starts to become a distraction you can close your eyes and call in Universal Love within and in the denser environment. As you become more connected to Universal Love, you shift your focus on the energy behind the form into pure love. The environment you are in or people you are in contact with that are not aligned with this expansive frequency of love can benefit by raising your own energy frequency above that of which you are experiencing. That will raise your consciousness to help you experience greater levels of appreciation and gratitude.

Some people get caught up in the denser energy because their thoughts start to judge and/or fear it. They lose their inner power to it by feeding that dense energy with their focus and become insecure. Putting too much attention on the distraction activates the human ego control. Some people become a victim to denser energy especially if they are sensitive to it. They find ways to protect themselves with shields, energy colors, grids, etc. these are great yet if you are doing it out of fear or insecurity you are only creating an invitation to more of it because your focus is on protection and fear around that of which is in a denser form. You experience deeper inner peace by embracing and surrendering the denser energies to Universal Love. Connecting to Universal Love prevents you from judging, fearing, or becoming insecure by giving your power to unpleasant experiences. Whatever you judge or fear only creates more of it in a variety of forms until you learn what is necessary from that experience in a peaceful way. By loving all parts of yourself and embracing that of which you experience with others, eventually any abrasive energy will not have a negative impact on you. Your connection to love is so strong, you don't even see or recognize the abrasive energy.

You start to feel the softer more gentle loving energy which enhances the nurturing and positive energy focus. You may start to realize how much power you have to negative energies. By shifting your focus from entertaining any negativity to happier thoughts and feelings, you feel peaceful. You realize that it is not who you are so you choose not to entertain it. You shift your perception from what you were judging or uncomfortable immediately into love and peace. As you take your focus off negative thoughts and the patterns it plays out and practice gaps of silence, thoughts of gratitude or on Universal Love, you experience more inner joy, love, and peace. If you entertain the human thoughts that are in resistance or discomfort due to a lesson you are learning or an adverse situation, it only feeds that vibration and brings in more of the same frequency. Freedom occurs when you let go and literally let the Universe be stronger in your daily life. Choosing inner joy and peace is the first step and committing to it is the second. You have to choose peace over being right, joy over the discomfort, and love over fear or judgments. The more you solidify this the greater the awareness becomes until it seeps into the subconscious and is automatically active in your life.

October of 2014, my Spirit Guides told me to let go of this armor I had around my heart. I had an armor around my heart in the earlier years that I felt was necessary to protect myself. That was an advantage and a disadvantage. The advantage is that I felt protected from any energy that was not aligned with the Angelic Love. The disadvantage was that I did not get to experience attracting the positive nurturing love on an intimate level that I wanted in human form due to the protection. I released the armor so that I could expand the energy of being in the body as an Angelic even more. I experienced this guidance sharing that I would experience lighter loving energy where love is prominent more than I did in the past.

The following day I went to this event. I had _expected_ to find others who also chose to enjoy life. What happened was not what I had hoped for. I experienced people in heavy drama conversations, focusing on their pain. The following day I went to another event optimistic. I had these high expectations that I would find people to play with. I again experienced people in heavy drama conversations, focusing on their pain. It took a toll on me. I was going out with this openness to meeting others who choose to LIVE life in joy, peace, and love and I was not experiencing this. It was so confusing. I knew I was expanding in the vibrations of love and I felt an even lighter playful energy inside. What I was seeing outside was still heavy negative energy. Towards the end of the 2 days, I got a message to go out without attachment to the outcome. A bit challenging when I chose to go out and play and what I was experiencing was people focusing more on their pain. I kept feeling that this is not where I am nor care to see anymore. I chose to surrender the attachment and enjoy life anyway, even if it meant by myself. When I went out into my daily activities, I focused on the Universal Pure Love Beings creating a stronger connection. Focusing on the love I was getting increased my confidence where I did not allow the outer world to become too much of a distraction. As I was strengthening this inside focus, I was learning to laugh and joke when it felt too intense with others. I would either change the subject or bless them and leave.

On the evening of the second day, I went to this event where we were to choose a book and flip open to a page to read. Mine came up as, "save the best for last." The edit version of it said, "we can become angry, fearful, or upset when we do not get what we want in the time frame we want it. Watching others who have attained what our hearts would like to have in life and feeling like something is missing, or wrong with us because we do not have it. We can become insecure blaming our self for reasons it is not happening such as, not being smart enough, pretty enough, rich enough, or young enough. We can blame people or conditions for not having the life desired. The only thing that stands in our way is insecurity, doubt, fear, judgment, and negativity of ourselves and others. As long as we deny or delay our good than we are not ready to have it. Only Source can truly provide what is best.

The Universe is the source of all. To open our hearts and be strong. To believe and have trust. When you honestly want for others, the good you seek for yourself, then you are ready to receive that of which you want." It was so apparent to me that a part of me was still judging and having discomfort around those with a negative close hearted energy. It was because I was "fearful" I would lose my center and thereby had to forgive those for where they are at and knew in a deeper way that I wished for them the great life too. I laughed as I realized that I could not take the old beliefs that were not serving me into this new energy and move forward with attaining my heart's desire. I was so happy to have this revelation and chose to embrace it with love and peace. I spent the day saying how much I wish the best for all and meant it. I was seeing how believing that someone or something other than myself can deny or delay my good, has kept me from having it. I had attracted exactly what I had believed.

I noticed the more I raised the body, the mind, and emotions, to a higher frequency, the more enjoyable it felt inside. It was becoming clear that the inside world was dominating the outside world with regard to the level of loving energy. That preparation from the time I dropped in and all these years since then to release what was no longer needed seemed necessary. I had to release enough of the denser energy so that I can experience more of the Angelic energy. I would have loved it if I could have done it when I dropped in, yet the body was not ready for it nor was Earth to hold the energy frequency. All of this was part of the Universal timing. In the midst of losing focus on this amazing love vibe, the Universal Pure Love Beings said, "which is louder in my life, human ego control which creates reactions and struggles or the Angelic Spirit which is a strong connection to the Universal Pure Love Beings?" It made me realize with confidence that if I forget and move into the human conditions, I am immediately guided and reminded to move out of that focus and thereby that control. I became so grateful for this realization and support. Anything that was not coming from love was no longer staying in my energy.

The following day Universal Pure Love Beings asked the question in a different way. It felt almost like a déjà Vu. "Do you want to let the human ego or Angelic expression control my life?" I, of course, said the Angelic expression. I felt the energy shift to my Angelic expression becoming more active and the human ego control losing its power. I felt light in the body, a deeper sense of inner peace, joy, and heightened love. I started to experience heightened energy levels of joy that continued into the next day. I kept the mind chatter to a minimal by creating silence gaps and shifting them to gratitude. I focused on appreciation, putting my attention on things I enjoyed. The human expression was experiencing a higher frequency vibration.

From the year I incarnated until 2014, I was strengthening the emotions toward more self-love, self-care, and self-worth. All this contributed to the expansive Angelic frequency of love, which brought greater clarity on my purpose on Earth. I knew my purpose was to assist in the awakening of human consciousness as an Angel and Medium messenger and being a conduit for the Universal Pure Love Beings to activate people's Inner Spirit. When you have a strong connection to Universal Love vs. your fears, limitations, and judgments, you experience a greater receptivity of the expansive love vibration. You're aware you are not controlling the process nor the outcome alone rather in partnership with the Universe. When your Inner Spirit is more active than the human ego control, your daily life has lots of unknowns. This is because you are not using the familiar mind stories that were active when the human ego was in control mode.

The familiar patterns and focus on the stories behind that created feelings of stuckness, repeated patterns, and stagnation in your life. When your Inner Spirit is dominant in your life, there are no familiar patterns and stories to attach to. All is coming from innovation and expansiveness. Living in the unknown becomes more of an adventure with life and enjoyment instead of fear or worry about it. You have greater confidence and trust. There's less domination with the human ego control personalizing or allowing insecurity, fear, judgment, negativity, and limitation to take over. That makes the unknown path more enjoyable because you know you are not alone and you experience greater levels of love in the process. It is so peaceful to have this in your life instead of feeding your daily life with worry, fears, insecurities, and frustrations. I was continuing to enjoy my connection with Sirius. Below are more highlighted dates.

July 3, 2014, at 2 AM I saw Sirius's UFO. I Felt lots of pure love

July 7, 2014, woke up and saw Sirius's UFO. He connected a cord from my heart to Universal Love and another cord attached from me to the man I will have a relationship with. I saw the energy of the guy. He also had cords connected the same way as me.

July 11, 2014, While napping, a UFO invites me in their ship. When I entered, they informed me that this particular UFO will not visit Earth anymore.

July 14, 2014, I felt Sirius's loving energy throughout the day.

July 16, 2014, at 1:11 AM and again at 2:22 AM feeling the energy signature of Sirius being real close. Felt lots of pure love

July 17, 2014, I felt Sirius's loving energy felt throughout the day

July 26, 2014, I went to a workshop that was heavy in drama. I started to feel overwhelmed by the drama. I left to take a break and sat in the car to relax. I saw an orb spinning over my car feeling so much love. During the lunch break, I stayed in the room to eat my lunch. They all left. I did this exercise of watching the grass and becoming it. I saw this collie, 2 little girls with golden hair and a family pass by in front of me. The collie went toward my right foot and I took a step back. As the family was getting closer to me, I was not able to move. I experienced the high frequency of love and observed their methodical slow walk toward their car. I watched in awe, the way the mom was kissing the dog and the husband lovingly kissing the dog. I saw how they walked very slowly passed me, putting the dog in their white truck. Very lovingly moving its paw and closing the trunk and getting in the car. They each closed their doors gently. The two little girls then got into the car. I was experiencing this love at such a high frequency, more than I ever felt in a human form. I knew they were aliens. I could not speak or move until they drove away. All I could do was feel this love so pure and high enter inside me. When I looked at the time it was 1:11 PM.

From August 1-11 2014 and August 14, 2014, Sirius's energy of love was getting even stronger. To feel so much love at this amazing frequency is beyond anything I ever felt on this planet. I wanted so much for him to appear in human form permanently to have a relationship with him.

September 11, 2014, at 1:11 AM. I felt Sirius's loving energy in my heart, feeling in love with him.

October 31, 2014, I saw the time on the clock as 4:44, which meant a spiritual calling of balance and strength. I felt the flip between the human ego control and my Angelic expression during swimming. It made me aware of how human time and ethereal time are so apparently different. human time is linear with past and future. Ethereal time is multi-dimensional where you can have experiences in various time warps. When the human expression aligned with the Inner Spirit's vibration, the flip occurred. The human ego starting the flip from its control to that of the Angelic expression was Universal timing and there was nothing I can do to change it. The flip experience for me was emotional freedom where I no longer had major emotional swings from joy to sadness or any other duality types of emotions. I felt more content, a heightened level of inner joy, and peace from the nurturing that was inside. All I had to do was tune inside, and I felt happy.

Feeling self-love was stronger now. When any human beliefs got triggered, it did not last long. The heightened nurturing love transmuted the energy before the human mind could analyze or the emotions getting caught up in it. I was not concerned about what others said or felt. I started to feel more of the nurturing energy which the Angels told me would amplify each month and become heightened in May 2015. Within the first week of the Angelic expression being more active, I started feeling this back and forth between the Angelic in charge and the human ego controlling. I felt the Angelic expression while swimming and afterward I felt the human ego attempting to take over. It was confusing to me and it became clearer as the day unfolded and I saw 222 on the clock which symbolized the spiritual meaning of combining the human ego and the Angelic energies into oneness.

October 11, 2014, I experienced an energy portal opening and a huge surge of high frequencies of love entering Earth. I define portals as frequencies of energy that shift from one vibration suddenly to another. I decided to meditate throughout the day to help bring it on Earth. I meditated at 11:11 and at 1:11 and felt this huge source of loving energy coming in. I channeled it all over Earth. It was amazing how much love and abundances I was feeling. I had this vision I experienced on December 31, 2010. I remember on December 31, 2010, I watched television witnessing countries being televised as they were celebrating the new year. I knew at that moment humankind had free will with the option to choose peace. Unfortunately, they did not. The angels told me to raise my energy and that the planet was going to go through a purification period. I thought that was only going last a year. It has been many years that I observed Earth experiencing a huge purification demonstrated by earthquakes, tornadoes, tsunamis, etc. I asked the Angels why this is still happening and they told me to teach people about compassion. Through struggle they would come into greater compassion and eventually choose peace. I wish people will collectively come together and choose peace.

As the days passed by, and 2014 closed, I was feeling Universal Love more and more. I became so aware of staying connected in a stronger way. Anytime I got a tinge of the human emotions wanting to control and going through frustration or any complaining, I shifted my focus to the Universal Pure Love Beings. I created these tools listed below to help with the expansiveness of the human mind, emotions, and body. By applying them on a daily basis, you will have the opportunity to develop greater inner peace, joy, and deeper love within and have less of the human ego attempting to control.

Mind: Imagine raising any thoughts up to the Universal Love. Visualize putting the thoughts in your hand, lifting them up, and surrendering them to the Universe. This will silence the thoughts.

Emotions: create a bubble around your body with an umbilical cord attached to the heart. Imagine Universal Love coming into the heart through the cord. This provides greater levels of peace, joy, and unconditional pure love.
Body: Take deep breaths in the parts of the body that you would like to relax. Breathe and imagine your body lifting up to help raise the vibration. This will help you free yourself of the heavy energy or any tired feelings you are experiencing

During meditation, I saw a vision around judgment. I saw how human ego creates duality thinking and judgment. How thoughts and emotions are detrimentally affected by finding things wrong and complaining. I also saw how the energy of appreciation, gratitude, acceptance, and love is freeing and nurturing because that releases the human ego from being in a duality type of energy. Judgment creates a feeling of missing something. It looks for things that are wrong, attempting to fix problems. Gratitude and appreciation strengthens the connection to Universal Love. When you choose love over judgment, you have a direct connection to Universal Love.

November 23, 2014 at 2:22 AM Sirius's UFO ship appeared. At 6:50 PM I felt so close in energy like I can touch it.

December 20, 2014, I felt the message to enjoy life vs. solve it.

December 22, 2014, In a dream, I saw this white orb approaching me. I communicated to the Orb saying, "have you arrived to take me with you?" The orb approached really close to me. This lady appeared and did energy work on the right side of my body.

In 2014, I started to feel the Angelic energy more fully within. I noticed that in the past when I was around others who are more in the denser energies of fear, insecurity, and negativity, I would go into a protective mode. I was personalizing it from a deep desire for friendship and people to play with only to find them still in their pain bodies and drama. That is when I started to feel uncomfortable and feelings of not belonging here on Earth would escalate. Since I was no longer into solving or fixing, I did not relate to the dense energies. There was still some more closing out with this lesson since it was still in my energy field when I went out. I knew there were some deeper patterns that required transforming. The challenge I was having with this was to become more comfortable with it. I had lots of opportunities since I had a purpose of assisting the awakening of the human consciousness.

December 24, 2014, at 10:40 AM, I was feeling the energy of love in my heart building. I saw an energy veil drop, and a huge opening with a vast amount of loving energy surround all around me. There was extremely high frequencies of love. I was experiencing how life is like an elevator and that I am raising the energy more in the body, mind, and heart. The next day, I was feeling the positive and nurturing energy of love even in the midst did not allow it. I chose to stay focused on this loving energy with gratitude and appreciation. I started to play more with raising my energy above that of which became uncomfortable for me. The Angels told me to do this about a year after I dropped into
physical form, yet I didn't know how or what it meant then.

I became aware how raising my energy as high as I can, prevented denser energy from coming in. I saw how energies of fear, insecurity, judgment, and negativity cannot reach that high so it cannot affect me. If I am experiencing thoughts or emotions that resonate to the denser energy then it invites that energy in more. I noticed that if I kept my energy on love, on an ongoing basis, that the denser energy has less power in the collective consciousness and within the human thoughts and emotions. With each day of awareness with this, it became clear how energies work on the physical plane. Judging the denser energies entertains them, fearing them contributes more to them, and allowing the negativity sucks you in. After a month of committing to raising energies to love, I started feeling the difference in regards to love, joy, and peace. I raised my energy and felt Universal Love stronger than ever. I would then drop that energy of pure love into the body. The more I did this, the more I saw how the denser energy didn't bother me as much. I felt happier and peaceful.

As I continued playing with energies at the different vibrations, I came to a deeper realization that the minute I put a thought focus on an area and feed it with emotions it became form. So I decided to create more positive thoughts. With that realization, I started to see how the human ego desires play out with this. If a desire was not aligned with my purpose, and I attempted to make it happen, I would experience conflict. I learned many years ago, that if a desire was not aligned with my purpose of being here, that it will not manifest in form. If it is aligned with my purpose and the timing is appropriate, choices and opportunities will flow organically. I also learned that timing plays a big role to manifestation. There are lessons in the form of obstacles that are necessary to learn, the readiness of all the people involved to come together, and the proper timing set in place for the synchronicity to occur. The Universe knows when, how and where it will occur, and who's involved when it occurs. I chose to believe more in the Universe and allow all to unfold organically. I knew I would get the proper messages and this deep inner sense of peacefulness with the decision to go forward..

December 28, 2014, I went to this event. The message I got from the Angels was to bring Angelic loving energy from inside to the world. I was still mastering how to be a conduit of Angelic loving energy in human form. I attended this event holding the energy of love. It was a confirmation how much easier it was to hold the Angelic vibration of love. I felt so much nurturing from Christ Love and it felt amazing. I then went to another event, I became aware of a judgment I had as I looked around and didn't see anybody celebrating life. I saw sadness, anger, and emptiness in the people at this event. I left feeling somewhat sad that no one joined me in celebrating life and the magic life offers. I became aware of how I looked outside of myself to have the same experience I was having inside.

By focusing on inner love, joy, and peace and taking that into my daily life experiences, I am allowing the mirroring to enter my life organically instead of searching and hoping it will be there. As I became stronger inside with my connection to Universal Love and knew that as my solid truth, I was ready to then share this heightened level of love as a channel. I was able to keep the "light" on to remind others of the choice to connect to Universal Love. It was not about preaching this rather being this. When I returned from the event, I went to check Facebook. This Message kept popping up saying, "a message from GOD." Each time I closed that page and reopened a new Facebook page, the message popped up. I decided to read it. It said, "put your computers and cell phones down and have a heart to heart connection."

At that moment I felt a deep energy release around fear of getting hurt in intimacy. The message of putting your cell phone down and having a heart connection was a message to connect more from the heart with love instead of fearing and protecting myself from getting hurt. I realized that was the reason I had been attracting what I didn't want to experience in relationships. It confirmed the message of letting go of the protective shield that I had received consistently and kept playing out until I made a conscious decision to let it go. When you get out of your own way and stay present in love that which is not resonating with love gets released. When you take it a step further and choose a higher vibration of love, then the body, mind, and emotions have to resonate at that frequency. Having protection from fear of intimacy was not in alignment so it got released. The fear was standing in my way of expressing my Angelic frequency.

December 30, 2014, I experienced an energy connection with the Avatars. It was my first awareness of this connection as they shared who they were. They shared how I was leaving behind the old world of suffering, which included, fears, judgments, and negativity. It felt amazing. I felt more connected to nurturing love, and life became more enjoyable. By me nurturing myself, the bond with the Universal Pure Love Beings got so much stronger. The outside world had less impact on my emotional well-being. I was not giving it as much power and control by identifying with it and the human ego emotions became less domineering. I was still strengthening this truth that I had awareness of. I did this exercise to help me strengthen this truth I chose to solidify. If I saw something in the outer world that was not coming from love, I closed my eyes immediately or looked inside with eyes open and reconnected with the Universal Pure Love Beings to help remind me of the truth of the inside world. This was a reminder that the inner world is my reality and that the outer world is temporary, based on past beliefs. The saying, being "in" the world vs. "of" the world became more realistic.

When any negative influences would attempt to cling on to me, I noticed that it was important to release it with loving energy. It became baffling to me why I had experienced negative influences so often all these years until I recently felt me raising my energy would free me of the negative influences. I trusted that these negative energies were there to teach me to strengthen the bond with Universal Love. The negative influences had lessons for the human evolution which when completed in the 2nd phase had no more purpose of being around. As an ultra sensitive person who picks up on energy, it was a challenge when I was around people I did not feel a vibratory energy of love connection with. It felt like something that was irritating me. The more the resistance or judgment, the stronger the pull into that irritation.

The more acceptance, embracing, and focus on self-care and Universal Love, the easier it was not to judge that irritation and shift it to compassion. When enough of the denser energies in the form of beliefs are evolved into higher frequencies, the Inner Spirit is activated. There is more of a oneness connection to the Universe. The result is being in the world without being "of" the world and others' depleting effects. Knowing this mentally and experiencing this are two different things. One is learning, and the latter is living the truth where you have spiritual freedom. I love playing with colors in the energy field. I imagined the body as energy, raised it and then engulfed it with white, pink, and gold light energy. As frequency of the body raised. I saw dense energy fall away at a higher loving vibration. I felt a softer loving energy inside the body. I felt a stronger connection to Universal Love.

.
People have asked me, "how do you know when the human mind,

emotions, and body become awakened enough to have the Inner Spirit become activated?" The human mind is complex, having many beliefs and limitations. Beliefs that are conscious and others hidden in the unconscious. Some beliefs activate the Inner Spirit and others put it to "sleep."In sleep mode, the human ego control will go into this fight, flight, or protect mode due to certain beliefs being challenged. When thoughts are overly active and you give it power, it controls your life, creating many complexities through its familiar belief patterns. There are beliefs that trigger the human ego control and those that activate the Inner Spirit. If the human ego is controlling a particular area in your life, you'll experience more duality living. In duality living, there will be both dormant and active beliefs that are not serving the Inner Spirit that get transformed through awareness and evolving them. The human mind will then play out the belief in the form of chatter through mind stories, creating emotional discomfort.

When the body goes into a fear mode filled with negativity and judgments, creating this domino effect of complaining or reacting. The human ego then reacts through a flight, flight, protect mode. Dense vibrations create limitations in many forms. This leaves you feeling stuck. You become stagnant, apathetic, and confused. There's a tendency to personalize others' behaviors when you feel insecure and in a protective mode. You may think people are angry with you if they're in a bad mood. You may feel you have to fix or correct others' behavior if they complain. Both are a lose-lose situation. You go deeper into the denser energies, feeling stuck and experience. more problems and discomfort until you make peace and take better care of yourself. By taking better care of yourself, you have compassion when others are in a bad mood. You know it is their lesson to learn and not to personalize their behavior. You're supportive and empathetic. This frees you to live your life with more joy and peace.

You create feelings of separateness with Universal Love when you allow the human ego to control your life and identify with it as who you are. When you give your power to any self-defeating beliefs and you continue to focus on them, you will experience many struggles. You may resist letting go of the self-defeating beliefs. resistance is futile. You may judge yourself or others who trigger these self-defeating beliefs. The stronger the human ego control, the greater the level of struggle. This creates a domino effect of more struggles and negativity you will attract. Habits and beliefs that are not aligned with your Inner Spirit attracts lessons, in the form of challenges to acquire greater wisdom, You become smarter "spiritually." Over thinking can get in the way, comparing situations and people from our familiar belief systems.

In our daily life experiences, as we keep our focus on love vs. judging any condition or person, we stay in the vibration of love. You thereby avoid attracting more negative influences. Focusing appreciation, love, and gratitude, keeps us aligned to joyful and peaceful living. Choose to celebrate life instead of commiserating, fixing or correcting the dramas in the world. You heighten the vibrations of love, joy, and peace. when you keep your focus on Universal Love. You become a role model to help others wake up. Staying connected to Universal Love keeps you away from focusing on what could annoy you. In other words, you go above the condition rather than underneath it, entertain it, judge it or attempt to fix it. If you feel hurt by another's behavior, consider the answers these 2 questions:

1) who are you working for Universal Love choosing to live in peace, love, and joy?
Or
2) are you working for the person who hurt you. Do you want to get even and hurt them back by wishing them harm, reacting, fighting, etc.?

If your answer is number 2, then you stooped down to the level of the person that you got hurt by. That only will make you more miserable and will not solve anything. If your answer is number 1, then connect to Universal Love in the heart, mind, and body and stand strong in that love. That may just wake that person up to their inner love. What a gift you gave them to "wake up" from their struggles, negativity, pain, limitations, etc. Doing number 1, shows you are coming more from compassion and love.

A Buddhist said if you do not accept the gift, it is not yours. If your focus is on someone's behavior and base your feelings on that, you are giving your power to that behavior and also judging it. By focusing on others' behaviors, you are participating on some level with it. You don't have to entertain it, by judging, teaching, fixing, teaching, giving your opinion, or letting it drain you from enjoying your life. That moves you out of inner peace, joy, and love and into a reactive mode. By focusing on love, you attention is there and not on the other person's behavior. When we are solid in love nothing can deflate it. It is like a tree that is in a storm. The strong trees stands strong and erect in vibrations of love and weathers the storm without it falling down. It may lose a few branches in the storm yet it is still strong. The weaker trees lose some branches, its roots soften in the soil and falls down. The stronger the connection to Universal Love, the greater the inner foundation with love becomes that strengthens inner confidence. That which is not aligned with love, will no longer have a negative effect and diminishes in power.

The human expression operates at the vibration frequency it is at. If your thoughts and emotions are operating at a higher vibration, you express from that higher frequency. The higher the vibration the greater the connection and partnering with the Inner Spirit. When thoughts and emotions are coming more from a dense vibration, such as complaining, judging, blaming, and sadness, you start to feel a disconnection with the Inner Spirit. You do not "kill" off the human ego. If you do, you die. Some want to hate it, judge it, ignore it, etc. That leads to is the human ego control becoming active in a greater way to protect and continue in the area you are resisting, fearing, or judging. Love is the only way. Love and embrace the parts that are not aligned with your Inner Spirit. The alignment creates a oneness connection to Universal Love vs. a separateness that creates struggles and problems.

The separateness activates the human ego control by attempting to over analyze to understand or solve it, or correct it. When there is human ego control, it uses familiar human belief programs instead of the Inner Spirit intelligence and Universal Love's wisdom. You may feel a deeper sense of frustrations, resulting in more mind chattering stories and more emotional discomfort. Surrendering the perceived problem to Universal Love, allows for enlightened solutions to come. Universal Love provides solutions way beyond what the human mind already knows. It is not about giving up rather letting go of the emotional discomfort and chattered stories. Allowing Universal Love to give you the solutions. Life is about enjoying not about struggles and pain. That is a limiting belief possibly out of a lack of worthiness or out of fear of the unknown, rejection, failing, and even success.

As you surrender the human ego control to Universal Love, you start an expansive spiritual journey toward greater freedom. It can seem challenging as you learn from the self-defeating beliefs so they get transformed. It's like you are in a cocoon getting ready to be birthed into a butterfly. Nurturing and compassion are key here so there is a stronger connection to Universal Love. Those beliefs that have been "asleep" in the denser energies of limitations, fear, and negativity will get transformed. When you feed these dense energies with your attention or claim them as your truth, you become fearful and insecure. Insecurities can hold you back from enjoying the abundances of love, joy, and peace that Universal Love only knows of. Having a commitment to self-care and self-love is necessary to break the addictive patterns that feed off each other. Once you commit, your path of self-discovery begins.

It's healthier to not associate with people who distract you from enjoying life. Exaggerate self nurturing so that you feel it inside. Build an inner sanctuary of love, joy, peace, and prosperity. The more aware you are of what your loving inner sanctuary feels like, the easier it becomes to stay focused on self-love. Be gentle with yourself. keep your attention on self-love instead of focusing on what you are transforming. That will keep you from slipping back into the insecurity and fear. When enough of the beliefs that were in a dense form get transformed, expansiveness starts to occur. For me, what was amazing is that the connection to The Universal

Pure Love Beings was even stronger and felt closer to my energy field. I started to feel a sense of freedom and a deeper level of love way beyond what was ever felt. Human love has so many conditions due to the attachment to the beliefs and the way the thoughts and emotions express them. With conditional love, when beliefs resonate with another person's beliefs, the human ego is happier and relaxes. When the beliefs didn't resonate there was potential conflict. Unconditional love has no attachment to the conditions. There aren't beliefs to compare, so there is no conflict.

I chose to wish a better life for all, even those I was hurt by, and I meant it. Those I felt hurt by or betrayed me, were teachers to help release the self-defeating beliefs and make me take better emotional care of myself. I experienced a deeper sense of forgiveness with those that I gave my power to and felt betrayed by them. I came into a deeper understanding that the areas they triggered were there to help me let go of that which is not bringing the inner peace, joy, and deeper levels of self-love. I became aware that feeding limitations, negative distractions, or self-defeating beliefs only held me stuck in the human emotions, making me feel lost, confused, fearful, and insecure. With a greater sense of confidence, I was able to recognize this and choose otherwise.

I did not experience the human expression going in one direction and I was in another direction creating that conflict and feelings of separation. Instead, they were one experiencing a deeper connection to Universal Love. That is the reason I felt lighter in the body and experienced this level of abundance that is beyond anything the human expression can imagine. It allowed me to have what I call more of a cooperative partnership with the human expression. The more love and prosperity the human expression felt, the easier it became with cooperative partnering. I felt more comfortable in the human expression since the energy felt lighter. I laughed more, played more, and experienced a deeper connection to the Universal Pure Loving Beings.

Univestations

When the human ego is more active, it strives for desired outcomes outside in a searching way. The human ego enjoys instant gratification and attempts to manifest things to supply the gratification. With the human ego controlling the manifestation process, there is setting goals time frames, working harder in attaining desired goals, and solving problems. Linear time is very active here with a past focus on "what if" you were smarter, made different choices, etc. in the areas of your life that you are not enjoying. Linear time is also active with the future focus wanting to have something different from what is currently happening. The human ego works sometimes really hard to make the desired outcome happen. Using the human mind and attempting to fix, control or make things happen only causes more stress. When the human ego control attempts to manifest, you experience human behaviors that are frantic and intense. There are attachments to outdated beliefs which keep you feeling stuck. The mind gets caught up in the stories creating uncomfortable feelings. You feel like you are paddling a boat upstream. Anything created from that place is not what you want. Your attention is focused on what is missing which only creates limitation. What gets manifested is more of what you don't want. The limitations.

Limitations arise from desired outcomes from an unpleasant experience or some goal. If you allow those limiting thoughts to run your life through storytelling and complaining, you will feel stuck in the energy of those limitations. Some take the storytelling and complaining to sleep, in their meditation, to Universal Love, and to others keeping their attention and focus on those limitations. By doing that, the Universe cannot help bring them the abundances, solutions, love, joy, and peace because they are attempting to solve it themselves with human ego control. They give their power to what they don't want which causes suffering because they are living in the lower vibrations. The story will create human emotional discomfort. Focusing on the lack of a desired outcome only brings up emotional sadness and apathy which creates blocks. This is where the separation occurs and the struggles and lessons were more dominant. The human expression habitually creates by default through the human programs. That only keeps you stuck in the familiar patterns.

Human ego controls when fear or an intense desired manifestation focus occurs. It may sneak in to control the outcome through force, attempting to get clarity on "how" to manifest the desired outcome or become discouraged and frustrated with the timing of what is not manifested. Focusing on "how" desired goals will manifest only creates more limitations. Limitations on not having it when you want it and how you would like it, only keeps you stuck in the "don't wants." You let go of a limitation focus when you let go of the focus on the "don't wants." You are letting go of what you are not enjoying and the boxed in feelings of restrictions. You feel and move more into freedom because limitations no longer have your attention. The Universe knows the how, when and where. When you focus on the energy of abundance and you stay open to allowing it to unfold with gratitude, you transform the limitations. You have trust and allow with receptivity and a deep knowing that all will come to fruition on Universal timing. The "how" is Universe's business. The 'how' and attempt to figure out is something to let go of the control around and be more patient with Universe's timing on bringing clarity with the proper steps to take. The boxed in feels like you have no power or choices to get more into the expansiveness and freedom of unlimited potentials that life has to offer.

Holding on to any attachments only creates the surrounding limitation. The stronger the attachment to the desired outcome, the harder the process becomes because your attention is on the searching. Human ego control shows through impatience with the arrival of the outcome and judging what you don't have. You become Insecure thinking you are not worthy of it or did something wrong, and that is the reason it is not in your life. You then feel stuck in a lower frequency which sabotages what you would like. If you focus all your attention on what is missing or don't have, you become stuck in that limitation. As a result, the outcome will be exactly that, a mirroring of situations that proves the unworthiness, lack, and mistrust as reality. You continue to not have it. This separates you from feeling the Universal connection to love and prosperity..

In the midst of what seems like waiting, focusing on gratitude and appreciation enhances prosperity consciousness and love. When you experience limitations, there are self-defeating beliefs that become more active and become reflected in life experiences and with people. That helps to see what self-defeating beliefs are dictating your life so that transformation and expansion into healthy beliefs can occur. Becoming aware of the self-defeating beliefs and choosing not to give them your power by stating them as truth frees you from their hold. It is best to nurture those areas in place of judging anything or anyone, so awareness with greater understanding occurs. When enough of the self-defeating beliefs get evolved, your Inner Spirit becomes more active. Creative visioning and innovations of what could come about is more effective instead of what was present in your life that you don't want to experience anymore.

Imagine you rush home after being stuck in traffic for hours. You have dinner to make, calls to return, an appointment to go to all in an hour. You are frantically running from one room to another, Making dinner in the stove, lights on in every room, television is on, and you get on the stair master to exercise. You blow a fuse and the lights go out. You become frantic forcing attempting to get the lights on. You get upset, blaming the lights for going off. Yelling at them and telling each one to turn on. You go to circuit box to reset the circuits. You go to the circuit box and flip the switch which turns the lights back on. The circuit box represents a connection to the Universe. You didn't ask HOW that worked or WHEN it would go on. You trusted flipping the switch would turn everything back on. All that stress from rushing, getting upset, blaming, complaining, etc only made you feel more frantic. It is the same thing with life. When you connect to Universal Love and allow it to deliver on its own time, you become more relaxed. You know that it's already done, and the Universe is orchestrating it for you. This is because the focus is not on the outcome and the timing of getting that outcome according to the human ego's time. It is on believing it is already complete based on Universal timing. Now imagine you let all that go and you stayed focused on Love and Prosperity. Breathe that in and feel that. Much more relaxing and peaceful yes?

I have seen some people get so caught up with their attention to the outer world of manifestations, the cars, money, etc. that the human ego sometimes gets so caught up in the getting more and more of things. There is nothing wrong with having material items if it brings joy and pleasure. It is when it becomes almost like an addiction where you are not satisfied and continue to get more and more without enjoying what you have. It then doesn't serve your spiritual evolution. Hoarding the material items such as money and possessions, doesn't help either because it is coming from lack and fear. When you start becoming addicted to success, you feel incomplete and thereby unhappy because you are attaching your identity to those things. When you have attachments, you feel imprisoned by them and they run your life to a point of never feeling satisfied. The human ego "driving" your life only keeps striving for more and more until you become aware of the pattern and choose to stop it. Even if someone has billions of dollars, they could still be coming from lack and fear of losing it. Usually, that comes from an upbringing of not having many possessions in life. There is an overcompensation to gather and possibly hoard it for fear of losing it. Material possessions are things to enjoy. You get to enjoy simple things like nature and the exotic things with complete detachments to the form itself.

You have to get out of your own way of letting go of human ego control and learning to flow with life through acceptance, appreciation, and gratitude. The Universe cannot help you if you focus on any unpleasant conditions through complaining or storytelling. Taking the story to sleep, in your meditation, and/or to others will keep you stuck in the limitation energy. If your focus is on what is wrong, the Universe cannot bring you the abundances, solutions, love, joy, and peace because you are attempting to solve it yourself which is human ego control. You will feel stuck in what you don't want which causes unnecessary suffering. The contrast can show you what you do not want so you can focus on that of which you do vs. complaining about what you do not want. Complaining about it only keeps you stuck in that vibration which causes greater confusion and stagnation. Challenges cannot be solved from a focus of complaining. In times when it seems that nothing you are doing is working just give thanks. Give thanks for all. The Universe provides through by being receptive with gratitude and appreciation. Giving thanks without attempting to figure it out, can get things resolved easier than when in a complaining mode which is a denser vibration. Focusing on gratitude and appreciation behind what you would like to experience drives the energy forward to a more expansive place of manifestations, which is "Univestations." Trust that the divine plan and outcome is already known by Universal Love and that something even better is coming. It is not about *not* knowing the next step rather knowing you are *aware it is coming from the Universal place of unknown. Formless to something new that the Universe is creating* vs. familiar repeated lessons that materialize in a variety of forms with the energy of what you don't want.

When you release enough of that of which is in the way of fully living in your own power, you will get the Universal clarity and feel complete with what you are learning. Eventually, the Inner Spirit becomes more active in that area and the human ego control subsidies. From this expansive frequency place, you will start to experience celebrations of life and not just experiencing one lesson after another. The Inner Spirit becomes more active so there is more of an aliveness inside. When there is a shift from human ego control to the Inner Spirit coming more in the forefront, you become free. You will see how the control was keeping you in duality living. As the Inner Spirit becomes more active, you feel heightened levels of joy, love, peace, prosperity, and vitality because you have a stronger connection to Universal Love. The process of fruitions begins on the ethereal realm in an energy frequency and then on the physical realm in form.

The Universe delivers based on the energy you are in. If your energy frequency is emulating at a limitation vibration, your manifestations will come at that vibration level. If your energy resonating at an abundance vibration, your "Univestations" will be at that vibration level. If the human ego is attempting to control an outcome, the vibration is at a limiting density until you surrender the control. A technique to surrender the human ego control is to imagine a white flag that you wave when you become aware the human ego is wanting to control a particular outcome that has not materialized as yet. Sometimes the human ego desires so strong that there is a driving pushing force that happens, and that creates frustrations, fears, and insecurities. When you surrender the forcing, which the white flag imagery symbolizes, you are able to let go of and stay more in the flow of trust, faith, and allowing. Your focus is more on receiving from Universal Love and choosing to stay attentive on prosperity.

"Univesting" was easy in some areas of my life and in other areas it was so confusing to me. The lessons I was going through to complete the 2nd leg was creating so much resistance. I wanted the 2nd leg's lessons completed and to move on to more of my purpose as an Angelic was getting stronger. This resistance was making the closure more challenging. The more I accepted the lessons, the greater I moved through them with ease. The more I resisted, the more I experienced the human emotions getting frustrated. Dwelling on why a manifestation was not here only made the human emotions active. I identified with them and started to feel confused, frustrated, and allowed the human emotions to put me in a limitation focus like I was missing something. I learned that human ego controlling the process only made things more difficult. Trying to understand the reasoning, controlling outcomes, over analyzing situations, trying to make a desire manifest. forcing outcomes, impatience, and self-doubt created emotional distraught.

I became aware of how the human ego dominated by pushing or controlling the process and attempting to make things happen. It put me in a state of limitations because I was not aligned with

Universal abundance. The was conflict between my Angelic expression and the human ego controlling my life. The results led to what I didn't want and undue stress. The attachment to having the desired outcome was a primary focus. This only hindered my confidence when it was not there within the timeframe. desired, and that only kept me stuck in limitations, sadness, fear, and confusion. As I let go of the human ego controlling the outcomes, I became more aware of the patterns and blocks. They consisted of limited beliefs that were holding me back, the timing being off because there were lessons to learn, and I was too attached to it without allowing Universal Love to deliver it. The confusion came from the human mind attempting to figure things out, like why it is not happening and what is wrong? Then I became insecure and unhappy, feeling incompetent. The human ego likes instant gratification, and I didn't feel it.

In the beginning years of my incarnation on Earth, I remember hearing Arc Angel Michael say let go of the human ego desire around relationships and friendships. It was one of the biggest challenges where there was more of a separation going on between the human and Angelic expression. There was a deep longing for friends and the mate and I was not experiencing them on the physical realm at a compatible Angelic frequency. In 2012. I was driving to California to explore moving there. I thought then that moving there would bring me greater opportunities for a mate and friendships of a higher loving frequency. I drove back to Oregon feeling discouraged and confused.

I knew the human ego was running this program and yet I didn't know honestly how to stop it. I kept hearing the message throughout the years from my Angelic Guides about letting go of the human ego desires. I would hear it in dreams, in meditation, reading about it, through people, and from the Universal Pure Love Beings. I thought that I was hearing LET GO of my Dream you won't get it. This only made the human ego want it more. What I learned was Archangel Michael was saying, Let go and let it be brought to you. I chose to trust that Universal timing was off because the lessons required evolving first. It was an eye opener to discover the more I held on to something or pushed to get the desired outcome, the longer it took to get and the more struggles I faced. It created a limited energy that literally blocked the flow with it showing up.

I chose to stop ask questions, which was coming from the mind and instead listen. The answers won't come from the human mind. They will come from the Inner Spirit and Universal Love. Surrendering the attachments to human ego desires is what freed me. When you surrender the control, you are better equipped to move into a state of acceptance with the process and Universal timing more. Letting go of the attachment to having it and allowing it to materialize in the proper timing, was more peaceful for me. I learned that it takes Universal timing for the creation to "Unifest," like a seed planted in a garden. We don't watch the seed grow or even really know when it will bloom. We know it will bloom and the time it blooms is what makes it magical. That is Universal timing. I enjoyed staying more in gratitude, and appreciation like I had it already.

I imagined plugging myself into Universal Love, like a plug going into a wall. I disengaged the human ego from controlling any desired outcome. When the connection was intact, abundances happened magically. Trusting Universal timing and not forcing physical time with any fruition allows creations to occur organically. Life was more enjoyable when I stayed present, instead of focusing on what I did wrong and why the manifestations were not happening. A serendipity attitude sees obstacles as learning lessons to educate the human mind. The human mind learns and the spirit mind teaches. The focus was on the process of enjoying life in place of forcing an outcome. If Universal timing was off, sometimes it was due to lessons that required evolving first. Life is more enjoyable when you stay present, and not focusing on what is wrong or missing. That only blocks the flow and delays the "Unifestations." With "Univestations," there is more of a flow with life, accepting, and allowing the Universal timing and not the physical time. There are times when it is necessary to just BE present in silence. Other times proper action comes with insight and clarity.

Fears and insecurities are the two biggest trigger points for the human ego to go into flight, fight, or protect mode. Fear of the unknown, fear of failing, fear of rejection and even fear of success are some of the biggest fears I met in my interactions with some people. Insecurity is one of the biggest reasons people look outside for something they feel they are missing. The search for love outside of you will never be fulfilled. All the searching will not find the nurturing because it is already inside. The more you love yourself the more self-esteem grows. All you have to do is focus your connection to Universal Love in place of connecting to the insecurity. The more you expand your consciousness into this realm the greater the love within. Are you ready for FREEDOM to live a life you would love even more?

It does take courage, commitment, and patience. It is really easy to get distracted with the void one can get into when you are in transition from the human ego controlling to more of the Inner Spirit being active. You could experience a longing to have the void fulfilled joyfully and peacefully when getting ready to leave one phase of life to move into another. When you put your attention off Universal Love and on "wanting" the void filled, the attention is on what you lack or feel is missing. Attempting to control it only makes it more difficult, creating what you don't want. This detrimentally affects your confidence, especially when you are experiencing fear and insecurity. Trusting and connecting to the truth builds inner power with regard to love and abundance. You continue to expand self-love believing you are an individual expression of Universal Love and that you are loveable; You increase your self-worth by affirming that you are valuable since Universal Love created you; and you enhance self-confidence by knowing you are a strong light of Universal Love.

Meditation and focusing on Love, Joy, and Peace, helps to calm the human ego from controlling. Remember what Universal Love feels like and focus deeper on that in place of the conditions. That frees the reigns the human ego has with regard to any form of control Then the Universe can work through you deeper and any conditions get resolved more efficiently. When you put your attention on Universal Love, your attention is not on self-sabotaging thoughts and emotions which could lead to judgment and personalizing. This is all human ego control. Instead, the focus is on Universal Love which leads to greater inner joy, inner peace, unconditional love, and prosperity. Close your eyes and feel this connection, the aliveness, and playfulness.

We came to Earth to become wiser by evolving more into the truth of being a spiritual being in a human form. When your Inner Spirit is more active than the human ego control, you are in new territory in your daily life filled with lots of unknowns. You have a greater opportunity to acquire wisdom from the necessary learning lessons which will activate the Inner Spirit in that area. This is because you are not using the familiar mind stories that played out more when the human ego was in control mode. The familiar patterns and focus on the stories behind that is what created the feeling of being stuck in a repeated pattern and stagnation in your life. At first, you may have discomfort with the unknown. The discomfort with the unknown is due to fear, insecurity, and the unknown itself. The how, when, and where from the mental stories attempting to figure things out before the clarity comes and the emotional discomfort around not knowing can trigger insecurities. Choosing to let go of any control around over analyzing or attempting to get the outcome when you want it, allows the Universe to deliver in a more playful way, whether it is clarity from an experience or some inspired action. Continuing to stay in the heart and embracing creates freedom of the human ego control. It also allows for a deeper connection to Universal Love. With every situation, you can either choose to experience it with joy and optimism keeping you in a joyful and peaceful place or resist which creates more struggle.

When the Inner Spirit is more active, there is more of a "we" focus choosing the highest good for all vs. a "me" focus, of what you can gain. You really come to a full understanding that you are not taking the possessions with you when you die. You take what is in your heart, the love, with you when you leave this planet. You become a direct channel to Universal Love and that will help improve the consciousness on Earth and the abundances that are available to enjoy. Your focus is on compassion and pro-peace instead of righteousness. Letting go of the righteousness is how you start to live more on purpose with your mission. When you partner with Universal Love, you feel empowered. It is more enjoyable to keep your heart on the belief of being worthy, your thoughts on gratitude and your focus on the moment listening for clarity and direction. Choose to focus on abundance and love.

With the alignment to Universal abundance, "Unifesting" occurs naturally. "Univesting" comes more from a spiritual place and allowing it to come into form in the physical realm consists of connecting to Universal Love, feeling the desired outcome, releasing it to the Universe and listening for inspired action. You grow and expand in the necessary areas as you enjoy the process of your daily life. You have this belief and confidence that the Universal is delivering instead of fear and insecurity from something you feel is missing. There is no searching or finding fault when something hasn't manifested in the time frame you wanted it to manifest. "Univestations" is where Universal Love provides and human ego doesn't have to actively work so hard or search outside to get something.

There is more of a receptivity to receive and allowing the Universe to bring it to you. You still take action and the action is guided by the Universe instead of the human ego. As you connect to Universal Love and focus on abundance, you become a magnet to the proper people and necessary experiences at higher vibrations of love and abundance. The emphasis on the "doing" and stressing becomes more of an "allowing" and inspired action. Your imagination is so strong with creating. If your imagination has doubt, worry, limitations, fear, anger, and insecurity then experiences play out in that energy vibe. If your imagination has belief, trust, abundance, confidence, and love, the experiences play out in that energy vibe. When the human ego starts to release control around attempting to make things happen, there is a mind game that plays out.

It moves from what the what "I believe" to experiencing more what the Inner Spirit knows. What "I believe" is coming from an attitude about a new belief that is maturing which allows for the fruition to materialize. The new belief is coming from Universal truth and a deeper partnering with the Inner Spirit. When the Inner Spirit is more active as it partners with the human ego there is a stronger oneness connection to Universal Love. The experience is beyond the "what I know" and "what I believe" mind game. The human mind is not playing out any role rather the Inner Spirit mind is. There is more expansiveness at higher frequency vibrations of love, joy, peace, abundance, health, and vitality. As the Inner Spirit becomes more active, there is no duality such as, doubt-belief, limitation-abundance, fear-trust, insecurity-confidence and anger-love. There is pure love, pure joy, pure peace and pure prosperity and "Univestations" happen in a magical flowing way.

There are no goals to set because Universal Love already knows. Universal Love is infinite, omnipresent, and omnipotent. When aligned to that, you experience prosperity consciousness. If the Universal timing is off, sometimes it's due to lessons that need evolving first. Life is more enjoyable when you stay present and not focusing on what is wrong inside that the manifestations are not happening. The blocks that are keeping you stuck in a self-defeating pattern get resolved easier as you stayed present with love, joy, and gratitude. Remember inner power is greater than outside which is part of the past. By fully opening up to the receiving, the limiting energy, emotional discomfort, and mental chatter dissipates. The focus is not on attempting to fix, correct, analyze or judge, bringing a greater level of wisdom and clarity.

Your focus is on believing and knowing it is already done and excited to see how the fruition comes about. Because the Inner Spirit is more active and aligned to Universal Love, "Univestations" occur organically. Life becomes playful, experiencing greater joy, peace, and love. The human ego desires no longer become the driving force which creates the struggles if there is a limitation focus, self-defeating beliefs, or human ego control involved. When the Inner Spirit is active, it already resides in love and abundance energy, "Univestations" thereby occur in a flowing way. Eventually, you don't even have to focus on what you desire for periods of time. There is a oneness connection to Universal Love, so the fruition occurs organically.

Living in the unknown can become uncomfortable. You are not using the familiar belief patterns to create. This is better than the human ego can ever imagine. You are living in the unknown using more innovation, creating, and envisioning new possibilities. There is a higher frequency that turns from an energy into a form, from unknown to known, where creating flows with ease. Human ego control comes into play when the human ego attempts to have some desired outcome manifested and thinks it has to DO something to make it happen. When you have a fear of the unknown, you allow the lack of clarity to trigger a longing to take some action. You become uncomfortable with the unknown and thereby attempt to make or force an outcome. When the Inner Spirit becomes more dominant in your life, there are no familiar patterns and stories to attach to. All is coming from an innovative and expansive place. Living in the unknown becomes more of an adventure with life and enjoyment and not fear or worry. You have greater confidence and trust. There is less domination with the human ego control personalizing or allowing insecurity, fear, judgment, negativity, and limitation to take over.

If there are areas that have fear around the desired manifestation, the human ego may somehow sneak in to control the outcome through force, attempting to get clarity with "how" the desire gets manifested, or become discouraged and frustrated with the timing of what is not manifested. The human ego becomes controlling from a lack of worthiness, lack issues and/or trust issues. As a result, the outcome will be exactly that, a mirroring of situations that proves the unworthiness, lack, and mistrust as reality. You enjoy the process when you let go of the control and allow knowing fruition comes on Universal timing. You have a greater level of self-worth, trust, and abundance. Your life starts to flow. The "how" is Universe's business.

As you start to master in love and abundance energy as your primary focus, you feel a stronger connection to your Inner Spirit and Universal Love. This is Oneness connection. This is when the Inner Spirit becomes more active. I call this, "the flip" between the human expression and the Inner Spirit. This is when the Inner Spirit becomes more active with running your life and the human expression gets to enjoy life more by listening and becoming educated from the Inner Spirit. You feel this expansiveness of heightened love, joy, peace, prosperity, health, and vitality. You experience higher self-belief and unconditional love within you. Living in Universal Love's energy of abundance and love continues to strengthen inner confidence. You become inspirational and a visionary of greatness as you allow the Universe to deliver what is best for you in your life instead of what your human ego desires to have in your life.

This brings about clarity and inspired action, making the process more enjoyable. This leads to something even better. You start to flow with life instead of resisting, attaching, or forcing things to come about. Eventually, you come into a greater knowing that the Universe is taking care of what the human expression wants. You get to experience a new life you are creating inside of you and you enjoy life more. The deeper you go with inner joy and letting go of the attachment to that you don't enjoy, the outcome and the stories, the greater the connection to the Universe. The Universe knows only pure love, prosperity, joy, and peace. It doesn't have limitations, conditional love, and unpleasant feelings. As you apply gratitude and appreciation daily, you start to feel happy, peaceful and loving inside. There is no limitation, fear, and insecurity in Universal Love. That is a human condition that you let go of through embracing so that magic of the Universe delivering comes with greater ease.

You don't have to worry about missing out on something or doing something because the Universe provides clarity on steps if you are to DO anything. Letting go and trusting behind any self-belief is necessary to live an enjoyable life. Everything comes from inside. True connection to Universal Love fulfills all. Instead of going to the Universe with a lack focus of demanding something, you live in gratitude and appreciation celebrating life. Staying Connected to Universal Love is where expansiveness is. You get to fill yourself up 1st and share from that place vs. going out to get something from the world. You connect to Universal Love, continually filling up so you don't get caught up in the chaos and feel lost/ You experience relationships and your life on a higher frequency vibration way beyond the human perception. Life becomes more of a playground because you are choosing to enjoy your daily life in place of pushing to get something which only leads to stress. You no longer allow outside circumstances, human ego desires, and situations control your happiness.

When you stay focused on Universal Love and connect to the abundance, there is a deep knowing that the Universe will take care of you. You have a deep underlining belief that all is already taken care of. The more you relax the reins of the human attempting to figure out or push the time frame and know all is well, the greater the expansiveness to abundance. Instead of planting the seed and digging it up as a metaphor, you plant the seed and know the seed will grow and flourish. You listen daily for guidance and focus on the feeling of celebration. You focus your energy on abundance, love, and trust vs. fear and insecurity. Insecurity keeps you stuck and fear puts you into limitation. This only keeps you experiencing what you don't want. You acquire a deeper level of compassion vs. judging others that are in fear without feeling you have to agree or entertain them. There is a letting go of all controls with the unknown and focusing on the present moment. Partnering with the Universe is more fun than feeling like you have to do it alone. The greater the connection to Universal partnering, the more receptive you become.

The Angels told me to enjoy the higher frequencies of love more. In the summer of this year, I was able to experience greater acceptance that Universal Love is the Source of all. Gratitude flowed and the human ego control became less active. I had an even stronger connection to Universal Love. I enjoyed feeling my Angelic Energy in the body, mind, and heart more without feeling pulled by any of the human ego desires. It felt great to come to a deeper realization that life is not about solving problems or fulfilling the human ego desires. I experienced Universal abundance within and enjoyed expressing that. Manifestations or what I call "Univestations" occurred organically.

I no longer felt I had to overdo and force desired outcomes. That was the human ego being in control mode which no longer was running my life. Human ego control creates limitations, blocking the flow. When the human ego control was active, I noticed I identified with the human expression, becoming more reactive and impatient. Holding on to the focus from a place of missing something, or thinking I did something wrong, only created an impatience that would lead to the don't want syndrome. That started the human ego control to become dominant and pushy. I literally saw how energy gets blocked from flowing when the focus was on limitations or feeling there was something missing. That woke me up that human ego controlling my life was not effective at all. It was making me feel miserable, and I was not enjoying my life It is one thing to learn lessons and another to suffer in them. We learn lessons and suffering is optional.

I felt calmer and more trust that I am taken care of by the Universe. I put more attention on creative projects like writing this book, inspirational stickers, and writing new articles. I found more activities to play. I found myself feeling happier and at peace knowing all is going to be taken care of. I felt excitement as I chose to believe the fruition was already done and celebrated that. The energy flowed, insights of wisdom came and I was pro-active with inspired action. Since the insights were coming from Universal Love and the Universal Pure Love Beings, I knew I could trust the guidance. The more I played in life, loved, and focused on prosperity, the easier my connection to living in Universal Love became. The greater the flow with allowing the "Univestation,." the more patience I was.

Oneness Vs. Duality

I look back on all these years and how duality living was causing so much chaos. It made life so complex because of the judgment, resistance, discomfort, fear, and insecurity around the denser energies. Giving my power to judging, fear, insecurity, and negativity immediately sucked my energy down right away making it more difficult to raise it back up. It was not the duality itself that was bad. It was my perception around duality that made it so difficult. I learned the more you hate something the stronger that which you hate becomes. It is an energy that becomes stronger in power because I was giving my power to it. The more I loved and embraced, the weaker it became because I gave my power to love. The more solid my connection to Universal Love the freer I felt to express this love in an amplified way. Universal Love's power and my attention to that made it easier for me to serve my purpose and enjoy life. I had been so determined to get along with everyone that it was making me miserable. I decided to accept and focus more on being self-loving so that I would feel free to express love anywhere without being concerned how they felt about me. Duality thinking and feeling brings about feelings of separation from Universal Love where the human ego is more active and controlling. You are serving the personality and attached to your beliefs feeding it with your power and attention.

When thoughts and emotions stem from duality and you give power to it, you experience more struggles. There are emotional reactions and judgments associated with the beliefs that are not aligned with Universal Love and abundance The human ego identifies with active belief systems and uses comparisons to associate how it feels and thinks. When the human ego associated the belief system with the condition or person as a favorable outcome there is a positive response. When the human ego associated the belief system with the condition or person as unfavorable a negative reaction occurred. With a oneness connection to Universal Love, our focus shifts from human ego to the Inner Spirit being more active. When the Inner Spirit is more active, there is no duality living. The labels of good and bad, right and wrong, happy and sad don't exist because all of that comes from judgment. We experience duality when we allow self-defeating beliefs to dominate the human thoughts and emotions. We also have duality when we experience a challenge that we perceive as a problem and complain, blame, and judge it. Duality creates emotional discomfort and confusion. Duality thinking experiences labels such as, right and wrong, good and bad, or positive and negative, which creates the chattering thoughts and the confusion. The human mind attempts to get clarity on some area. If duality thinking gets fed, duality emotions become active such as happy and sad or angry and love.

Anytime the mind creates using duality thinking that in itself creates conflict and struggle. I experienced the human mind associating with judgment through its labels, resulting in conflict and struggle. This can keep you in a loop of feeling stuck in a pattern based on an outdated belief that is not serving your overall well-being. You feel hooked in, affecting you emotionally and mentally. The pattern is keeping you hooked in because you are not releasing it fully. You are putting attention on it, talking about it, complaining, feeling victim to it, and holding on to it like it is who you are vs. what you are experiencing. Putting your attention on the self-defeating beliefs keeps you stuck in a linear timeline of past and future in place of the present moment. The memories of what you don't like, keep you fearful of staying stuck and the future of not getting the desired outcome causing greater fear and insecurity. Allowing that denser vibration to keep you captive only creates more of what you don't want to experience.

I was aware that feeding the self-defeating beliefs created a denser energy. A mirroring effect like a hologram would occur where others and situations in that same energy field were present. There was more problematic experiences where I felt the human expression take over to solve and feed it with more drama. By no longer choosing to entertain the denser energies and releasing enough of them, I was able to experience my Angelic presence in the human form. This provided for responsive love and more playful energies to emerge in me more deeply. I started to feel greater abundance from being connected to the Universal Pure Love Beings in an omnipresent and omnipotent way. There was more of a flow with life creating greater ease with life. That which was not part of the expansive energy started to come up in the form of beliefs. I saw them as energies vs. as beliefs which allowed me to let go of the focus and fully release them. This made it easier to move through that of which was no longer necessary which eventually led to more abundance and love with daily experiences and with people I interacted with. As the experiences in the 2nd leg started to move away, I was able to experience more of the new energies of abundance and heightened levels of love to form into all areas of my life. It was a slow process which became clear in March of 2016.

The human eyes see what the human thoughts perceive based on programs in the form of beliefs. Energy is formless so there are no programs in the form of beliefs just energy until the energy turns into thoughts. Thoughts can come from a oneness with Universal Love or a separation out of a judgment. Training the mind and emotions to experience the unseen energy with love before it comes into a thought, will help ground the higher vibrations of loving energy into the human expression. A great exercise is to go into nature and focus on the tree, seeing the tree's form and then formlessness with it from a place of pure love. Then express that loving energy into the world with others. I continued to express the heightened levels of love from inside and became a channel of Universal Love. I went to this event and noticed as I raised my energy and focused on love that the people looked lighter, less dense in their human expression. I learned to have a stronger focus on the higher vibrations of love instead of giving my power to denser vibrations by putting my attention there.

I wasn't entertaining any focus, conversation, or judgment around these dense energies. I felt more confident and freer to express since I felt Universal Love inside. I was strengthening my focus on Universal Love as an Angelic in the human form. I chose to stop giving my power to the external world, so I wasn't pulled into the denseness.. I knew feeling insecure or fearful would only weaken my connection and create a feeling of separateness. If I felt insecure, I would rely more on others for comfort and support which only kept me feeling lonely and isolated. I was coming from loneliness instead of wholeness and connection to Universal Love. Each time I felt emotionally insecure, the body felt denser and became more lethargic. I would focus on Universal Love raising my energy. I felt heightened levels of love and became more secure and the body felt lighter and more vibrant.

I was strengthening self-empowerment by raising the human expression above this energy line that would allow me to feel a lighter and more loving connection. I would raise my vibration high enough to go above the energy line and once there. I created a strong connection to Universal Love. The Angels told me to do this when I first dropped in. I didn't know how to do it then. The human emotions had too many self-defeating beliefs consistently triggering insecurity. The thoughts above this line are positive and prosperous. The emotions have pure unconditional love that is more playful. Any energies in contradiction to this frequency of love would either go into the light or get transformed to purer loving energies. As I went above this energy line, I noticed some energies leaving and going into the light which made the body feel lighter in frequency. When I absorbed Dense energies in the body, it felt heavy. I felt tired when the body held onto dense energies. Sometimes denser energies would become attracted to the light and cling on to it to learn. When the vibrations were at a high enough vibration the density was not able to hold on. Fear keeps us stuck in dense vibrations and love is freedom from the hold it has on us.

When we connect to unconditional love, we move away from dividing our self and we experience greater love. Love increases confidence and we feel more empowered. Judging or resistance moves us away from love and more into fear, separation, and insecurity. You can focus on being an energy of unconditional love and then download the energy into the human mind, emotions, and body. When you chose to "be" love vs. look to get love, you have a stronger bond to Universal Love. The human ego is not in front driving your life. As your Inner Spirit becomes more active, you experience life in a magical way. There is a sense of neutrality, peace, joy and calmness. You are aware of the human mind programs and choose to focus more on the Inner Spirit's intelligence. What's amazing is that the old stories are no longer dictating your life so you make smarter decisions. The great news is as you experience lessons to evolve and become wiser you make choices that are for your highest good. Freedom reigns that allows you to move on to the next experience and have a deeper more loving connection to Universal Love.

Focusing your feelings and thoughts on Universal Love in the midst of challenges vs. hating or judging them, is the greatest step you can take to freeing you from giving power to the condition. The steps I found helpful is to let go of judgmental thoughts, and move into silence. Sometimes using imaginary clouds where you put the thoughts on them helps pull your attention off them. Focus your attention inside your heart. Ask Universal Love for love to come inside the heart. Feel the positive and nurturing from within vs. the outer world condition. Choose and commit to being happy means to embrace that which is not coming from joy. To choose peace over being right. To choose to respond with feelings of love vs. react in anger. To embrace vs. resist. To accept instead of judge. I experienced becoming free of the emotions dominating by embracing the uncomfortable feelings and nurturing them vs. judge them, shove them down, ignore them, or resist them.

Through observing the discomforting emotions and embracing them, I was able to learn from them and transform them to joy. Resisting or pretending they didn't exist only fueled them, making me anxious. Freedom is truly letting go of the attachment of the self-defeating beliefs as they are transforming. Instead, I put my attention on the new healthier beliefs. I noticed people embracing life more when they were having fun experiences. There was more judgment and resistance with the unpleasant experiences. This only kept them stuck in that energy. You become unstuck, by letting go of the attachments to the stories around the beliefs no longer serving your highest god. You experience freedom as you let go of the resistance and embrace what you are experiencing

Quieting the mind chatter and embracing the emotions helps break the duality pattern. Sometimes surrendering it humbly to Universal Love is all that is required. Eventually, clarity comes with greater wisdom. You experience a positive perspective when you perceive obstacles as challenges which are opportunities for wisdom. Having a problem mentality is when you find things to complain, judge and blame. Being optimistic makes learning more enjoyable. Lessons become easier because you feel appreciation, think gratitude and have patience while listening for inner guidance. Eventually, you become more solid in the connection to oneness living. This heightened level of love is unconditional love. You experience self-love, self-care and sharing from a "we" perspective with others in your daily life.

When you are one with Universal Love, you are experiencing and shining love. There are no attachments to the personality. There is only Love. A freedom to shine that love and not be hooked in, pulled down, swayed or reactive to the temporary world and the human conditions. The pureness of this love resonates throughout the body, mind, and emotions and a flow with life provides for deep inner peace. There is a feeling of Unconditional Love and you enjoy sharing instead of a conditional love that gives or receives from one's beliefs. Acceptance with complete trust and faith replaces fear and judgment even in the midst of the unknown with daily life. Living in the unknown is where the magic begins. It is like you see from your 3rd eye more than the human eyes. The 3rd eye being in-between the 2 human eyes which is where your Inner Spirit resides in the mental realm. Life is flowing with a oneness of joy, peace, and love.

There is more of an ease and flow in your daily life instead of experiencing struggles. Life is so rich and full no matter where you are, whom you are with, what you are doing and how you are doing it. Daily life and the process of attaining outcomes are more playful vs. focusing on getting through it to get the outcome. By believing you are the body, thoughts, and emotions, you create duality thinking and feeling which is separation. Duality living occurs until enough of the self-defeating beliefs have evolved than a connection to oneness occurs. As a walk-in, I instinctively knew I was not the human expression, rather using it as a vehicle to experience life. This made it easier to release the addictive patterns and get support from the Universal Pure Love Beings by raising the frequency to create a oneness connection. Through awareness I was learning how to bring more of a oneness connection to Universal Love at a higher vibratory frequency.

By focusing on Universal Love vs. the conditions or the dislikes, you discover greater inner power. Giving you power to the condition or dislikes only hooks you back into judgment, fear, negativity, and insecurity. The human ego control becomes active wanting to analyze, correct, and teach, out of fear or insecurity Limitations arise and you feel stuck.. Universal Love frees when you allow and surrender the attachments. By being open and receptive to Universal Love flowing through you as an individual expression, you experience heightened frequencies of love. It is so important to set healthy boundaries. Know when you give your power away and when to walk away from that of which feels draining. Staying in the energy that is not healthy will only suck you in if you are not strong enough to bless it and walk away. Eventually, you will be so connected in strength to Universal Love that it won't pull you down.

Another approach I enjoyed doing was to raise my energy above the body and send love to the human expression. I Imagined stretching the 3rd eye over the human eyes. That will silence the mind chatter. Then I imagined the heart getting bigger and filled with pure love. This deeply relaxed the human ego. This heightened the frequency energies of love, positivity, prosperity, joy, and peace. If there were any dense energies, they would fall away peacefully. Each day I would meditate and focus on love, joy, and peace. I would put my attention on Universal Love. I would allow Universal Love to come inside deeper by opening myself up more to receiving. If I felt tired, hungry, was experiencing too much negative stimuli, and I gave my power to it, I felt hooked into that energy where I was not able to physically move. I started to feel disconnected to Universal Love. When this disconnection started to occur, I would have discomforting feelings and my energy would start to drop into lower vibrations. These lower vibrations of fear, negativity, limitations, judgments in addition to the insecurity, made the human ego control active.

I learned to somehow physically move the body to break the hold it was having on me. I would then leave the situation and focus on something that I enjoyed and can show gratitude and appreciation. When my energy started to get higher, I was able to reconnect my attention and feelings on Universal Love. Shifting my attention off the condition and people and putting my focus on what Universal Love feels like reconnected me to the higher frequencies. Universal Love connection cannot be broken. It is only a temporary sensation of separation because the human ego is going into protective, flight, or fight mode and thereby focusing thoughts and feelings on lower vibrations instead of Universal Love. It is a fear of separation, losing connection to Universal Love, that triggers the human ego to go into protective, flight, and flight mode. By remembering it's a <u>temporary</u> sensation of separation, the human ego control calms down quicker.

When I was experiencing lessons around any beliefs that needed to evolve, I learned to shift my focus of seeing the condition and the people involved as an energy of love. This helped me to see what the pattern was and not put my attention on the condition or people, which could distract me from seeing what was necessary to learn. The more I chose to focus on appreciation, gratitude, and love the easier it became to shift my focus off the story about the belief. That strengthened the oneness connection to Universal Love. This allowed me to completely release the self-defeating beliefs that were not serving and I experienced freedom. You become attached like glue to that of which you hold your attention. From that place, more struggles occur and lessons because you remain attached to the self-defeating belief. This makes you feel "stuck" creating lessons until you fully decide to let go of that which is no longer serving. The letting go is not always a physical letting go of some form rather an internal letting go shown through reflections with other people. Once you let go and focus on the feelings of expansive love, joy, peace, prosperity, health, and vitality with gratitude and appreciation, you experience true freedom.

Mastering a connection to Universal Love comes with keen awareness. Solidifying inner focus over outer world attention and energy depletion by giving your power to it. Filling the inner world with love and raising its vibrations provides for more love. You stop looking outside for what you feel don't have and instead, you know it is all inside. You are receptive to Universal Love. The level of love and abundance is far greater than the human expression can conceive. You can have a connection to Universal Love by closing your eyes or imagine your eyes closed, call in Universal Love. Open your heart and feel the love, joy, peace, and prosperity enter. Nurture yourself and fill yourself up with so much love to enhance self-confidence. From that place, you can then shine love out into the world. It is not about looking outside for love, money, health, or whatever else you are looking outside for. It is about knowing the truth of love, peace, joy, prosperity, and health is already inside through the connection to Universal Love where no lack occurs. The more receptive and greater your self-worth, the more you allow Universal Love to give.

Keep the mind quiet and off what is bothering you or keeping you from gratitude and appreciation. Connect to Universal Love and breathe. Focusing on any unpleasant condition only feeds it and attracts more of it in different forms. Bless any unpleasant conditions, embrace it, release it, and put your attention on Universal Love. That allows Universal Love to solve any challenges you are dealing with by giving you clarity so you can take inspired action. You get to flow in your daily life feeling happier and confident. Be grateful for the unknown, the formless, allowing it to materialize without figuring it out, attempting to make it happen on your time frame or other control tactics. That is human ego control and you won't get the highest and best outcome from that place. When you experience a solid connection to Universal Love and fully feel it, you see others from a place of pure love. You don't connect with your human personality as who you are. You know you are here on Earth to learn lessons to evolve and enjoy life experience. What you give your power to, you become one with. Give your power to Universal Love you become one with. Give your power to outer world condition, you become one with that.

2015 started out as a magical year. I felt it finally leading me into the 3rd leg of my life. The last leg consisted of me applying everything that I received in the cellular memory in the 1st leg and latter part of the 2nd leg when I dropped in. For the first time, I felt me going into the 3rd phase of my life free of the other expression's energies, what the Angels called the 3rd leg and the last one. I knew the negative influences around the other expression were complete and would move on so I could live my Angelic purpose more effectively. The human expression having a lighter frequency of love made it easier to raise the form up to a higher frequency energy line. I started to have greater feelings of joy, love, and peace instantly. I was so in awe. It was crucial to raise my energy above this line I was experiencing to feel greater love, joy, and peace in the body, mind, and emotions. I became optimistic that I would attract experiences that resonated with that on the physical plane. Enough of the self-defeating beliefs got transformed, so I was able to experience elevating above the energy line to the higher frequencies. In 2015, I was establishing a deeper connection of oneness to Universal Love. I was developing a deeper love connection with the Avatars and Sirius. I was feeling Sirius daily now. I discovered that the Avatars and Sirius were part of the Universal Pure Love Beings. Below are dates that stood out in our interaction.

January 1, 2015, At 12:32 PM, I saw Sirius's UFO ship come from behind the clouds really close. I was able to see the ship as it was going in and out of the clouds. I sent loving energy and felt loving energy returned. I was in awe that the UFO could feel my connection from out there and reply so fast. I heard the Angels tell me to remember I'm an Angelic being vs. associate with the human expression feeling that is who I am. The human expression is a vehicle used to live on Earth.

January 2, 2015, in the early morning, I felt a huge energy releasing related to the outside world no longer able to control me. This was necessary for the connection to Universal Love, to become inseparable. To be a complete channel of Universal Love and express that wherever I go. The human emotions being in charge was dissipating where it had less pull on my energy or attention. I felt a metamorphism going on at 6:30 PM. It felt like bubbles inside and a cocoon feeling that lasted about half an hour. I closed my eyes to meditate and saw a vision showing Christ's journey on Earth. I saw how he was expressing more of his spirit in the human expression. He was seeing through the eyes of Universal Love, not through the eyes of protecting himself from others' pain and that I am going in that direction.

In a dream, I saw a small circular UFO appear by my window. It attempted to come inside the door which was slightly opened. I was unsure of their intentions and moved away at first. I felt their loving energy. I decided to enter their ship. The male energy that was visiting me from 2012-2014 was there. I asked him where he and the rest come from and he said he could not share. I asked him how old he is. He said 1 year and told me in a human age, it means millions in age. I asked another question, and he replied by asking me if I am an alcohol drinker? I said, "no I am not." He said I ask lots of questions. I asked if he is the one that visited me from 2012-2014, where we had an intimate connection. He said yes with a smile. I asked if he did this with others too. He said yes. I shared how I thought he was my partner. He replied saying, "uncomfortable; that is awkward." I explained the reason for my questions was to find out if he was my partner vs. asking this straight out. I shared how I'd enjoy meeting everyone else on the ship and he smiled. We walked around and I saw how everyone was peaceful. They had white hair. I got this huge clarity that these peaceful beings are part of the Universal Pure Love Beings, in addition to the Angelic Realm, who were downloading the pure loving energy. I then wake up.

January 3, 2015, I felt the death of Sirius as an intimate partner. I fell back to sleep feeling really sad.

January 4, 2015, I awakened feeling Sirius in a different way than that of an intimate partner. More like nurturing love. I felt this message that said, "the next step is shifting the human mind to that of the intellectual mind and using that more. This eliminates the judgments, suffering, and the attachments of the outer world conditions. I am to focus more on the intellectual mind." There was a transition period where I was bouncing back and forth between the emotions getting active and my connection to oneness. This lasted for a few months until the oneness connection became more solid. The only time the human ego became active, is when there was a lesson to evolve or when I was around negative influences and I gave my power to it. I felt this intensity that brought my energy lower and more in fear and insecurity. Because I learned how to recognize this, I was able to quickly shift to my Angelic frequency quicker by surrendering the human emotions to Universal Love instead of entertaining them. The human emotions calmed immediately, and the energy got transmuted instantly bringing great insight.

I surrendered enough of the human ego's free will to the Universe to strengthen the partnering bond, making it easier to express the truth of love, joy, and peace. The focus was not about putting the human emotions first rather filling the energy of Universal Love first inside. Then taking this filled energy of unconditional love and nurturing the human emotions. It was much more relaxing and empowering. There was no driving force attempting to force things to happen; no pushing of time that would create more limitations; and no insecurity from feeling incompetent, or that I was doing something wrong because a certain desired goal didn't manifest as yet. The human emotions were not as active anymore. I experienced more calmness. Oneness occurs where there is more of an Inner Spirit and Universal Connection that is more active in your life and the human ego benefits tremendously from it.

Oneness is pure unconditional love, pure joy, pure peace, health, vitality, and prosperity. Oneness shares this pure love, joy, peace and prosperity. When the focus is on Universal Love and you share from that place, you are not giving power to that of which is not Universal Love. You feel more empowered because of the connection and the oneness you have. You see anything that is not connected to Universal Love as an illusionary movie, not real and bless it with compassion vs. entertain it. Anything that has human ego control attachments, will keep you at a lower vibration until you learn from that experience and evolve it.

January 21, 2015, being happy was really ringing true in my life and I was grateful. I kept feeling the message from the ethers to enjoy everything I do with positive focused energy in every moment. I kept singing this song that popped in my head-"if you are happy and you know it, clap your hands."

January 30, 2015, I felt a greater sense of freedom from the negative energies and negative influences. The 27-year cycle is finally closed with the second leg which had all the ancestral energies. I started to feel a greater sense of freedom that allowed me to live in the world with greater confidence and joy. I was very excited. This freedom reminded me of trees that have been through many storms. The stronger ones stood tall, and the weaker fell to the ground.

February 8, 2015, at around 12:12 PM as I rose my energy, I felt and saw a dark type of energy go into the light. I knew that symbolized the negative influences moving out of my life. There was more freedom inside the body. I started to feel the human ego emotions moving to a higher lighter vibration where I was feeling Universal Love more deeply within. This is how the process of strengthening the connection in the human form to the Universal Love started to become clear.

March 3, 2015, I went to this event. I heard Angels say to keep my focus on abundance which will help to attract what I would like in my life instead of focusing on what I don't want.

The next morning, I started focusing on the energy of love. I was focusing on what it felt like to love things I adore and noticed the human heart opening to receive. I didn't feel comfortable walking around saying I love you to people. I didn't feel that was coming from integrity with the high regard with intimate pure love that I chose to express. By staying in the energy of love, I shined love and saw others' Inner Spirit. When the human ego was active love had a tendency to come more from a conditional place because of the belief system. I saw people's beliefs, experiencing a variety of emotions and thoughts that were more limiting. I was feeling myself as an Angelic having a spiritual experience in human form. That felt more authentic than me having a human experience or the human ego becoming more active attempting to have a spiritual experience. Both have more duality and human ego control being more active.

March 8, 2015, while driving, I Saw a billboard sign at a grocery store on the way back from downtown Bend. It said, "you don't seek happiness you find it inside." It confirmed the messages I was hearing from the Angels about continuously raising my energy and filling up with unconditional love.

March 9, 2015, I saw another billboard sign at the same grocery store that said, "you can't use the clicker to change the world. Be love and the world will transform."

March 14, 2015, I went to my favorite sacred nature site. I got messages there often while meditating. I heard this beautiful message about having more inner confidence and with that, I am able to feel more love inside instead of getting it fed from others. I saw this female named Julie approach me who I initially met at Natural Grocers in Bend. I felt we had a lovely conversation. We both agreed to contact each other and enjoy walking in a park. We exchanged numbers. I called leaving a couple of messages within a month's time frame about taking a walk. I never heard from her, so I blessed her and moved on. She approached me with this guy asking if I was the person she met at the grocery store. I answered yes. I asked why she never called me back. She made up a bunch of excuses about a break-up and a new job and then she said her phone deleted my phone number and name. Her friend looked at her shocked by her responses.

When she left, I felt lots of sadness around rejection coming up to be released. I cried and then I saw a vision when the body was 2 years old where the rejection was first experienced. The image of the 2- year-old and the energy around rejection transform into a loving energy. I realized that is when the protection shield started. I saw them returning from their walk and he was rushing ahead of her upset like he didn't want to have anything to do with her. As I left the sacred nature site, I heard the message that the human ego was transcending and my Angelic expression was coming forth more. Then I felt this death with these foster parents that the other expression had lived with in a foster home in New York from the age of 12 until 17.

May 3, 2015, at around 4 pm. I was feeling disoriented and sad. At 4:45 PM, The other expression became really strong inside with me in the human form where she was experiencing the age 2 again and not wanting to live on Earth. She became aware of how important it was to forgive that time in her life so she could move on more peacefully. She didn't like living on Earth and wanted to be with her husband. She again felt the feelings of not enjoying Earth. She went into forgiveness and then I heard the Angels say that she was free to go. She said, "we did it. We are free now." She thanked me for helping and said she will see if she can help me with the partner I would like to have a relationship with. She said she really wants to help and then went into the light. At 5:01 PM I felt this deep sense of freedom.

May 14, 2015, I felt my energy shifting more and experienced feelings of worthiness. I felt my Angelic Guides. They said I had 25% remaining energy to clear and activate to a higher frequency. Then I saw the date June 16 with lots of spiritual light. They said to let go of feeling I had to do anything. To stay open to allowing what is necessary to unfold and continue to focus on nurturing. Continue to believe in the abundance. I knew I was clearing and purging emotional energy so I continued to trust the process.

June 9, 2015, in the morning for the first time, I actually felt the soul mate talk to me in human form and hug me. I said, "what took you so long? and he said, "I attempted to get to you sooner and this was the best time." I felt so connected to him and asked him to find me. I gave him my address and laughed hoping he would come and knock on the door.

June 18, 2015, I saw a billboard sign by a hospital that said, "stay positive." I smiled knowing that was another sign for me to remember to stay focused.

July 5th, 2015, Today was the other expression's birthday, I got confirmation that I'm moving into my Angelic purpose. The ancestral energies that the other expression was born in was permanently complete. When I incarnated, I had felt so encumbered by the emotional insecurity, the lessons the other expression didn't complete, and the negative influences. I went into a meditative state. I started to go through an energy door and immediately felt my energy become lighter and positive. I felt the human expression connected to Universal Love. A week after going through the energy door, I felt the shift where the Angelic mind became more active with a stronger connection to Universal Love. I felt enlightenment of the human mind. As this was happening, I experienced the human mind moving away from judging and moving more into compassionate love.

The Angels told me to put my focus and attention on the 3rd eye in between the eye brows and connect to Universal Love. They said there is less focus on the human mind analyzing and judging what is on the outside world. The stronger the bond energetically to Universal Love the easier it was to channel this higher frequency of love. I felt like the human mind, emotions, and body got taken into a divine light and it became easier to feel and experience this frequency in the physical realm. This helped the human ego control to let go of everything at an even deeper place and flow with life in a more trusting and playful way. I started to care more about letting my love shine and not about getting anything from the outside world. From this place of vibration and focus I became aware that nothing can hurt, distract, affect my energy, or bother me, The more I stayed in the higher frequency of love and strengthened my bond to Universal Love, the easier it became for me to share love without being pulled down by others' judgments, fearfulness, and negativity.

The more I strengthened my confidence by focusing intently on the Universal Pure Love Beings and Universal Love, the less power I gave to the outer world distractions and the human collective consciousness. By focusing my attention inside on love, joy, peace, and prosperity in addition to the Universal Pure Love Beings and Universal Love on a consistent basis, I felt happier. I didn't experience any suffering from conditions, people, situations on the outer world nor did I feel I had to care-take. When the conditions of the outer world did get my attention, and it became a distraction, I learned to surrender it more with peace and love. There was no attachment to any desired outcomes of what I would like the condition to look like or on how the person should behave. There was no story around the way a person should behave, such as," if only this thing didn't happen or this person behaved this way, then life would be so much better."

Allowing the chattered story of a desired outcome will only create more of the limitations on what you don't want more into your life. You become free of judgments with outer world lower frequencies when you let go of choosing to suffer. The negative talk, judgments, insecurity, or limitation is a form of suffering. Rather than personalize others' behaviors or entertain them, which leads to judgments, negativity, teaching, etc. you see it from a place of love, acceptance, and compassion. It is really easy to blame the outer world for how you are feeling inside. When you blame, what follows is the verbiage of wishing or attempting to change something. You may say "if only" followed by a statement that states if the person, condition, situation, etc was the way you would like them to behave, you would be happy. That is a victim consciousness approach.

It takes your power and creates apathy, feelings of sadness, mind chatter around wanting, fixing or correcting. None of this works because you cannot fix it since you are not broken. You cannot solve a human belief program that makes you feel stuck in the mental story. You surrender the attachment to the mental story, learn the lesson, and become enlightened. That transforms the human belief program. By claiming healthy boundaries and stating how your inner world is happy no matter what the outside world shows you, you have more of a connection to Universal Love because your vibrations are more aligned with joy, love, and peace instead of blaming, judging and hating. From this place, clarity comes and when the timing is right and you learned what was necessary from the experience, you will get to move on to the next step through inspired action.

As you fill up with divine love and share it as a beacon of light, you don't get depleted by denser energies. Your inner focus is stronger than getting something from the outside, no matter where you are, who you are with, what you are doing or where you are. By focusing on your connection to Universal Love, self-love and self-worth increases. Self-love and self-worth are your solid foundations. Universal Love is great and loves everyone, therefore everyone is love. Every situation will either be a lesson to become wiser and more connected to Universal Love or to celebrate the feeling of this connection. The greatest steps you can take is to clear your mind and emotions of any distractions that are in the way of your inner connection. Don't allow anything that is not aligned with love, joy, peace, prosperity, health, and vitality distract you from your connection to the truth of Universal Love.

It takes commitment, awareness, and mastering to a point where it becomes solid inside. I remember going swimming one day on a vacation in Lake Tahoe. While swimming, I felt this heavy energy all of a sudden. I looked up, and I saw the pool guy. I was wanting him to leave. The Angels told me to raise my energy to higher frequencies of love, download it into the body, and channel it around the pool area. I did that while I continued to swim. I focused that energy all over the pool area. I continued to enjoy my swimming. When I got out, the guy ran from the complete opposite side of the pool to get the gate opened for me. His energy was lighter and he smiled at me. When I was leaving to head back to Oregon, I saw the guy hiding by the pool door watching me load my car. He looked so sad and I felt he was sad that he could not feel that love the way he did when I was swimming. I sent him a telepathic message that it is all inside him.

This reminds me of how Jesus sat by the tree for 40 days focusing on his connection to the truth of Love. He didn't allow the enticements or others to affect his connection. This is such a true inspiration for me because it reminds me of the truth in living from an inner world of reality vs. an outer world of illusion and feeding it with your power. When you take the inner world of self-love, inner peace, and blissful joy out into the world you remind others of their own oneness with it. If you start to go into self-doubt, you are allowing your inner peace to get affected by the outer world. You could develop unpleasant feelings that keeping you from feeling inner joy, peace, and love. You start to feel separate from your connection to Universal Love. The connection is lost in the mind with chatted thoughts wanting to fix, correct, teach, and judge. Or possibly moving into the past with your familiar beliefs programs or future with not wanting to deal with the current situation. Then the human ego control comes into play with the fight, flight, and protect mode. Making life feel unsafe where you want to hide, escape or avoid what you are experiencing.

Having higher self-love, self-confidence, and self-worth created a solid connection to Universal Love. I experienced positive thoughts and appreciation more often in my daily life. There was no past comparing with projecting beliefs in situations or with people. I felt greater peace in the midst of all situations because I chose to experience an inner world of tranquility and compassion with each experience rather than allow the outer world to affect my sense of calmness. I chose joy as the prominent focus and laughed when I was around others who felt too negative. The stronger the connection, the greater the *being* of love, joy, peace inside. The weaker the connection is, the greater the *doing* of wanting to teach, correct, fix and judge. If you put more attention on the strengthening the inner world, you have less attention on wanting to *change* the outer world through activism. You are able to *transform* the world by being a role model. You are responsible for your life make it a fun, loving,

peaceful one. Live life, love fully and walk in tranquility. When you express love, joy, peace and prosperity the energy is contagious where others feel safe and can choose this too. When you express doubt, anger or lack of peace, that is also contagious. Others can feel threatened or unsafe by it if their self-worth, self-confidence, and self-love is not high enough. Freedom comes from within. Love comes from within, Joy comes from within and Peace comes from within. TRUE FREEDOM!!!!.

August 7, 2015,I experienced a loving spirit entity. I asked for her help and she said yes. She stretched the energy of the 3rd eye chakra over the human mind and eyes making it one eye. I started to see love as an Angelic expression even more. The next morning, I felt myself moving through what I considered a vibration portal. These portals are like energy veils. When I finish lessons in one energy veil, I get to move into another expansive vibration. As I went through the vibration portal, an energy veil got lifted. New lessons within that vibration portal would emerge. The lessons were easier to move through and felt lighter and more playful each time I went through a new portal. It required me to strengthen my hold to the higher frequency energies of love. I experienced a stronger bond to Universal Love, which resulted in stronger self-empowerment and self-love. It was getting easier to hold the higher vibration as I went out into my daily life instead of getting pulled into other denser energies. I was putting attention on inner love in a stronger way and gave my power to that vs. focusing on others pulling my energy down.

Shifting vibrations to more expansive love vibrations requires commitment, focus, and courage. The courage comes from fully letting go of the old beliefs that are no longer serve you. The focus is about keeping the thoughts on silence and/or gratitude and the emotions on appreciation, compassion and love. Rather than focusing on changing a situation or person, focus on transforming the self-defeating beliefs that are triggered by going inside and becoming aware of that belief. Embrace that belief and choose a healthier loving belief that is more expansive than that contrasting belief. Once you experience a oneness connection to Universal Love, you don't want to go back into duality living filled with so much pain and struggle. Oneness is feeling Universal Love's unconditional love, joy, peace, prosperity, and vitality at heightened frequency levels.

Your Inner Spirit is active and your connection to Universal Love is more solid. As you experience a oneness connection, you initially may put extra attentive focus on how you think, how you feel, and what actions you take. You experience a little "fear" that you may lose this connection, becoming even more alert and focused like a hawk on your thoughts and emotions. In some ways that can serve you because you are using discernment and commitment to stay connected to Universal Love. If you allow yourself to feed the "fear" of losing the connection, you may start to feel a separation because your underlining focus is on the surrounding limitations. Trust and faith play a huge role here. Relaxation and enjoying the process of solidifying the bond strengthens the connection, not fear, anxiousness nor being over-cautious. That is a human ego controlling type of behavior.

You come into a deeper inner place of enjoying and celebrating life. You rise above the fears, negativity, and insecurities and choose unconditional love, positive focus, and empowerment. You embrace the negativity, fears, and insecurities vs. judge them to stay free. The activities you choose and the people you associate with come from a place of celebrating life instead of commiserating in it. You enjoy the simplicity and the richness that life offers, like nature, the sunshine, the ocean, and the mountains. Life becomes an adventure, not a chore. You don't have to wait until you die to enjoy life. You can choose to enjoy life now even though there are things in this world that are not aligned with that. The Universe knows what it is doing and although many things may not make sense to you. You trust that all is well and taken care of. You bless that which is not aligned to Universal Love.

TRANSFORMATION ANGEL WALK-IN'S PATH

You become this beacon of love and light, that just by being around others, helps to remind others of their own awakening and Inner Spirit activation. Of course, there will be some that are not ready for it and become either scared or resist it. This is due to them still in their own "sleep" mode and living in that mode in a denser vibration. This denser vibration will come across in behaviors that come from limitations, fears, negativity, and judgment. You cannot make someone wake-up to love. When and if they are ready, they will. By being a channel of love, you help them whether they recognize it or not without saying a word. If this occurs the best approach is to bless them and walk away. Playing the teacher role, especially without them asking, will only get you sucked into their stuff and keep you from enjoying life.

Remember, you are not responsible for others' behaviors and their choices. If others are receptive to Universal Love, then it is a win-win situation. If they are not ready, then your best approach is to leave. If for some reason you cannot leave the situation, choose to accept where they are without entertaining in their energy or in a conversation or judging them. Universal Love is always stronger than that which resists it. Staying committed to choosing peace, love, and joy, will strengthen the loving frequency vibration inside. You are now on the path of expansiveness.

On August 27, 2015, I did an Event via phone at 5:25 PM. I called in the Universal Pure Love Beings. Everyone including myself felt a pure loving energy in a huge way. After the event was over, I saw feminine energies coming in like I saw in the ship on January 2nd. They said there is a flip between human ego control and the Inner Spirit starting. The Inner Spirit is becoming more active and I will start to experience joy as an Angelic vs. the human ego experiencing the drama and struggles.

In meditation, I saw a vision flashback of me being told I'd be a light beacon shining it to help others wake up. Then I got an email with an angel message saying time to shine and come out of hiding as a confirmation. I was grateful that it was becoming easier for me to live on Earth with the different vibrations. I was still feeling some closure with the ancestral energies of the other expression. That seemed confusing since I thought I was complete. At the same time experiencing my Angelic Energy in the human expression. The Angels told me to stay in my heart and not in the mind to analyze it. I felt my Angelic connection inside the body, mind, and heart, giving me more confidence. Whenever the mind attempted to figure out what was going on, the insecurity and emotional discomfort with the unknown became active.

I wanted to know what was going on with this dissipation of the old energies. I knew that was the human emotions and thoughts wanting to control. It was much more enjoyable to stay present with the downloads of new energies. The more I focused on self-love the easier it was. The more attention I gave to the old energies the more frustrated I became. Being happy was more important than feeling frustrated. I became aware that what I was experiencing was what I call ghost energies. Thoughts that I was still experiencing the other expression's life since the human expression was so familiar with that. What a relief to know that was what I was experiencing. The more I trained the human emotions to focus on being happy and turn away from that of which is not aligned with that, the stronger I felt inside.

Knowing this is not enough, it was about the human expression actually *feeling* this consciously and eventually it turning into an unconscious experience. I remembered by raising my energy that as it reached a certain vibratory level, my Angelic frequency became stronger. With the ancestral lessons completed, I started to experience a sudden fusion between my Angelic and the human expression. I felt this relief with a strong conviction that I'm not interested in entertaining any form of negative energy nor being attracted to it anymore. This energy had started when the body was born into a negative influential family. The pattern never got broken. I lived my life so concerned about hurting people's feelings or in fear of catching the negative energy that I didn't take care of myself. It would have served us better if the other expression resolved this in her younger years. It was obvious that was developing stronger positive self-love. I experienced a flashback memory of the other expression's mom wanting to take her with her when the mom died and she told her she had to stay to learn about becoming emotionally stronger. She and I succeeded since my confidence was getting higher.

This year I experienced a flip between the human and the Angelic expression. The human expression was less dominant and my Angelic expression became more active. Life became more fun. The human collective mass consciousness played a secondary role and the Universal Love consciousness played a primary role. This role was about a formless energy of love and abundance that penetrates into the human body, mind, and emotions and expressing this with others. For the next few weeks, I was feeling the higher vibration of oneness and observing the mind confused as it was going back and forth between oneness and duality. The human ego was becoming less involved. There was more of a surrendering going on where I was able to rise above and out of the body fill up with love and go back into the body shining it out into the world. I saw movie clips in the mind on duality living as I kept affirming love, peace, and joy in the midst of what felt like inner chaos. My energy moved through a veil where I felt and saw Unconditional Love through the human eyes with all situations, people, animals, and nature.

September 23, 2015, In a dream, a UFO ship came to visit me. The ship resided in a cloud. Sirius told me his ship is requiring repair, so he is returning home. I didn't want him to leave.

Oct 1, 2015, I felt the Universal Pure Love Beings come in the physical realm behind this veil that was in front of me. As I put my focus and attention in front of me, the veil expanded, and I was able to feel these loving beings more fully inside. I felt the body ascending energetically and simultaneously all the energies that were not aligned with this energy was transmuted. I felt at first the human ego resist. The minute I started to embrace the energy the more nurturing and comfortable it felt inside. This loving energy was pure love. I had no feelings of fear or insecurity. It was very expansive and peaceful. As these energies came more fully in the physical body, I noticed the energies surrounding me also started to shift. I learned that I was no longer attracted to places where energy healings occurred. I felt pulled more into places where my energy felt more expansive.

The human ego and my Angelic expression becoming one with a higher frequency felt different and much more peaceful and loving. For the next few months when I witnessed others giving their power to the human ego control, I actually saw how they descended into lower vibrations. They went into a state of confusion, fear, anger, and insecurity. They felt lost and disconnected. I focused on Universal Love and became a conduit channeling love in the midst of this. Letting go of the idea that I was responsible as a teacher and as my purpose to educate those in duality helped me move more into my purpose. The Angels told me a few years after incarnating to let go of the teacher role and "be" love instead. It took many long struggling years to release the care-taking program during those earlier years when I incarnated. The Angels guided me to places to become a conduit for Universal Love to express through me.

November 16, 2015, I saw the UFO ship passing by confirming that he was back. I was so happy.

November 22, 2015, at 5 PM I felt the UFO Ship. I felt energy in my 3rd eye and throughout the mind as images. It reminded me of the dream where I visited them. As more people awaken to love, we will see the world from a totally different energy vibe. Where the Inner Spirit rules Earth and not the human ego. Then Earth will live in a greater balance of love and enlightenment. Earth is evolving so fast. Many are becoming enlightened at a rapid rate. I believe human ego's free will is going to lose its power and won't have a choice except to have a great awakening. The Inner Spirit will become more active and we will have greater love, joy, and peace. When one is "asleep" in their world of density, they don't know anything else or any better. Once there's an awakening, their life starts to transform and they become more solid in the higher frequencies of love. From that recognition, their life transforms.

Their human ego's free will subsides and the Inner Spirit becomes one with the Universal.

In the early years of my incarnation on Earth, I experienced the vibrations of the human expression. I often felt insecure, disconnected from Universal Love and thereby felt lost. I would immediately quiet the mind and calm the emotions. I then asked the Universal Pure Loving Beings to clear any energy that was keeping me from my connection to Universal Love. It was amazing how I get clarity almost immediately on what was blocking me from feeling the connection. It was easy to release attachments to outside conditions or people behind any belief that was creating the confusion and emotional discomfort. Now that I am more connected as an Angelic in the human expression, I feel a greater connection to Universal Love. With my vibration being at a higher frequency, I feel more confident and love inside the human expression.

There were times I would surrender the attachment by giving it to the Universe. That helped me resolve challenges easier. I did not attempt to figure it out by myself. I experienced other teachers who reminded me of the truth of Universal Love and the direct oneness connection. Universal Love filled me up with love, joy, and peace, not the conditions, people or tangible stuff on Earth. The Love within and connection to Universal Love was full and rich and nothing could take that away in energy, emotionally, mentally, or physically. This year I mastered the awareness that putting any attention on conditions in the outer world only created an emotional attachment to those conditions. When the conditions were favorable, I felt happy and when they were unfavorable I was unhappy. I learned to shift more to the inner and less to the outer world. I finally broke the pattern of going outside for love and surrendering more to receiving Universal Love's. care and love was becoming a natural occurrence I had known all this on some mental level. I was not getting it fully on an emotional level due to the power I was giving to the human emotional frequency.

We live in a world that has both negative and positive energies. asking a conscious choice to live in joy, the negatives no longer had as much of a pull on my energy. Anything that was not aligned with positive vibrations no longer was of interest. Simplicity enriched my life. The transitional shift from one vibration to the other became easier once I reached above the energy line where my energy didn't get depleted and drop into the lower energy vibrations. Places like nature, lighting candles, soft happy music, baths and creating a room that was soothing in colors and smells helped make life more enjoyable, triggering positive feelings and thoughts. Not entertaining life around negative stimuli assisted with breaking any negative patterns. The more I embraced them without entertaining the negative whether it was thoughts and emotions or with others, the greater the releasing of its hold. It was also important not to judge or resist the negativity. I Sent it love and blessings and chose happiness. Any activities I attended resonated with the choice of joyful living.

Strengthen the positive energies was one of my main focuses. In my journey into my connection with oneness, I discovered that when the focus was on one "With" Universal Love, I felt this sense of separation and insecurity. The "With" here means side by side, duality vs. oneness, where you separate yourself with human and the Inner Spirit and form and formless. When I connected more from a place of one "in" Universal Love, I felt a stronger connection. One "with" Universal Love allowed for the human form of separation of negativity, judgments, fears, insecurity, etc to appear. Being "in" Universal Love radiates love with greater power and strength within. It was like I was living in Universal Love's house and channeling this love wherever I went.

Journey From Human Consciousness to Oneness

Some start their Earth school experiences as a human expression having a human experience filled with insecurity and fear. With the human expression wanting instant gratification, the human ego control became heavily involved incurring many life difficulties. By feeding the difficulties, some experienced drama and addictions around self-defeating beliefs. They incurred insecurities and fears. It is like dreaming while walking through life because some are living in their illusions, the self-defeating beliefs they give their power to as being their truth. Some are not even aware they are a spiritual being in physical form. They identified more with the human expression and the belief systems. They have attachment and controlling issues around the beliefs. Survival was the primary focus. Surviving relationship challenges, financial bills, work, and daily life. Life feels more like a roller coaster. Many highs and lows with mind chatter and emotions. Life is full of challenges with transforming the beliefs due to so much domination with the human ego control.

A choice comes initially from a place of love or judgment. We either live life experiences from fear and Insecurity or love. When we judge, fear or become insecure with anything we take that in and learn from it. When we have areas in our life that have fear based beliefs attached to them, we experience that part of our life from a vibration that is at a limited frequency. The beliefs get pushed and if we move into fear instead of embracing them, we get stuck in an insecure place. We allow the conditions in the outer world to amplify our inner fears or insecurities by not facing the conditions with a choice of peace and self-love. We thereby get stuck in a fear and insecure vibration. When we have a dependency on the outer world, we create a habit of giving our power to it. Giving our power to negative energy, only initiates expectations around desired outcomes we would rather experience. We look to the outer world and people more and more to feed us. When it is not met, we become disappointed and that can create dependency with people, situations, and experiences.

We take in both positive and non-positive energy. With the non-positive, we experience some outdated beliefs and if we feed it we attract more of it and feel stuck in those experiences. We become insecure or fearful in that experience and that is where the judging comes into play until we make peace and then we are free. We may attract more and more negative energies feeling sucked down into the lower vibrations and stuck in that.

Some go through their whole life protecting themselves from negative influences. Through the protection they end up attracting more negative influences. This is because there is a subtle fear, judgment, and insecurity hooked into it. Personalizing causes the sticking of glue to that of which is unpleasant. They become attached to that energy so they attract more of it. When they decide to face it head on with confidence and love, they release the energy hook and the attachment and they are free. Embracing the unpleasant situations, conditions, and people immediately "unglues" us from that experience, person, and situation. By embracing what we are feeling inside, we see the outdated belief for what they are, illusions that get played out by giving it our power. We can move through them and complete what it is attempting to teach. Then we can move forward in our life endeavors with greater self-love. Anytime we look outside for something to fill the inside with, we create a dependency with it.

We want to fill up a void we are feeling inside. When we fill that void with Universal Love, we don't look outside for it rather we go outside to share the fullness we already have inside. The lessons are complete and they move forward with greater awareness and love. They move out of the shadow and more into the light of love where they actually live life instead of fearing it. They no longer give their power to the human conditions, which include self-defeating beliefs and lower energy frequencies. As we free enough of the negative energies through love and peace we start to move more into the positive and life takes us more into lighter energies where we attract more positive influences. When enough of the self-defeating beliefs transforms, the human ego control starts to lose some of its power. More awareness comes into the consciousness, through evolving the human personality. We transform from a problem-oriented focus to that of Universal Love solving with inspired clarity and action. we shift from seeing our self and others' negative manifestations to that of more positive inspired "Univestations."There is an awareness of knowing he or she is a spiritual being having a human experience. Some challenges with human ego control may still occur, yet the awareness of the self-defeating beliefs gets released quicker. There is a duality type of living still filled with lots of contrasts to transform. Expansion occurs as outdated beliefs get transformed quicker and the thoughts, emotions and the physical body ascends in frequency. During this transition, there is both a feeling of connection to the truth of being a spiritual being, feeling empowered and flowing *with* life.

Other days there is a feeling of disconnection and inner conflicts. The human personality processes self-defeating beliefs and transforms them to healthier beliefs. The commitment to being happy will out way the feeling of entertaining drama when you are going through lessons. There's a commitment to love, joy, and peace in all situations and interactions with people, instead of judging, blaming, or complaining about the unpleasant conditions. You realize Earth is temporary and the outer world conditions thereby are temporary. You know that reacting to unpleasant perceived experiences creates more of it in various ways. You experience a shift in perception from a problem-oriented focus filled with judging, complaining, and blaming to a challenge-oriented focus filled with opportunities for growth and wisdom. Instead of attempting to fix, correct or play teacher, it becomes easier to let go and choose inner joy, peace, and love immediately. The focus is on surrendering that which is not serving You intuitively know that Universal Love will take care of you. There is trust and faith in the unseen and unknown. When that happens life feels freer and happier.

Sometimes in the midst of your daily life, you experience a person or situation that feels invasive or unpleasant. If the human mind blames and judges the person or condition, you give your power to it. As it chatters away, eventually you feel it affecting you emotionally. Through keen awareness of this, you can decide to ignore the outer condition and situation and instead focus on love. You have keen awareness of being a Spiritual Being in human form vs. identifying with the condition or person. The condition has less power or control over you. You experience rising above almost like you are out of the body and shining love. Rising above the situation allows you to feel higher vibrations in place of the human ego controlling through a fight, flight, protect mode.

Instead of giving your power to others or conditions that are bothering you, you focus on nurturing the human emotions.. Focusing on the conditions and allowing it to upset us only keeps you stuck in it. Instead, you can come to trust and know that the Universe solves through insights and inspired action. The easy part is to stay connected to Universal Love and listen for guidance. Trusting in divine timing, being patient, and focusing on gratitude is much more enjoyable than attempting to force certain outcomes. You get to live life with inspiration, love. and joy and to stay aligned to Universal Love and prosperity. You live life by getting yourself in a deliverable mode and continuing to enhance self-confidence, self-love, and self-worth. You get to choose to have a positive, grateful attitude, a joyful heart, and allow Universal Love to deliver.

We sometimes can get so caught up in wanting to see the physical creations of what we would like to experience because we dislike what is in our reality that we end up creating limitations. The more we entertain the limitations by focusing on what we don't want and storytelling around it, the longer it stays in our life. This unpleasant reality comes from a past focus on something we outgrew or no longer serves us. Yet if we know that we are choosing something different and know that what is here is temporary, then we move into acceptance of what is. We can choose to strengthen our feelings around what we are imagining and live in greater joy in the present moment. If we use imagination in a focused and stronger way, we become more empowered inside. The outer world has less control over us. By focusing on what feels great inside and what brings us joy inside, we start to feel good no matter what. That is what I mean by outside conditions having less control over us and instead our feeling good taking precedence.

The great part about acceptance and focusing on embracing that of which you are not enjoying is that it helps to move your emotions to a happier state. The lessons become opportunities in place of dreading them. The more you put your attention on inner joy and love, the less control the outer will have because you are not giving it your power. It is freeing to see the energy get transmuted when you embrace it. This is what I call spiritual freedom. The Inner Spirit takes over and transmutes the energy replacing it with unconditional love that is so beyond that of which you have released. You have to love yourself enough to know how to train your thoughts to focus on thoughts that uplift your emotions to a place of greater joy. If you don't feel you are worthy, your focus and attention will be around hardship and struggle. If you feel you are worthy, your focus and attention will be on self-love and playing. It is as simple as that. Knowing Universal Love as your true source of direction over the outer world conditions empowers you to make healthier choices.

Conditional love takes over when you put too much trust in the physical world for your happiness, peace, and love. You have *expectations* of getting something you feel is missing from outside sources. Expectations sets us up for disappointment because there is human ego control attached to wanting a certain outcome to occur or a person to behave in a certain way. That only leads to more challenges where the human ego desires come from a limiting and frantic place. You expect them to behave in a certain way for you to feel happy, peaceful, and loving. This only makes your life miserable because no one can ever meet that expectation 100% of the time. They have their lessons to learn and their connection to source to strengthen. The best approach is to strengthen the connection to self-love.

When you have a sensitivity to others' energies, through keen awareness in the early stages it is manageable. You become aware early on whether you are coming from love or giving your power to the outer world conditions. If a person or situation is there to teach you a lesson for spiritual development and you see the contrast from a place of love, you move through the lesson with greater ease. If you see if through judgment, limitations, victim consciousness, negativity, fear or insecurity, you move through the lesson with struggles. Both will teach you, yet the love focused approach is more enjoyable. You are not giving your power to the lesson as your truth of reality. You are evolving it to a heightened level of love and spiritual maturity. This is the way to a deeper connection to Universal Love. Judging it keeps you stuck in it. Embracing and accepting vs. resistance and rejecting, allows for a deeper connection to Universal Love. With the choice of feeling happy, you don't allow the condition to make you reactive. You focus on feeling good and shifting your focus from judging to that of inner nurturing. Reacting causes more unpleasant emotions and thoughts which worsens the unpleasant condition. You remain neutral to the temporary experiences vs. reactive. You continue to focus on being receptive to Universal Love and abundance and allow it to "univest" organically.

If you notice your energy is low, stay with it by being an observer vs. participating in any mental story. Stay present and embrace the experience. This helps release what is necessary so you can raise the energy back up. In conditions with denser energy or negative behaviors from people, it is really easy to go into a protective mode. You lose confidence as you move away from self-love. Connect to Universal Love and embrace the dense energy with amplified love. Embrace the dense energy with amplified energies of love to transmute it. Stay focused on love, peace, prosperity, joy, and Universal Love. Gratitude, appreciation, and self-love are one of the quickest ways to increase the vibratory energy. Avoid entertaining drama based conversations with others, by changing the subject, accepting where their consciousness is, and blessing them with love. You can interject saying you choose to enjoy life and this conversation isn't conducive to enjoying this experience.

We can get so concerned about hurting other's feelings that we listen to their drama and get discouraged when we give our power to it. Set healthy boundaries and honor your choice of how you would like to live your life. If something is not serving you or is making you unhappy shift your attention on something you enjoy. Take better care of yourself. We all deserve a happy life. It also helps to stay neutral vs. giving opinions. When you give opinions, you're pulling in your beliefs and comparing them with what they are saying. That is what creates duality, such as, I agree or not agree, I like or dislike, and I accept or judge.

Freedom comes from within. Love comes from within, Joy comes from within and Peace comes from within. TRUE FREEDOM!!!!.

The human ego becomes secondary and the Inner Spirit becomes primary in your life. You know you are not the body, mind, and emotions, therefore, the beliefs, emotions, problems, or challenges, have no power over you. You live life from a higher vibration of love experiencing greater love, self-confidence, joy, gratitude, peace, abundance, vitality, and health. When you know you are spiritual being using the body as a vehicle to get around, you don't attach to beliefs, emotions, or thoughts, which is duality living. The Inner Spirit is energy, not a physical form. When you emanate the pure energy of love, joy, peace, prosperity, health, and vitality all gets heightened in that vibration frequency. As the human emotions become softer and receptive to love, the energy of love becomes more alive. If you get so caught up in over giving or in expecting to receive you are missing the true meaning of love. Love is not about getting or giving it is about sharing. The only way to share is to come from a full place. A full place of inner love that only comes from one's inner connection to truth to pure love. That pure love is unconditional and nurturing. There is no agenda or conflicts that arise from this place. It is so pure and nurturing that it fulfills all and provides for greater confidence. From that place, you are better equipped to share gratitude, compassion, acceptance, joy, peace, and authentic love.

The stronger the connection to Universal Love, the greater the inner *being* of love, joy, and peace. The weaker the connection, the greater the *doing* of wanting to teach, correct, fix, and judge. If you put more attention on the inner world, you have less attention on wanting to *change* the outer world through activism. You can *transform* the world by being a role model, an example through your actions and words. As Mother Mary says, "Invite me to that of which is pro-peace not anti-war" You are responsible for your life. Make it a fun, loving, peaceful one. Live life, love fully and walk in tranquility. When you express and share an energy of love, joy, peace, and prosperity the energy is contagious where others feel safe and can choose this too. Expressing and sharing from an energy of doubt, anger, or lack of peace, that is also contagious. Others can feel threatened or unsafe by it if their self-worth, self-confidence, and self-love is not high enough.

The Inner Spirit knows and the human ego attempts to figure out. When you completely let go of the human ego controlling life and the Inner Spirit becomes more active, it is naturally connected to Universal Love. You express higher frequencies of love organically. Attention moves from the "me" self-absorption focus to the "we," unconditional loving focus. This is not saying to discount yourself or not take care of your own well-being. Rather, the opposite. To take care of yourself means to connect to Universal Love for all inner needs, including nurturing love, inner peace, joy, desires, health, and vitality. Through meditation, you get to silence the human chatter and calm the emotions to a place of peace. That makes it easier to connect to Universal Love, be fed with love internally, and then express that wholeness to the outer world. When we are not fed inside, we tend to look outside with a belief we are missing something. This creates neediness and more of what we don't want in life.

This reminds me of a story someone shared about how Jesus sat by the tree for 40 days focusing on his connection to the truth of Universal Love. He didn't allow the enticements or others to affect his connection. This is such a true inspiration for me because it reminds me of the truth of living from an inner world of love in place of giving power to the outer world. When you take the inner world of self-love, inner peace, and blissful joy out into the world you remind others of their own oneness with it. It is imperative to hold the energy of love with confidence. You lose a connection to Universal Love with self-doubt and fear created by giving your power to the outer world conditions. The connection is lost in the mind with negative chattering thoughts wanting to do something such as fix, correct, teach, over analyze, or judge. Or possibly moving into the past with your familiar beliefs programs or future with not wanting to deal with the current situation. The human ego reacts through the fight, flight, protect mode, making life feel unsafe and wanting to hide, escape, or avoid. By evolving the emotions to a healthier place of self-confidence, self-love, and self-worth, I was more effective in making a solid connection to Universal Love. Life became filled with acceptance, gratitude, and appreciation. There was no past comparing with projecting beliefs in situations or with people I interacted with. I felt inner peace because I chose to take the inner world of tranquility and compassion to each experience. Joy was my prominent focus, and at times laughed to lighten up any situation that seemed intense. Choosing inner joy meant no longer entertaining others' drama.

Then at some evolutionary point in life, there is an awakening and awareness of the Inner Spirit becoming more active. You realize you are not the body, thoughts, and emotions. The body is a vehicle to live on Earth where it experiences thoughts and emotions based on human programs from beliefs ingrained in the conscious and subconscious. With the Inner Spirit being more active, life is full of heightened frequencies of joy, peace, love prosperity, health, and vitality. You become aware how you gave your power to the body, thoughts, and emotions and how it was running your life. The conscious choice of letting go of the human ego control initially created a split between duality and a oneness connection to Universal Love. With a oneness connection to Universal Love, there is more confidence and empowerment. When there was more of a split with the human ego attempting to control there was more insecurity, negativity, limitations, and fear. Leaving you feeling dis-empowered and not knowing what choices to make. There is a knowing now that receiving love directly from Universal Love and the Inner Spirit is stronger than that of humans because human love is conditional and Universal Love and Inner Spirit Love is unconditional.

As the Inner Spirit becomes activated, there is a realization to being a spiritual being having a spiritual experience in a human form at heightened frequency levels. All is inside and thereby creating comes from inside. Universal Love and the Inner Spirit are solidly connected. The Inner Spirit's heart nurtures the human heart which amplifies the energy of love. There is an energy of love expressed way beyond any human energy of love has ever experienced because there is an unlimited amount of love with the Inner Spirit and Universal Love. There are experiences of heaven on Earth in a human form filled with heightened levels of prosperity, joy, love, peace, health, and vitality. The body has higher frequencies, feeling lighter and can hold the expansive energy frequencies better. Material creations occur naturally since the Inner Spirit knows of abundance.

Life becomes more of a playground than that of fearing or being insecure in. We feel so taken care of in our connection to Universal Love that the suffering becomes more obsolete. As we keep our thoughts and focus on that which is positive as well as staying in appreciation and gratitude, we connect to greater levels of joy. We move out of a fear and insecure dominating vibration where life seems like one struggle after another, one problem to solve after another, and one thing to commiserate after another to that of freedom. Freedom to feel and express love, joy, and peace unconditionally and knowing that Universal Love is inside of you. The expansiveness overpowers anything that is not aligned and it gets released. You get to experience feeling optimistic in all situations and letting Universal Love give you the specifics, such as what form it will take, where it will happen when it will occur, and with whom you will experiences with. Life becomes full of new beginnings each day. Pure love and positive energy are expressed in a deeper more profound way.

Awakening the human personality to the point of realizing my

Angelic expression helped me to see why I had conflicts with being in the human form. The human personality was so strong that I identified with it as who I was which only created the density and conflict. Fear and insecurity came from a human condition. A feeling of separation between self and Universal Love. My connection as an Angelic expression in the human form provided freedom. The Inner Spirit being active doesn't strive for anything outside because it all comes from inside. No more searching outside with this feeling it is missing something using controlling tactics, feeling insecure and fearful. That only created more of the limitations. Love brings freedom from feeding the fear and insecurity. As the human ego control subsides and the Inner Spirit takes over there is more of a positive, abundant consciousness. Having a strong connection to Universal Love is omnipotent love. This omnipotent love is like being a bright light in a dark room. Each day, I meditated opening up for the human expression to experience divine love. I cared more about my connection to Universal Love, expanding in higher frequencies of inner love. Self-worth became the solid foundation. Universal Love is great and loves everyone, therefore life is great.

Every situation will either be a lesson to become wiser and more connected to Universal Love or to celebrate the feeling of this connection. The greatest steps we can take is to clear our mind and emotions of any distractions that are in the way of our inner connection. Have healthy boundaries by not allowing anything that is not coming from love, joy, peace, prosperity, health, and vitality get in the way of our connection to the truth. It takes commitment, patience, and mastering being present to a point where it becomes solid. When there is a deep connection to Universal Love, the world becomes friendly and feels safe. When we give our power to fear and insecurity people, places, and situations can feel unsafe and uncomfortable. Especially if we are in an unfamiliar area physically or within our own comfort zone. It is easy to get sucked into the fear and insecurity wanting to hide from the world when things don't feel safe. When there is a feeling of not feeling safe, it is coming from us giving our power to that which is not coming from an awakened state of love. We don't have to fear or give our power to the condition or person. The connection to Universal Love is empowering and so vast in love, helping you feel empowered. You become a beacon of light reminding others of this truth. We get to become this light of love, no matter where we go, who we are with, what we are doing, or where we are. We become a role model for those who are giving their power to the outer world conditions and people resulting in inner fear, insecurity, and negativity. Inner heightened levels of self-love transforms any insecurities and fears we experience.

When we come from a full place of inner love, our mind has more gaps of silence and our heart is receptive and creative. This provides a oneness connection to Universal Love with ease. We are able to express in an innovative optimistic way. A loving and abundant perspective supports us in living a more fulfilled life. With every experience and each person we meet, we either give our power to love and abundance or judgment, fear, and limitation. Keeping our energy high is crucial to staying connected to Universal Love. Eating healthy, meditation, exercise, rest, walks in nature, baths, happy music, staying positive, and surrounding our self with other positive people are examples on how to keep our energy high. It is so much fun to wake up to the realization that we are a full expression of Universal Love encompassing pure love, joy, peace, prosperity, health, and vitality. All else is a dream, an illusion, that we gave our power to and therefore played out continuously until we realize it was a lie. We played it out in chattered stories where we talked about our suffering, wanting comfort and solutions.

Even the positive stories can have an impact if the experience, person, or condition is no longer around . We end up missing and feeling and empty without it.. We played it out in our emotions feeling unpleasant feelings and giving our power to the unhappiness or to the happy feelings that got hooked into the outer conditions. We played it out by entertaining the news, movies, books, etc Then we go to classes, events, take seminars,. We take classes, seminars, vacation to spiritual locations, go on retreats, go to metaphysical centers and churches,, read books, listen to educational radio shows, look for Gurus and therapy to solve this lie attempting to find answers when it is already inside. The more we believe in it and attempt to fix it, the more it stays alive in our life. Our freedom from this comes into reality when we realize we are living illusions of suffering and that Universal Love is not the cause of this. Our relationship with Universal Love is the solid foundation for our joy, peace, love, prosperity, health, and vitality from within not from outer conditions. We *share* love with others vs. looking for it outside to complete our incompleteness.

With expansiveness comes greater ways of shining the light of love, joy, peace, and abundance. You get to play big in life. Playing big means experiencing abundance in place of limitation. Expanding the energy of the human frequency is both an adventure and filled with challenges due to lots of growth and acquired wisdom. When the human expression is operating at a denser energetic frequency, life plays out with more limitations. *Thinking* thoughts of abundance will not work because it is coming more from practice vs. believing. When enough of the energy frequency gets expanded inside, you get to *experience and behave* from more of an abundant place. The Universe can only express through the energy frequency with which you are allowed. The Universe mirrors the frequency of which you are operating from. For example, If your belief systems are similar to that of a glass of water, you get that amount from the Universe. This is limitation. If your belief systems are similar to that of an ocean, you get an unlimited amount which is prosperity.

if the mind has limited thoughts and unpleasant emotions the Universe has very little to work with and mirrors that reflection back in the physical realm. You experience this in different forms so you can see the contrast and how you are playing in it. If you are receptive, express gratitude, self-love, and appreciation, the Universe has vast amounts of energy to work with and can express the abundance easier. The abundance comes in a variety of forms. Energy is easier to expand in frequencies of love, joy, and peace. When the expansive energy turns into form, you experience heighten frequencies of that form. Whether it be a new job, relationship, money, or self-love. With a strong connection to Universal Love and choosing to celebrate life, you experience an expansive shift in consciousness and emotions. The human mind uses lots of familiar programs from stored beliefs that it checks in and analyzes, compares, and sifts through to see if it supports an outcome. When we awaken to the awareness of being happy, we experience fewer struggles from unpleasant conditions and we move away from judgments, fears, and insecurity.

Playing, laughing, having fun, and feeling joy, opens the heart chakra and expands the aura. An open heart and a grateful heart is certain to strengthen the connection to Universal Love. As you stay aligned to Universal Love, you become heightened with love, joy, peace. and prosperity. The human deficiencies no longer take the dominant focus of your life. This is where you get to experience true spiritual freedom. The more solid the connection, the greater the impact has on you and others. It allows you to invite others who are also aligned to Universal Love to join you in the party by enjoying life. The more you choose to enjoy life and align to Universal Love, the less you get caught up in the fear, insecurity, negativity, and limitations. Just because others choose drama talk, you don't have to join them. Feelings of joy, love, and peace you get directly from Universal Love, allows your energy of love and positivity to outshine. You become both free and a strong leader when you can strengthen the inner power and connection to Universal Love and shine that out with confidence, love, positivity, peace, and joy.

Choose peace over righteous responses, respond with calmness vs. react, show compassion and love over living in fear, and believe in yourself with confidence over insecurity. Doing this helps keep your inner sanctuary loving, peaceful, joyful, and abundant. Focusing all your attention on Universal Love, including your energy for those who are sensitive, helps you from getting sucked into any distractions you may perceive as unpleasant. The more you master this the stronger the connection to the vibrations of love. You get to live as a light of love in the world. The Bigger the contrast, the greater the need for inner strength. Like a tree in a storm that remains strong and beautifully still. If you give the contrast power you become attached, resulting in struggles. Attempting to force a different outcome or judging it, only prolongs the negative impact. You focus is on what you don't want and become unhappy. Through nurturing and focusing on thoughts of gratitude and feelings of appreciation, you get to experience a positive perspective. Your energy starts to rise and reconnects to love vs. fear and insecurity.

When I first incarnated into the body, I knew I was not the body, mind, or emotions rather experiencing the human expression. I found it really easy to get sucked into the human personality, getting lost in self-defeating programs. I thought that was who I was, by falling "asleep" in those self-defeating programs. I call that having a human experience so I could learn from them and evolve them. When I gave them my power, I became lost, confused, and insecure. I didn't know how to keep the connection to Universal Love solid when lessons took over. The emotions had become so caught up in the fears and insecurities around the programs. I kept experiencing the lower energy vibrations. When the human mind was not chattering, it was easier to connect to Universal Love. That allowed the energy from the Pure Expansive Loving Beings to flow into the human mind free of clutter and download energy which turned into instructions that the human mind can understand. When the human mind was chattering away, there was an energy block. It stopped the flow and created confusion and a feeling of separation.

The energy downloads felt stronger when enough of the self-defeating beliefs got transformed. The self-defeating beliefs caused the human ego to go into control mode when I gave it power. The attention was on that vibration where the human ego was wanting to have a desired outcome experiencing unpleasant conditions that were there to learn and evolve. The more fixated the focus was with the unpleasant condition, the denser my vibration became. This made it harder to get the messages from the Pure Expansive Loving Beings, which caused the feeling of confusion and separation. This transition from one vibration to another was like a caterpillar moving through the cocoon to become a butterfly. Becoming a free Angelic Spirit took lots of courage and patience to awaken the parts that were dormant and activate the energies to a higher vibration. I learned the act of surrendering the human ego from going into control mode. I learned to shift from reactive mode to compassion, from flight and fight mode to love and surrender mode, and put all my attention on Universal Love. I continue to stay in gratitude and appreciation and feel blessed to have the Universal Pure Expansive Loving Beings in my life that made it easier to transform.

When we let go of the mental attachments and embrace the emotional discomfort, the human ego becomes relaxed. The control mechanisms become dormant. These attachments which include, fixing, figuring out, analyzing, judging, and limitations dissipate. As we let go, which feels like surrendering, we become free from the density and allow a stronger connection to Universal Love. This letting go of the outer world conditions affecting your inner peaceful sanctuary is all about. Being in the world with the vibrations of unconditional love in place of reacting to the conditions of the world. You become more aware of being aware. It is like you become aware of the thoughts, feelings, and sensations of the body and have compassion and unconditional love. Through this awareness, transformation occurs where the areas that are not serving the Inner Spirit gets transmuted to higher frequencies. This is the path of deep awakening to love.

Awareness of the energy behind the beliefs takes it a step deeper because the mental thoughts don't go into figuring out or analyzing the situation. There is no resistance. Resistance is futile, and it doesn't serve. You feel like you are stuck in quicksand and cannot get out. It is the fear of the unknown that can start the resistance. Using shoes as an analogy. You know the shoes with the holes in them are not wearable. You are familiar with the shoes. You don't know if a new pair will be as comfortable so you keep the old shoes. Even though they are not as comfortable. You feel more from a place of love instead of analyzing. The awareness of being aware becomes heightened through the connection to Universal Love. You get to watch the energies move from the human expression into pure nothingness and replaced with omnipotent love.

Chapter 9

Transformation

In 2016, I was experiencing the body's energy acclimatizing to the Angelic frequency. I had experienced both the Angelic expression being active and then the human expression being active. Both were taking turns. I had temporary energy sensations that felt like a glimpse of this higher vibration and then it would disappear. I was getting energy downloads 2 times a day now. I knew there was nothing for me to really do, except to stay allowing the downloaded energies to replace the outdated energies that were moving out. In the summer, I experienced a huge transition from human ego control to the Angelic expression becoming more solid in the mind, heart, and body. I felt this oneness connection through the crown of my head with Universal Love shooting inside. I kept hearing from people who I met say I am a huge ball of light. One guy kept taking pictures of me and staring at me at this event in October I went to.

I was able to see more clearly how the personality was active in others. Their communication and behaviors showed how they were allowing their beliefs to run their life. Their healthy beliefs demonstrated more unconditional love as they expressed it in a positive, happy, and vibrant way. They had so much inner love that their body showed it. I also saw how others had more of their self-defeating beliefs dominate their life. With them, they expressed more negative behaviors and unhappiness and they looked exhausted. They were holding on to so much dense energy and their body showed it. My connection to the Universal Pure Love Beings became more sacred. Below are some special interactions I had with them.

January 19, 2016, the Universal Pure Love Beings downloaded energy that was so profound that I felt it all over the body. Throughout the years I would feel it in the heart and mind. Now I was feeling the pure energy in the body. I kept hearing them tell me to focus on love. It felt very nurturing and different.

January 25, 2016, I felt the Universal Pure Love Beings' energy inside me in a huge way this morning. They were downloading huge amounts of loving energy. They told me that this was to help attract more joyful experiences and not the contrast that I was experiencing. They told me to keep embracing and loving everything I experience to help loosen the contrasted energy. I had a dream that night where I was given a white feather which meant a fresh start. When I woke up, I found a white feather by my bed just like in the dream. I was quite amazed how this feather got here since my bed is a Tempur-Pedic. The white feather symbolized a true confirmation of the new life I was feeling. I never saw a feather in a white color that was so pure and it felt magical to hold. The next few weeks I experienced the human consciousness becoming more expansive where the thoughts were less active. I experienced higher energy frequency thoughts becoming more active. Thoughts of gratitude, love, and joy.

February 4, 2016, The Universal Pure Love Beings told me that I am in a gestation period. The readiness of the physical body and the environment are necessary for the birthing of the new life. They told me to allow it to occur and let go of feeling I had to do anything to prepare. I felt excited because I knew a birthing of a new life was coming. I was feeling a shift of vibrations from one life experience to another. I experienced the other expression's life no longer having a strong hold on me. I was feeling the new energy yet it was not clear how it would look on the physical realm. I was living in an unknown and choosing to stay in trust. There was no familiar past to compare my life. Life was a daily new beginning filled with a choice of love over fear.

February 11, 2016, the Universal Pure Love Beings shared, "when people are operating from a higher expansive frequency their heart is more open and pure than when they are living more in their mental human ego stories." I saw a vision on how Universal Love has no suffering only pure love, joy, peace, prosperity, health, and vitality and anything that is not that is a temptation and lie. I felt freedom finally from all those lies I bought into that had led me to protect myself.

February 16, 2016, I experienced a spiritual vision and a sensation in the body of the other expression's energy being fully released from the body. I felt so much swirling energy that I had to lay down. I was in a funnel of energy. Any energy that was not aligned to the new life got lifted out of the body. It made so much sense why I was experiencing the conflicts throughout the years. Now that the human expression was at a higher frequency, the energy of the other expression got released and mine was coming in more fully. I had a dream that night where I saw Scorpions and Paladins in a room. The dream showed me an experience I had in the year 2006 where they came to me and asked me to help them with their species. They now were helping me by transmuting any remaining energies that were not resonating to my Angelic frequency. I woke up feeling gratitude with them helping me.

February 27, 2016, I received a message from the Angels telling me to raise my energy even higher, connecting stronger to Universal Love so I can experience more positive frequencies. They said to become confident, verbally say positive power statements to continue to train the human mind, and amplify love. That night I had a dream where I rid a small negative entity through intentions of love, peace, joy and prosperity. Universal Love dissipated it. I saw a sign that had the word, Gretchen. They told me that meant inherent courage and endurance to accomplish "The Impossible Dream." They told me I hold keys to the material world, but with this gift comes high spiritual responsibility.

March of 2016, I experienced my Angelic energy in the emotional field. This freedom of experiencing Angelic love in the emotions in place of the human emotions of duality was so peaceful. My connection to the Universal Pure Love Beings was so much more enjoyable. The more I held to the truth of pure love and brought that into the human expression, the greater confidence and ease I felt on the planet. The human expression had experienced so much emotional abuse that it became so tired and protective. This protection got replaced with a vulnerability and trust in the Universal Pure Love Beings taking care of me. This allowed me to feel safe and free to live my daily life with greater joy.

March 6, 2016, I felt a shift from human ego controlling the human form to my Angelic frequency being more active. In the past, the human personality was making the decisions coming more from the human belief systems. I didn't resonate with the personality anymore. I felt my Angelic expression of pure love inside the human form which felt peaceful and content. I was not relying on human beliefs anymore. The connection to Universal Love was providing the answers. There were less mental opinions. It got replaced with compassion and blessings of love. Love started to replace any sense of fear or insecurity.

March 12, 2016, I received a message on how the human ego cannot solve at the level Universal Love can because Universal Love is at a higher frequency. Surrendering unsolved challenges to Universal Love makes life more playful and life flows with greater ease. Expressing from human ego to human ego comes more from a limited point of view to learn lessons and become enlightened. Human ego to Universal Love is omnipotent. Both serve a purpose in life. Anytime we go outside for something we feel is *missing* in our life, we move away from the connection to Universal Love. This only brings the human ego into a control mode, experiencing insecurity, negativity, fear, and limitations. Human ego to Universal Love helps to create innovations beyond the human's perspective. When you Bring Universal Love in all situations and with all people, you experience higher frequency levels of love, joy, prosperity, and peace.

March 26, 2016, the Universal Pure Love Beings downloaded a new energy grid inside the body. They said that it is an energy of expansive oneness. I felt it was necessary to keep my eyes closed making it easier to avoid mental chatter. I felt the body shake for a few minutes. While my eyes were still closed, I felt this sense of excitement and then I saw a spiritual vision of the Universal Pure Love Beings appear in human form. They were smiling at me. From this day forward I feel and see them daily.

March 30, 2016, I had a dream and saw a UFO ship fly into a bigger UFO ship. The bigger UFO ship had circular bubbles around it. I affirmed that any remaining human ego control be lifted out of the energy field of the body. I asked the Universal Pure Love Beings to help me with this.

April 1, 2016, I saw a UFO ship. I felt outdated energies in the 1st chakra by the tailbone get transmuted. The fist chakra symbolizes the core root of the personality. I felt this deep sense of freedom.

April 7, 2016, I received an Angelic message that said let others know to BE love and not to live in fear based protection. Fear closes the heart where you get sucked down into negative energy.

April 12, 2016, I felt the Universal Pure Love Beings. They told me that enough of the human emotions got cleared away for me to live more from an Angelic energy in the heart. They told me to continue to nurture the emotions. They said the Angelic expression _shares_ love while the human emotions _desires_ love. Sharing love is whole and complete while giving and receiving has a tendency to come more from an expectation or conditional place. Sharing love has a higher energy frequency of love. They said with this pure form of love I experience empowerment and will share that love without any expectation of return. Giving and receiving love is a human expression based frequency which incorporates belief systems that trigger the conditional form of love and the expectations of how to give and receive it.

April 30, 2016, I had a dream I was on this very small piece of land with this female. I shared how the relationship I have been ready for is coming to get me and she agrees. We fly up into the sky to a chair with gold pieces of straps over it. I sat down and felt this amazing nurturing love and then I woke up. I noticed my connection to Universal Love shifted from taking breaks and tuning in to fill myself up to that of _being_ full of this love and channeling that love. I felt even greater love and optimism. With the connection to Universal Love, there's a "we" mentality where the "we" includes all in expressing divine love. The "you focus" keeps you separated experiencing more self-absorbed behaviors.

May 6, 2016, While swimming, I again experienced my energy moving more into my Angelic frequency. Two hours later as I focused inside, I felt more of the Angelic Energy and very little of the human expression's energy. The personality belief system was losing more power. Many decisions were made at this human frequency way too long leaving me feeling confused and unsure of myself. Operating at a higher frequency encompassed more abundant energy. I felt more peaceful, joyful, and loving. The Angels told me to stay in gratitude with everything. The 3rd leg of my life was moving me more into expressing these higher vibrational thoughts and emotions. I didn't resonate anymore with denser emotions like fear, insecurity, negativity, or limitations.

May 8, 2016, I had a spiritual vision in the form of a film clip with the two lives parting. The other expression and mine. The paths parting allowed me to step in even more fully into the human expression and acclimate to it being my energy. I was allowing the experience to organically unfold, by staying in my heart and feeling the experience. I didn't analyze or attempt to figure it out. I enjoyed the vision and the experience simultaneously. It was like watching a movie and at the same time participating in the scene.

May 15, 2016, The Angels told me to continue to give my power and attention to the 3rd leg being created. That will keep me in the higher frequencies of love, joy, peace, prosperity, health, and vitality. To keep raising my energy above any unpleasant condition. To not give my attention and power to the old life I was closing out. I committed to focus my attention more on the possibilities of my amazing new life that was unfolding. The more I shifted my focus off conditions and people who could irritate me if I allowed it and put it on Universal Love, the happier I felt. It was like planting a seed and nurturing it with food, love, water, and attention as I allowed it to grow. I kept nurturing the human emotions to continue to feel love inside.

By putting attention on higher frequencies of love and choosing to stay in joy and peace, you become one with that connection. There is freedom from the denser vibrations because life is full of heightened levels of love, joy, peace, prosperity, health, and vitality. A connection to Universal Love is what heightens these expansive vibration energies. When the Inner Spirit is active, you experience heightened frequencies of energy first. That energy turns into gratitude and abundant thoughts; happy, loving, and peaceful emotions; and you experience more vibrancy. Love, confidence, positive focus and abundance replaces insecurities, fear, negativity, and limitations. That night, I put on an event where I channeled the Universal Pure Love Beings living energy for the participants to activate their Inner Spirit. I had a dream where there were huge amounts of UFO Orbs flying all around me. I felt enormous amounts of love. When I awoke I felt the Angelic expression so fully in the body, mind, and emotions.

May 24, 2016, In the morning, during my meditation I affirmed love throughout the mind, body, emotions and energy field. The more I affirmed love, the greater the energy became. I raised my energy above the human collective consciousness and saw a portal open. I went into the portal and experienced heightened levels of pure divine love. *I then saw the Angels and shared how I didn't understand why I had to go through so many years of experiencing dense vibrations and the suffering from it. They shared that it was to learn about compassion, to become more empowered, and to learn so I am able to help humankind better.*

May 25, 2016, I saw the clouds make a heart and 2 eyes. I was talking to a friend about my interactions with the mate I'm getting ready to meet. I started to feel him. He was communicating so clearly like he was in the room. It was amazing. We were sharing how fun it will be when we finally meet in physical form. How wonderful our life together will be. We talked about a vacation together and all the activities we want to experience together.

May 26, 2016, During my meditation, I felt the guy I am going to saw a dove land on the railing outside and during a walk I saw 5 doves fly to the right of me. I heard doves when I took a walk.

May 27, 2016, I awoke to a bright light that shot in the room. The room was so bright. I felt this enormous energy of love. I looked at the time it was 1 AM. I saw the UFO right in front of me passing very slowly by. I sent love to it. I had so much energy buzzing through me. I stayed awake for a while enjoying the energy. I watched the UFO ship with its beauty passing by. I felt so much love inside. I would love for the planet to experience this so we all can live in greater love and peace.

May 28, 2016, I went to Newport beach in Oregon. While walking, I channeled Universal Love. I walked for two and half hours feeling so much love. I saw Love and Joy written in the sand during the walk. I experienced so much love and everything looked beautiful. On my way back, I was getting thirsty and tired and became a little delirious. I was not sure where I parked and became amazed I walked as far as I did. I started to have feelings of fear that I would not find the parking spot. I communicated to the fear sharing how I could go up to the hotels to ask where the lot I parked at was. I told the fear to calm down and that the fear is an illusion since I could get help with finding the parking spot. I told the fear I trust Universal Love to guide me to the parking spot. I asked Universal Love for help and instantly saw the people who parked next to me. I was standing in front of the place I parked and they confirmed it when I asked them. I thanked them.

I noticed my energy was lower due to the fear I had experienced. I learned that when I am in a true love connection, everything is beautiful and when not the human ego becomes more protective with a tendency of judgment, fear, limitation, and negativity. The vision I saw of beauty turned into the mind having thoughts, opinions, and judgment. The streets didn't seem pretty. I saw sad and happy people walking. Everything shifted when I fell out of the energy of love. It was fascinating to become aware of how the human mind experiences life with the different levels of love. The higher the energy frequency of love the more gratitude and enlightened beauty we express. Whereas, the lack of love, fills the thoughts with more judgment, lack, fear, and negativity.

June 3, 2016, I felt high vibrations of love and heard a message about putting my attention on my heart. To stay out of any mental chatter. I heard to continue to keep my focus on love, joy, peace, and prosperity. I started to feel and see the Universal Pure Love Beings' energies all around me. There was a thin transparent veil and I could see them. I felt so loved. Their energy was so nurturing and playful. They had this innocence of unconditional love, joy, and peace. I was so grateful for them being in my life.

June 4, 2016, I felt high frequencies of love this morning and again I heard to stay in my heart. This time, I felt it also in the mental realm. I felt the Universal Pure Love Beings move my energy more into the heart which shot energy into the mind. I felt some limiting energy. These limiting beliefs came about after the birth of the body and were deeply ingrained. I felt the energies behind the beliefs. As these energies were coming up to be released, I focused on Universal Love and surrendered them with gratitude. I felt inner peace that went instantly into the heart. The Universal Pure Love Beings helped me clear the other expression's father's energy in the first chakra, by grounding more into the physical body. I was initially hesitant about grounding and then decided to do it. I felt and saw this limiting energy moving out of the 1st chakra. I experienced lightness in the body and happier thoughts. The energy of the father never fully got released in the past years that the other expression tenaciously worked on because fear was feeding it. That explains why she and I had experienced emotional abusive relationships.

When we hold on to the energy out of fear and/or insecurity, we have a hold on it like it is truth. Holding on to a belief as truth brings more of it into our life as experiences to confirm that belief. By releasing the energy behind the self-defeating beliefs, we experience the limiting energy as an illusion. We come to know that it is not our truth, which allows any limiting energy to become replaced with healthier beliefs more organically. You experience unnecessary struggles when you focus on the limiting energy and give it power. This creates mental chatter and emotional turmoil. Shifting our focus on Universal Love helps to break the pattern which brings us greater joy.

June 5, 2016, I experienced spiritual visions of what masculine and feminine energy feels like and how it can control desired outcomes. I saw how the masculine human energy expressed as wanting to make something happen. The mind became overactive with attempted to figure things out and set goals. I experienced deep desires to push time frames around desired outcomes to manifest sooner than they were. I experienced more impatience and frustrations as a result of the control around time, goals, and manifestations. Then I started to experience the feminine human energy becoming more active. I started to experience more of an allowing with desired outcomes to come about.

By surrendering the outcome I wanted to the Universe, the Universe delivered the fruition within minutes. Trusting the Universe and allowing the flow of the creation is what brought about the "Univestation" of it on the physical realm. There was no man-ifesting which had more control. In place, was more Universal delivering the vision as I stayed in the abundant energy around it. The vision I had helped me to understand the transition between human ego creating and my Angelic expression creating. I experienced a partnering with my Angelic frequency in human form and Universal Love as more "Univesting" than manifesting. Energies such as prosperity, love, joy, and peace were the primary focus around any form created and materialized in the physical realm. There was no focusing on a goal being created through a visionary process. That would best be described as a vision board, where you cut out pictures and focus on that. For me, it was more of an energy like feeling love, joy, peace, prosperity in my daily experiences. The forms materialized in daily experiences that resonated with the energy of love, joy, peace, and prosperity. The Universe knew what I wanted.

I started feeling a deeper sense of prosperity, inner joy, love, and peace. Higher vibrations of nurturing energies were coming inside the heart. The mind was not active with figuring out rather experiencing this sense of gratitude and expansiveness. I was feeling calm and playful in the human form. The focus on what was missing in my life created the unpleasant emotions and thoughts. Celebrating life by living in the Universal Love realm heightened frequencies of joy, peace, and love. The limiting energy which felt like something was missing from the human ego desires got replaced with a sense of abundance.

Human ego control reminds me of the Wizard from the Wizard of Oz. The Wizard pretended to portray a powerful being more than it actually was. It scared many people and was successful in portraying this huge powerful, mighty being. When the Cowardly lion, Scarecrow, Tin woodman, and Dorothy found out it was actually a man, the Wizard became embarrassed and weak. It no longer was a powerful force that controls. That is how the human ego control can work. When we give it power and let it control our life, we can become weak from any self-defeating beliefs and empowered from the healthy beliefs. In both situations, we are giving our power away to an illusion, the personality. We can believe it is alive and rules us. Yet in actuality, we are the one that is powerful. We as a spirit being living in the body experiencing thoughts and emotions that relate to the personality. We can decide whether we choose to live from a certain belief or not. When we can realize that we are not the thoughts, emotions, and body. We experience them, thereby we can become free of their control. We get to live life as we always dreamed.

The personality can become very enticing. Anytime you put your attention on the past, mental chattered stories, or your emotions on unpleasant current conditions and feed it, you identify with it as who you are. It takes over and you start to relive the experiences in your current life. The unpleasant memories and conditions have a hold on you if you are feeding it with your focus on fears, limitations, negativity, and/or insecurities. The best way out is to focus on forgiveness and self-love. Forgiveness is a way to move past the pain around the memories and free yourself of the hold it has on you. Self-love helps to move your vibration to a higher vibration, where your attention and focus is more on love vs. the pain of the memory. Ideally, if you can shift your attention away from the past and future and into the present, you can choose to enjoy life. Then you are vibing at a higher frequency of love, joy, peace, prosperity, and vitality. The present helps you stay away from focusing any attention on past unpleasant memories or current conditions and allows you to enjoy creating from the moment. I also find it helpful to bring forth wonderful happy memories and successful experiences into the present to support positive living now. We don't know what the future visions will actually bring so that could end up being a distraction and a tactic for the human ego to control.

Staying present is an effective way to becoming more empowered and enjoy life. When you feed your daily life with positivity, love, joy, peace, abundance, and vitality, you start to live life more from a higher frequency. This prevents you from getting sucked down into unpleasant experiences, energies, memories, and feelings. You shift more into acceptance, trust, faith, and stay connected to Universal Love. Your life becomes more of a playground instead of fear based living. Staying present allows you to become instantly aware and shift your attention off any unpleasant experiences and more on love, gratitude, and joy. This keeps your energies at a high vibratory rate.

My Angelic expression being more active in the human form made it easier to let go and let Universal Love lead me in life. This included lessons I was learning, clarity, and inspired action. Allowing Universal Love to lead, made it more peaceful and joyful. I was more receptive in love and definitely more relaxed because the human heart was open and filled with higher frequencies of love. I enjoyed the journey of daily life more too. The truth of love and prosperity replaced any fear, insecurity, negativity, or limitation. I knew awareness was the biggest clue to moving from human ego control to that of my Angelic expression being alive and active in the human expression. I learned that by being present with any thoughts and feelings and choosing love, joy, and peace supported my empowerment and connection to the truth. The truth of Universal Love outweighed over any thoughts the personality was experiencing. It became easier to shift from being the observer of thoughts and emotions to Universal Love. I didn't feel it was necessary for me to figure out what was going on. I trusted Universal Love would be a better teacher than the human thoughts and that I would get more effective results with my life. My connection made life even more enjoyable. Since I was not allowing the personality to run my life with what was going on in the outer world, I felt even more effective with what Universal Love instructed me to do.

Unpleasant thoughts or conditions had little to no power over me because I chose to not allow it. I chose to focus more on my connection and being happy, peaceful and loving in my daily life. I was aware of the thoughts I just didn't give it much attention. I shifted any chattering thoughts to gaps of silence. The focus became stronger on my connection to Universal Love. That is how the human mind became more aware of the intellectual mind. That is when I started to experience my Angelic frequency even more in the human form. The intellectual mind is more expansive with unlimited abundant frequencies and innovative thoughts. It doesn't rely on beliefs. It connects more to Universal abundance. I felt greater freedom from any fear or insecurity. I was aware that they were just programs running through a voice command. By not putting my focus or attention on, fear, or insecurity, it became weak. I became more empowered within the human expression.

The human mind sees through its beliefs where it compares. gives opinions, judges, or accepts. In the process of evolving them, you get to decide whether you want them to run your life. When you raise your emotions into higher vibrations of love, you experience more from the Inner Spirit's eyes and Universal Love. There are no conflicting human thoughts or unpleasant emotions. You experience heightened energies of love. When the human thoughts are more active, you miss out on more opportunities of love. When you allow a joyful heart to lead, you get to experience life from a new perspective with greater opportunities of love. Limitations, fears, insecurities, and negativity from any actively running unresolved beliefs get transmuted quicker through embracing instead of analyzing. Analyzing prevents you from enjoying life as fully as you can because you are allowing past beliefs to dictate and continue into your present life. When you lead more from a joyful heart, you feel more empowered and live in the present moment. Any conflicting beliefs get resolved more effectively because you are aware and can embrace them as they arise. You get to choose to let them go with love and confidence knowing that is not a truth according to the Universal Laws of love rather a lie that is living and running your life.

June 14, 2016, I got confirmation from the Angels that one of the clients I was working with reached a fork in the road where I was starting to feel I was to stop working with her. She was attempting to pull my energy down for a few months. I kept doing everything I could to help her stop, including sending generic emails to the group and verbalizing instructions on how to focus more on the heart and not on my energy. Nothing seemed to work. I knew that something had to change because I was losing interest in working with her. I asked the Universal Pure Love Beings to assist.

June 15, 2016, I went to this Native American Ceremony. The group went on a spiritual journey in a meditative state where I met elders that put a necklace of courage on me that had wings of hawks. That got ingrained into my heart. They did a ceremony, and I smoked a pipe with one puff. During the water segment of the meditation, I met young elders that appeared and we went swimming in this lake. I felt lots of love as we went into the spring. I saw me walking down the aisle with my future husband experiencing lots of joy. Then the elders came back and blew white smoke into my heart purifying it. I went up into my Angelic Realm and heard welcome home. As we imagined going into next year's summer, I heard a voice tell me that I have an Angelic mission to complete with the planetary evolution. As the meditation ended, The natives said to ground that experience. My energy felt heavy as I got out of the experience.

The next few days, I experienced lots of agitation and incomplete energies. I prayed for help because I knew something was not aligned. I was experiencing lots of dense energies in the ethers, wanting me to play the savior and caretaker with their life. I was feeling frustrated by this energy attempting to drag my energy to a denser vibration. I told these energies that I was not their savior or caretaker and they are responsible for their life. The energies left. I was able to bring my energy to a higher vibration. I decided not to go to grounding types of events. This got confirmed when a speaking engagement abruptly ended that resonated with shamanic energy. At first, I felt confused by the email and didn't understand what was going on. Why was he not interested in me speaking? It didn't make any sense. The guy in charge of bringing in speakers didn't return my calls or reply to my email. We never met since it was his predecessor who set me up to speak and she quit. The Angels told me that this door was closing because I didn't belong there. That was not part of my purpose where my Angelic energies would be received. When I heard this message, I felt relieved and blessed the experience.

June 18, 2016, I woke up feeling this dense emotional energy. It was attempting to pull my energy down into a lower vibration. I said out loud, "I am not your savior or caretaker and you didn't want my help." I felt these energies leave, and I closed an energy vibration hole beneath me and started to raise my energy above it. The Angels appeared and showed me the lower vibrations in energy format asking if I am choosing to no longer work with that energy vibration and I said yes. They pulled the energies out of me. I felt lighter and more freedom. I found out it was the client that I that talked about on June 14. I no longer was able to work with her and she was still in my energy field. The Angels told me she had other lessons to learn that were not aligned with my purpose. That night at 12 PM, I got an email from that client specifying that she no longer wanted to work together, asking all her testimonials be deleted and signed off with the word peace. I felt relieved that she ended it so that I can have a peaceful closure. The next few days was transformative where energetic doors were closing and my connection to Universal Love reigned.

June 19, 2016, I saw 3 UFO ships in a "V" shape. There was so much love that my body was tingling. The Universal Pure Love

Beings cleared the energy around the native ceremony. I saw the native energy leave, and they pulled the ingrained symbol off my heart. I felt my energy go back up, and I started to feel happier. I received a message from them that I was to stop putting myself in places that asked you to ground your energy, which includes Shamans and Native American ceremonies. We had different missions in life and it was not compatible with my purpose. I started to leave groups and visualized myself leaving this vibration with love and peace. It felt challenging and at the same time freeing. I heard this message that said, "step more fully into my higher vibration frequency."

During a channeling session that night, I heard a guided message, "there is a graduation into the next chapter in life, leaving behind all the drama." Stepping into the Angelic expression more fully meant freedom. That of which was not aligned was closing abruptly and falling away. It was uncomfortable and emotionally challenging. I had to stand strong in my empowerment and not personalize the doors that were closing as rejection. I chose to look at it as a form of celebration. Standing strong in the commitment helped to anchor in the higher frequencies more fully. I looked up the Spiritual meaning of a "v." "V" means *Universal Love is taking care my life. My prayers are heard. The Angels are with me. That doors to my old life are closing so that I am prepared to walk into the new life with greater ease. That some setbacks or delays are pertinent pieces of the puzzle for me to complete the last chapter of my life.* This is so true.

The next morning I woke up, and I felt so much emotional, needy energy. I didn't know what was going on. I felt the intensity and stayed with it, embracing the energies. I didn't let the energy of insecurity run my life by calling people and talking about it or by allowing it to make me feel dis-empowered. Out of nowhere, I felt the energy downloads I was getting from the Universal Pure Loving Beings all these years become active. The Angelic energy activation in the human expression transmuted the needy energy. I felt excited, energized, and empowered. I never got to experience the nurturing from a birth mom so that energy of confidence was something I didn't have when I incarnated.

The other expression had to learn to build inner confidence and nurturing inwardly. I took on what she learned and from the energy downloads to support an even higher level frequency of emotional nurturing and love. I got that from these Universal Pure Loving Beings. I would compare this to a child that was born into loving parents that adored and empowered the child. When there is a true connection to Universal Love, you don't go outside looking for love or higher frequency places. You find it inside and share that with others. Prior to me feeling this inside and knowing this truth, the emotions were searching outside for nurturing. There would be a longing for emotional love and a searching outside for people and places that had felt high in frequency. Now that I was feeling more emotional nurturing inside, there was less of a feeling like something was missing. I didn't feel I had to protect myself from others. I chose to share my love with others who knew how to share love authentically. When you have Universal Love fully in your heart and you feel empowered, there's no insecurity, limitation, fear, or negativity. Pure love and self-empowerment replaces that.

While relaxing, I experienced spiritual movie clips showing my life on Earth from the time I incarnated until now. I saw how I was having the courage to partner more with Universal Love and my Angelic expression. Deciding not to play the savior role freed me. I had put so much energy on "saving" people based on what they wanted from me as an Angelic. In the midst of this, I discounted the human emotional needs on some level. The human expression felt deprived of feeling the higher frequency of love because it felt trapped from playing the savior role. I was not able to express my Angelic expression fully because of this which led to inner conflicts between the two vibration frequencies. On some level, I had confusion with regard to my purpose as an Angelic. I felt like I was responsible for the awakening of human expression. I learned to have discernment on who I chose to work with. They had to have an honest commitment and readiness to their spiritual awakening to work together and have an open loving heart. If they were not ready, then working together was not an appropriate fit.

With my Angelic expression more fully in the human form, that of which was not aligned closed and fell away. I experienced energy doors abruptly closing which felt uncomfortable. Staying strong in the commitment helped to anchor in the higher frequencies more fully. When that was complete, I felt free to move into another expansive energy vibration. By deciding to partner more with Universal Love and my Angelic purpose in place of playing the savior of what people wanted from me, helped me to move more into my Angelic energy. By choosing to walk in higher vibrations of love, I freed myself from allowing others that were not committed to higher vibrations of love to drag my energy down. Standing strong in self-love dominated more over feeling responsible for other people's lives.

There is a fine distinction of self-directed leadership where it is necessary for others to do their part in taking care of themselves and not leaning on me or others to do it for them. I became strong in my connection to oneness. I was living life with stronger healthier values. I was feeling empowered which heightened the vibrations of love. I was feeling these higher vibrations of love so strongly in the human expression that life was becoming more mystical filled with greater levels of joy and peace. I noticed when I was around people who lived more in duality mindset I was able to turn my attention and focus toward Universal Love. This shifted my energy away from any potential judging to compassion, acceptance, and love. This solidifies the statement, "whatever you put your attention in on long enough, you become one with." Universal Love was stronger than the duality mindset.

With all the messages I was getting with regard to meeting the twin flame and actually feeling his presence, I discovered the human expression wanting to force the time frame. It was so subtle how the human expression, was feeding this and attracting people who were single and just engaged to show the human expression to trust Universal timing. There was a part of the human expression that was losing trust. This became clear through people I attracted in a 2-day span. I noticed one day a picture of the twin flame and an affirmation about meeting him kept falling off the wall by my altar. I had it attached to a picture of Christ Love. Each time I put it up, it would fall back down. When I became aware of the human personality wanting to force the time frame, I was able to break the pattern. Letting go of the personality desires and putting my focus more on aligning to Universal Love, helped me become aware in breaking the pattern. The picture stopped falling off the wall.

I decided to "Let Go and Let Universal Love run my life." Universal Love knows what my heart chooses to experience in life. I felt peaceful as I let go and trusted Universal Love to deliver. If there are any parts of the human expression running your life in a limiting, negative, insecure, or fearful place, you will attract people and experiences that will vibrate at that frequency as lessons attempting to show you the pattern. Becoming aware of the pattern helps to evolve those areas and you don't continue to attract more lessons in those areas. When there is a direct connection to Universal Love, both the human expression and the Inner Spirit have this amazing cooperative bond. The human expression feed off the Inner Spirit. The human expression receives love from the Inner Spirit and that love gets amplified by Universal Love. You experience deeper confidence within and you radiate that through your mannerism.

June 27, 2016, I saw a circular UFO ship where I live that set off the security alarms. They kept going on and off for a half an hour. I felt a higher frequency of love inside the body. My ears started to ring which meant they were communicating something to me. The sound was their way of getting messages to me. The message was to focus on my heart and keep loving the human emotions.

June 28, 2016, I woke up feeling the human expressions and saw spiritual visions of hearts. 5 hours later, I went for a walk. It was a sunny day, and I was thinking how nice it would be to have the beloved partner next to me. I saw a big cloud in the shape of a heart. To the right of the heart was a small heart and underneath that was a shape of an angel. I heard real loud to let go of the energy and the attachment to the timing of meeting the twin flame. I knew I had to let go of the feeling of me "missing" out on having the mate in the physical realm so that I can allow Universal Love to bring it to me. I embraced the energy around "missing" and focused on gratitude and appreciation continuously throughout the day. I decided to trust Universal timing even though I had disappointments around the timing of his arrival.

July 1, 2016, I woke up and felt lots of negative energy. I was not aware of where it was coming from. I rose my energy above it and imagined white light on it. I felt Universal Love inside. The higher I rose my energy, the more I felt and saw the Universal Pure Love Beings. I had a deeper awareness with getting hooked into negative vibrations. I would feel these negative vibrations and if I gave it my power, I got sucked into it. I would express at that level, including negativity, limitations, fears, and insecurities. When I rose above that energy and connected to love, everything I saw started to come from that vibration, including positivity, prosperity, love, and empowerment. Things that were bothering me stopped bothering me.

I started to love and embrace all that would have annoyed me if I allowed it. I was experiencing so much love that all I chose to do was love. They were showing me this pattern to help human humanity with. We have the choice on how we live on this planet. We can live in the vibrations of drama and experience life at that level. We can live in the vibrations of love and experience life at that level. Life is more of a playground filled with so much joy, peace, love, prosperity, and vitality in heightened levels of love. You experience freedom from all the energies that have kept you stuck in insecurities, fears, negativity, and limitations when you say no to that and yes to love. Like mother Mary says, "Invite me to that of which is pro love."

I had visions of this transition from one vibration to another which initially was confusing. I would experience the human thoughts focusing on complaining, judging, limitations, negativity and the emotions feeling frustrations for no reason. My Angelic presence took over as it stood firm and confident with a focus on positivity. I would embrace the thoughts and emotions with love. When we let go of an outdated belief, we experience what feels like a void. We can use positive imagination in the midst of a temporary void and fill it with loving energy. Surrender anything that is not aligned with feeling happy and love to Universal Love. This will help to stay neutral. I became aware of this split feeling shifting more into a oneness at a higher vibration of love. My role was to hold the "high watch" around love.

Through this transition, it became easier to silence the chattering thoughts knowing to focus on gratitude and embrace the human emotions to experience more self-love. This is how oneness became more solid with expanding vibrations of love, joy, peace, prosperity, and vitality. I socialized in places where I felt higher energies around love, joy, peace, and prosperity. This included more time in nature, meditation, bird watching, swimming, gardening, uplifting music. and singing. When the vibration shifts from a negative realm to a positive realm, my perspective shifted in the human expression. Rather than have conflicts, I experienced more harmony. Rather than feel like two people were living inside the body, I experienced more oneness living. I saw through the eyes of Universal Love.

When we experience life in a drama based vibration and then decide we no longer choose it, it takes courage and commitment to break the energy cycle. The human ego is use to being in that vibration. You are breaking a pattern of attraction. Continuing to say no to entertaining or participating in the drama and saying yes to being happy and loving, will eventually break the habitual pattern. Then you experience true freedom. Developing higher self-love, self-awareness, and self-confidence, coupled with forgiveness, and compassion with those that expressed at the denser vibrations are the ways to take care of yourself. Expressing love and compassion and experiencing empowerment helped to break the pattern of getting sucked into the denser vibrations. When I was around those that had negative or judgmental behaviors, I would take my attention off them and focus on Universal Love. I knew if I put my attention on them, I would have a tendency to judge and get sucked down into that vibration. I kept choosing to come from compassion knowing they are doing the best they could with where they were currently expressing. I chose to stay confident and be strong enough inside to say no to allowing that vibration to pull me down.

Staying connected to Universal Love and taking that into our daily life environments provides for higher love connections. If we go out looking for that connection, we are going out with a limiting belief that something missing or lacking inside. We feel we have to go outside to find it to fulfill what we feel is not inside. We won't find it as a solid internal connection. We may experience it if we are around high vibration energies. That is only a band-aid approach because we again have this desired expectation of something we want in our life that we feel is missing and looking for it outside of ourselves. If we connect to Universal Love first, we become whole and complete in love. We fill ourselves up with this complete form of omnipotent love and abundances and take that out into the world. Now we are more empowered. It does not matter if what is in the environment matches. If it does match, we celebrate with it and if it does not match, we still stay connected to Universal Love. There's no feeling of missing or searching going on.

If an environment feels dense and all of a sudden you feel pulled into it, it could be as subtle as us allowing your energy to get sucked down by becoming a sponge to that energy you are in. You could be giving your attention to it through opinionated thoughts from that experience. You could be allowing your emotions to get hooked in and becoming reactive. All of this is a form of attachment. They all have some form of expectation because you are looking to experience some outcome from that experience. If you are not feeling inner peace, love, and joy, you became attached more to the story of something missing. You can shift through self-love, by clearing the thoughts and connecting to Universal Love. Love is always the answer to all.

When we embrace or come from compassion, we are able to detach from getting caught up in the energy vibrations. It is easy to get sucked into these energies if we have any subtle insecurity, fear, or lessons around them. Getting sucked into these energies teaches us lessons to empowers us. When we reach an energy vibration of self-love, self-confidence, self-awareness, forgiveness, and compassion around any condition that we are either learning from or detaching from, we become free.

We cannot free ourselves from what the lessons are teaching us when we judge any of it by focusing on what is wrong. Attempting to solve it, understand it, analyze it, fix it, correct it, or change it you will only stay stuck in it. We stay stuck in what is wrong with the condition as we fixate our attention there. In order to move beyond this, it is necessary to clear any thoughts and move our energy into self-love. To put our attention more on Universal Love. When we express love with conviction and empowerment, we move away from self-doubt and what's wrong. Focusing on what is wrong with the conditions of our life keeps us feeling separate from the oneness connection to Universal Love. Christ says to love all. This includes what we perceive as enemies and unpleasant conditions in our life. Love is always the answer. Feeding hate with hate is not the answer.

For me being confident and loving was important in my life. Being insecure sucked me into denser vibrations where I would become irritated. Being an ultra sensitive, it took commitment and lots of focus to strengthen the vibrations. I had to move passed the hate and blaming the denser vibrations. That was my way of playing the victim. Forgiveness, compassion, self-confidence, and love provided freedom and greater self-confidence. The more I focused on Universal Love and loving the human emotions, the easier it was to stay in the energy of love. *Wanting* happiness and love is different from *choosing and committing* to being happy and loving. Choice and commitment are coming more from empowerment. "Wanting" is coming more from limitations and missing. People's behaviors expressed at a denser vibration came into my life either to make me stronger internally to love or they needed love. I no longer committed to play the teacher role. Instead, I chose to just *BE* love in place of feeling I had to *DO* something about their behaviors. The Angels kept confirming this, including in my dreams, in meditation, and through channeling messages to me. I am so grateful for the Universal Pure Love Beings' energy downloads. I trust and love them completely.

The body became ready to feel more of higher frequency vibrations because it released enough of the ancestral energies and self-defeating beliefs. The energy shifted to more expansive awareness and a deeper connection to Universal Love in place of limitations, negativity, judging, insecurity. I started to feel the Angelic presence more fully in the human mind, where there were heightened levels of prosperity, love, peace, and joy. I got to celebrate life more fully. I chose peace over righteous behaviors if someone did something that seemed disturbing. I chose peace over allowing chaos to bother me. I chose neutrality, peace, and love. My connection to Universal Love became stronger. The human thoughts became more silent in peace, joy, and love. The mind of Universal Love has no problems. Universal Love knows solutions, joy, peace, prosperity, and vitality. Imagining positive possibilities and conscious focusing on what is "right" with the world replaces imagining the worst scenarios.

Knowing I am not the human thoughts helped me to train the human mind to see infinite possibilities in the mind of Universal Love. The human mind partnering with the spirit mind sees innovative solutions, bringing about expansive awareness. As the human mind started to focus more on positive thinking and possibilities, life became more enjoyable. I felt more inner joy by imagining possibilities in place of worrying, focusing on what is missing in life, attempting to make things happen, and analyzing for understanding. Acceptance and allowing the imagination to see life from what I would enjoy experiencing became more dominant. I celebrated life more, experiencing peace, joy, love, and abundance on heightened levels.

July 5, 2016, I went to the Oregon coast and then to my favorite site for a birthday celebration of the other expression. I decided to camp out overnight and see if I can experience the Universal oneness connection like Christ had at such a profound level that he became awakened to Universal Love and became the messenger. I read that he surrendered the human mind completely to God, and that is how his awakening occurred. So I set off to the beach with the same intention. I was having mixed feelings for some reason on driving to the coast to experience this.

On May 28th when I went to the Oregon coast, I was feeling such a high with love. I had seen the words love and joy in the sand as I took a two and half hour walk. This time, I experienced heavy energy. It was the complete opposite. I arrived at the coast feeling high and noticed I was starting to give my attention to the heavy energy. I was so surprised that the energy was completely the opposite of what I had experienced in May. I said out loud, "I guess me looking to the environment here at the beach to match the love I was feeling inside is an expectation." I then said that I am better off taking what is inside and sharing it in my daily life. If I get a frequency match in the environment or with others than we can celebrate together. If I don't, then I won't become disappointed since I am not expecting it. I knew I was complete with coming here and said that out loud as well. I became surprised when I saw a spiritual vision of the ancestral energies going into the light. I am guessing they came to celebrate the other expression birthday. I decided that celebrating July 5 was no longer necessary since it was not my birthday.

I decided to leave and go to my favorite sacred site and stay there overnight instead. When I arrived, I experienced such high levels of love way beyond what I experienced there before. I said a prayer out loud that I would like to experience the profound connection that Christ experienced when he surrendered his human mind to God. I said I would like to as well, in a deeper way. I already knew I was not the mind, body, or emotions rather experiencing life through the mind, body, and emotions. The vibrations became so high, I couldn't sleep. I was feeling energy beyond anything I ever experienced. I started to feel the human thoughts and watched them evaporate into nothingness. I stayed present and observed.

There was no way I was sleeping no matter how much I attempted. I had way too much energy going on that kept me wired. I experienced such a connection in the human form to these higher frequencies of love that I was experiencing at this sacred site. Freedom to share love beyond any fear of it. Freedom to know even deeper that any form of limitations, fears, insecurities, and negativity which is the personality holding on to some illusion. The illusion becoming real in some form by feeding it with attention and power. I knew that was not my truth. My truth is the connection to Universal Love and through this love, I get to experience positive abundant thoughts, happy loving feelings, and an energized body. The thoughts are there, yet I don't give them my attention or power through fear or insecurity. I don't allow them to pull me into judgment or negativity. I am sure this is the step toward what Christ was experiencing. I even felt Christ at the sacred spiritual site. My life was shifting to something beyond anything else. The expansion keeps getting better.

July 12, 2016, I experienced huge amounts of white light energies. The light shot through the mind and shook the body. I kept affirming how I release all human ego controlling my life. How I choose my Angelic expression to become more active with the truth of knowing I am an Angelic expressing in human form. I experienced unlimited Universal Love. An expansive vastness of energies running up and down the human body that kept triggering lights in the mind. The mind experienced bursts of energies that triggered an awakening realization of the truth of divine love. Love that kept expanding into other realms. The mind was traveling through different realms throughout the Universe. I was seeing stars and experiencing the unlimited and vastness of space. I became aware of a new way of perceiving and living life.

I felt my Angelic expression in the human form in a deeper way. I had a deep inner realization of how I was allowing the human ego to still control on a subtle level. I was aware of how I used tools such as, affirmation, visioning, visualization, and meditation attempting to honor what human ego wanted to experience and acquire in life. Sometimes the human expression would tell the Universe what it wanted. It was only when the human expression got exhausted with the subtle forcing that it surrendered and allowed Universal Love to lead. I became aware of these tools either working for a short amount of time and then stopped working or not working at all, making me feel incompetent. It felt more like a band-aid than a genuine solution. The energy download I experienced today woke up the mind to letting go of control period. I felt heightened loving energies inside the human expression. This is my truth. I became aware that through love and connection to Universal Love, life happens more magically.

July 14, 2016, I saw 2 angel wings in the sky and the word love in the middle. I saw a spiritual vision of the human ego dying on some level where it was no longer dominating my life and my Angelic expression becoming more active. I saw the human expression and the Angelic expression on two separate energy levels. The first level showed the Angelic expression having a human experience where the human ego was actively controlling.

The second level showed the Angelic expression having a spiritual experience in human form where my Angelic expression was more active. I was moving more into an Angelic Spirit having an Angelic experience. The first level had denser energy which symbolized how the human ego moves through lessons to evolve creating incremental higher energy vibration alignments to Universal Love vibrations. Once it reaches a certain energy vibration, the human ego loses control and the Inner Spirit becomes activated and starts to take over. The human mind no longer ran my daily life. The human mind being the beliefs and the thoughts associated with those beliefs. The Angelic energy was doing more of the communication and less of the human chattering around opinions and beliefs. My connection to Universal Love became my form of spiritual guidance where I would get my teachings directly from the Universe. I was either hearing, feeling, and/or seeing visions of inspired instructions at a Universal Loving vibration. The vibration in the human form was becoming more of a match to my Angelic frequency.

July 17, 2016, I spiritually pulled to drive to Mt. Shasta. When I got to the top of the hill where the mountain resided, I pulled off to the side of the road. I closed my eyes and felt energies going into the mind. It looked like spider webs shooting out creating grids of energies. I knew these were energy grids that would bring more peace and love on the planet. It was fun to experience this.

July 21, 2016, Throughout the day I kept affirming being an Angelic in the human form. This is unlike having a human experience as an Angelic. As a human experience, I felt more separateness from Universal Love's frequency. I felt unconditional love at a higher frequency that is pure and joyous in the Angelic expression more so than in the human form. When I meditated I rose my energy and felt some human dense energy go into the light. I realized how the human dense energy was blocking me from coming more fully in the human form. The more I focused on having an Angelic experience vs. human experience the lighter the energy felt inside and happier I felt. When the human expression was more active, there was so much struggle and attempting to manifest at more prosperous, positive, unconditional love vibrations. The more the human ego attempted to control this, the more I attracted what I didn't want. I realized that the Universe brings me the "Unifestations" in place of the human expression attempting to manifest at the vibration it was at. That will never suffice compared to what the Universe would bring.

July 22, 2016, while volunteering at a hot balloon event, I saw 3 stars in a "v" shape. I noticed the stars had unusual energies coming from them. Were they distant UFO ships or stars? At that moment, I received a channeled message to continue to focus on the Angelic mind versus the human mind by expanding the consciousness energy beyond the mediocre to excellence. I felt they were distant UFO ships. The mediocre is where the human thoughts dominate having opinions. The Angelic mind has more oneness connection to pure love. I kept expanding the energy and aligning it more with the main star that seemed more like Sirius so that I could see if there were any more messages. I felt this surge of loving energy running throughout the body. After that I knew were complete with their messages.

July 24, 2016, I put on a monthly event. The Universal Pure Love Beings told me to create an energy triangle in the front of the heart with silver light and in the back of the heart with gold light. I did this for all participants, including myself. I saw energy shooting through to the center. I had no idea what it meant until July 28th when it became clear. Removing the protection shield off the heart chakra in the earlier years and being open to receiving the pure loving energy made it easier for me to feel the energy downloads. I chose to become vulnerable and at the same time have healthy empowered boundaries. I experienced freedom from what felt like chains in my heart to feeling more nurturing.

Protecting my heart the way I was, comes from a victim consciousness. It says something about not wanting to get hurt again and thereby creates walls. That keeps us from experiencing healthy forms of authentic love. Setting healthy boundaries and having a strong conviction on what I chose to experience in my life was more important than fearing being hurt. The fear keeps us in hiding and healthy boundaries, love, and empowerment we get to enjoy living life. Having a strong connection to Universal Love and choosing to become consciously present each day, is a healthy way of taking responsibility for our life. We are not responsible for others' lives and their lessons. Being supportive without caretaking gives us freedom to live our life more fully. Caretaking only enables and creates dependent relationships.

July 25, 2016, I saw lots of doves. I was spiritually guided to create a wedding card invitation. It felt so right to prepare for meeting my beloved partner. I sent a copy out to a friend and we both celebrated the date of 2/14/17 as the wedding date. More doves appeared on July 26, 2016. I saw a vision reappear that occurred 10 years ago where Christ came and had lots of doves around me and him. He said that the timing of the guy appearing will happen on Universal Love's time and not mine. That it would be worth the wait. Seeing this vision and the doves felt like a sign that he is coming and will soon appear in my life.

July 27, 2016, I felt Sirius's energy of love which was enormous. The more I focused on this energy, the less power the old life had on me that the other expression lived in. It was moving out of my energy field and this soft pure nurturing love was taking over. This level of love was everything I knew as truth. I learned many lessons about emotional empowerment, including strengthening self-love and self-worth.

July 28, 2016, a little after 3 AM and saw Sirius's ship and 3 others in the form of a "v" shape. They looked like huge stars that I chose to believe were the UFO ships because the stars were flickering on and off with their brightness. As the morning progressed, I noticed anytime I had thoughts that started to find fault with someone, this energy in my heart would become active and I would see the triangle like the one on the 24th. I started to feel this enormous energy of love and thoughts of Universal Love and gratitude. The critical thoughts evaporated into thin air. I felt so much love. I looked up the spiritual meaning of a triangle. It said, "The triangle, having 3 sides, represents true wisdom. It can symbolize the body-mind-spirit connection."

When we put our attention of Universal Love, both in thoughts and emotions, we move away from any opinions, judgments, fears, limitations, and insecurities. Any time our thoughts go into what is wrong and we shift from there to Universal Love, we start to feel pure love and thoughts of gratitude. This replaces any complaining, blaming, or any righteous behaviors. Duality occurs when there is an attachment to a self-defeating thought or emotion where the human expression identifies with the belief as truth and gives it power. This makes the self-defeating belief more active. Focusing more on Universal Love releases the hold to the fixation on the mental thoughts or emotions. This trains the human expression to let go of the resistance or judgment. As you embrace and surrender the attachment, there is more freedom. Attachments and resistance only keep you stuck in what you don't want. By embracing and accepting the experience, you are able to let go of the surrounding constraints. Focusing on outer world conditions that you don't enjoy or would make you feel uncomfortable, only activates the human expression more. This created more duality which leads to unpleasant feelings and opinionated thoughts. The more you focus your attention on Universal Love, the more joy, love, and peaceful you feel. You are able to move through what you are experiencing quicker and more efficiently. Then you are complete and feel inner peace.

For many years, I felt how important it was to keep affirming that I am an Angelic having an Angelic experience vs. a human experience. This solidified the oneness connection to Universal Love. The more I affirmed and felt this, the less I felt the denser energies of duality. With this oneness energy being at a higher vibration, the human expression was able to enjoy more nurturing and pampering love. With duality there were more conditional and protective types of love, feeling disconnected from Universal Love. The more I opened my heart to love and sharing, the greater the connection felt. Experiencing this connection led to freedom from the constraints I was having with feeling love. With this higher frequency vibration, I was more aware of limitations, fears, insecurity, and negativity and didn't give my power to them. I continued to bless those that I saw in the experience without feeling responsible for their life and their lessons they were learning. I continued to strengthen my connection and know my truth of love, joy, peace, and prosperity.

July 30, 2016, sometime shortly after 10 PM, I awoke feeling higher energies. I saw Sirius at the opposite end of a line of 3 stars that had lots of energy. They were different from the other stars nearby since they were bigger, brighter, and I could feel some energy coming from them. I felt myself being pulled forward through a time warp and an energy portal. I felt asleep and then woke up again at 2:02 am. The line of stars turned into a "v" shape and Sirius was at the opposite end. I felt peaceful.

July 31, 2016, on my way to my favorite sacred site, I set an intention to release anything that was in my way of the new life coming into the physical realm. I donated money to the sacred site. I experienced this energy of prosperity coming into the human expression and barriers being released. Then I drove to Belknap Hot Springs. I walked for over an hour and surrendered energies around the old life. I affirmed the energy of self-love. I felt energy leaving my body and the body getting lighter. I felt happier, peaceful. and nurturing energies. I walked thanking the trees and water for being in my life. I experienced a vision of how the other expression and I both went through so much emotional abuse. Protecting our self from getting hurt all these years provided for a stronger connection to Universal Love. I developed a sacred bond with Universal Love. It was my intimate relationship that I knew more than any human relationship.

August 1, 2016, at 2:26 AM I woke up and saw Sirius on the opposite end of an upside down "v" shape. I felt enormous energies of self-love coming into the human expression. It was so nurturing and pampering. It was way beyond anything I have ever experienced in the human form. I expressed love and savored it.

August 2, 2016, at 2:26 AM I woke up and saw Sirius on the opposite end of an upside down "v" shape. There seemed to be a pattern going on here now for more than a week. I felt loving and nurturing energy coming into the body. The "v" shape seemed to mean heightened energies of love coming from them.

August 4, 2016, I woke up shortly after 2 AM and saw a line of stars and Sirius across from them. I felt my heart breaking open energetically and saw a deep separation between the human emotions and the Angelic expression. I focused on the truth of Universal Love. I kept calling in prosperity and nurturing love at this higher loving vibration. Some energy started to leave the heart and was replaced with this higher frequency energy of love.

I felt a deep inner peace and openness to this expansive pure love in areas of the heart that required more nurturing.

August 5, 2016, the Angels told me to raise the energy of the first chakra where primal energies get stored to solidify the downloaded energy of love and prosperity. I visualized a white light on the tailbone to purify the energy and then imagined the chakra raising in frequency. The energy in that chakra became receptive more to love and prosperity. I felt limiting energy leave the body. That continued for a few days. I also received a message reminding me to not personalize other people's behaviors. To not take it as a personal rejection or judgment. That only creates an attraction to more of that. The Angels told me to bless it all. To focus my attention on Universal Love and stay receptive. A few days later I had a dream where I met a Fairy Angel and she asked if I was ready for the relationship to enter my life. I said yes, and she shifted my energy to a nurturing vibration. Lots of energy from the last 19 years left. I was experiencing a purification in the heart. I felt pampering and loving energies coming inside.

August 7, 2016, at 3:26 AM I saw 4 stars in a square shape and Sirius was directly across. The bottom left star was shining brighter than the other 3. I felt an inner death with the life I was living. I continued to nurture myself with loving energy, listening to soothing music that felt nurturing. This helped move the insecurity that was coming up. I felt the Angels appear and clear energy cords in the mind that required transforming. I felt this deep freedom. The more I focused on prosperity consciousness the easier the higher loving frequency solidified. That night I had a dream where I crossed over a bridge and I experienced a higher vibration that was different in my current life.

August 8, 2016, I went to Belknap Hot Springs and walked for close to 2 hours. I felt lots of energy around money being transformed to an energetic vibration of prosperity and sharing. I let go of residual energies from the other expression's ancestral family around hoarding and lack. The energy of sharing also moved into love with others. A comfortable feeling of sharing love came over me as I started to express love toward others during my walk. Some were receptive and smiled at me. The fear of getting hurt by others' unconscious behaviors was transforming through my awareness of self-love.

August 9, 2016, I woke up with this realization that any form of fear around others' behaviors only attracts it into my life to confirm that lie. I experienced a deeper understanding that I am not responsible for other people's behaviors only mine. When others behaved negative or unloving, I no longer took it as I did something wrong. My awareness of not being responsible for others' behaviors broke that pattern. I became aware by choosing the truth of self-love and Universal Love. By choosing to take care of myself and not to judge. I am responsible for keeping my energy connected to Universal Love and to allow prosperity.

Surrounding myself with love and positivity amplifies more of this energy in my life. I saw a spiritual vision where I had become aware of being bombarded with so much negativity. I was not taking efficient care of myself by amplifying the positive and nurturing love. I gave my power to the negativity, and it sucked me down into the dense energies. I became so insecure that I started to have a deep fear of people. I had to strengthen and develop greater empowerment. My connection to Universal Love greatly helped where I no longer allowed fear and insecurity to control me. There were so many self-defeating beliefs feeding off each other. It was like an onion that peeled away one self-defeating belief after another until I got to the core belief. Transforming them brought a deep awakening inside where for the first time I felt my heart open to receiving love from others. Fearing others who had negative and unloving behaviors was no longer dominating my life. Higher frequencies of self-love made it more comfortable being around others.

August 11, 2016, I woke up after 2 AM and saw stars in the form of an upside down check mark and Sirius opposite of this. I noticed the human logical part of the mind becoming overactive with wanting to figure things out in this new chapter of my life I am in. I got clarity from the Universal Pure Love Beings that it was necessary to expand more of the feminine side of the mind. This is the right side, where it experiences more gratitude, trust, love, and acceptance. The logical side of the mind that attempted to figure out, have an outcome look a certain way, analyze how to make that happen, and the human ego wanting to control it all was no longer active in my life. That was not an effective approach. The human ego was no longer in charge.

I observed the human ego continuously surrendering the control and it subsiding in the midst of attempting to make things happen a certain way. This check mark being upside down for me meant that I was looking upside down in life with what was wrong in a certain area of my life. Letting go and allowing Universal Love to guide more with experiences in life made more sense. There were lessons and completions going on in areas of my life. Acceptance, in place of attempting to understand provided greater understanding. This understanding comes more from the Inner Spirit versus the human belief systems. This greater understanding thereby educates the human mind which provides for greater wisdom. Through acceptance there is more peace and confidence. Focusing on love and trust made life flow more in joy and peace.

August 12, 2016, I awoke at 1:46 AM and saw 3 stars in a semi-circle and Sirius. Throughout the day I saw, heard, and felt doves. I became aware that when my energy felt like it was moving into a denser vibration I became more fearful. The energy felt negative and the human ego felt threatened. I observed this with compassion and love. I saw how the human expression immediately went into a form of judgment as these energies being bad and not safe. The more I focused on embracing the feelings around this, the more the human ego let go of the protection. Then I was able to shift it to love by embracing the fears and protective energies. The fear dissipated and I felt peaceful. The semi-circle meant I was 1/2 complete of a lesson. I was becoming more comfortable with this form of energy that felt negative. Being aware of the human expression protection made it easier for me to shift into love quicker instead of letting the fear be fed with protection or judgments. The unique formation of the stars provided messages for me in this continuation of expansiveness.

The next day I the ancestral father's energies left the body in a deeper way. I felt lighter. I started seeing spiritual visions of how I was experiencing getting emotionally judged and personalizing it because of the fear of negative and unloving energies being played out. The energies played out due to the belief of getting hurt. Through embracing and loving the energy, it helped to raise it to fully transform, to more nurturing and positive energies. I was getting hugged by people all day. I focused daily on self-love, nurturing. and positive energies to keep my energies at a high frequency. The Universe operates on vibrations and matches with more in different forms. The more we love and accept, eventually we free ourselves from the chains we feel around certain lessons.

August 15, 2016, for the first time I saw a circle of stars. throughout the day, I kept feeling how important it is to stand in my truth of love. I was experiencing this truth throughout the day. When I went to sleep, I had a dream and heard that energies that I feel as negative are just another form of energy not to fear it rather accept it for what it is. I woke up feeling a void inside. It felt like a limitation. I imagined positive energies filling up this void and new energies, new perspectives, and new beliefs coming about.

August 17 and 18, 2016 I felt lots of expansion and energy opening up on the right side of the mind. It felt very nurturing. My creativity started to heighten. I started to feel an even stronger connection to Universal Love. On the 19th, as I focused my attention on gratitude and love, I felt this playful, loving energy emerge in a more solid way. I didn't allow those who had an active left brain which got expressed as over analyzing, judging, limitations, and chattering thoughts distract me. I chose to continue to stay with this creative and playful, loving energy.

August 21, 2016, The Angels told me to continue to have a positive focus in the midst of life changes. To laugh and enjoy life. To align the vibrations of love and prosperity more to

Universal Love. The Angels told me that which is not aligned with this will eventually fall away. I kept feeling energies fall away throughout the following weeks that were not at a higher vibration of love.

August 26, 2016, I saw Sirius in a line of stars. While swimming I saw a heart shape and dollar sign in the sand. Later I met this guy with a pink shirt coming out of a Porsche and go to the bank teller machine. As I approached the teller machine, he started to flirt with me saying he took all the money and I flirted back. I said, "well now what am I to do?" He smiled and commented that it was the weekend. He waited until I got out of the bank. All of a sudden I became shy and insecure. He waved goodbye and left. After he left, I was aware that the dollar sign and pink shirt symbolized our meeting. Pink being the color of love and the Porsche being the symbol of money. I had no idea where this insecurity and shyness came from. I felt like I made a mistake by not continuing the conversation and asked Universal Love to orchestrate another meeting where I would make sure I was confident. The Angels told me he was a messenger to help me build my self-worth. I felt a huge gift from him in our 5-minute interaction. I became aware that a guy with a Porsche could indeed be interested in someone like me that is Angelic. I had a belief that said, a guy in a Porsche would be more interested in a materialistic person. Yet he was different. He was funny, playful, and had a loving spirit. I felt I could have a relationship with someone like him.

August 27, 2016, I saw Sirius opposite the stars in a form of a smile. I knew they heard my prayer about the guy. In the early morning hours, I felt more closure around the old expression's life. It felt like every part of me was dying. I stayed with the feeling and embraced it without attempting to figure it out. After a few hours, the energy became lighter, and I started to feel more peaceful. I knew if they could help me with this, they will.

August 28, 2016, I saw Sirius and another ship opposite the stars in the form of a flag. I never saw this before. I went to visit this church to see what it was all about. I heard the pastor's sermon on fear and the focus of faith. He shared how important it is to become confident when experiencing inner fear. To have faith in the unknown. He focused all of his conversation on solving fear through faith. I left getting a huge insight. When people are in fear, they focus on struggles, attempting to fix and solve the problem. This only leads to the mind focusing on stories and what they don't want. They end up feeling lost, sad and stuck in what seems like a rut in their life. When we focus on love and celebrate life, there is more of a connection to Universal Love creating in the midst of the unknown. Our perception shifts from a problem-oriented mentality to that of challenges where possibilities and positive solutions come about from Universal Love through insights. We allow the Universe to create and deliver and we stay open with excitement, inner confidence, and a knowing it is already complete. The human ego control is not orchestrating anything so there are no struggles, fears, limitations, or problems to solve or fix.

August 29, 2016, The Angels told me how important it is to keep raising the vibrations of love and stand in this truth of love and prosperity. The higher the frequency, the greater the positive outlook on life. The greater the positive outlook, the greater the inner joy and peace. There is more of a flow with enjoying life instead of fixing, solving, and complaining about life.

August 31, 2016, I felt lots of energy going into the mind as I woke up affirming positive energy and love. All of a sudden the body started to shake. I was feeling lots of energy. I started to feel more confident. That night I had another dream that perceived negative energy as just an energy. The following day, I had a huge revelation that I felt about a belief that negativity is not out there to hurt me. It is just an energy. I was taking in that energy because I was feeling it was going to hurt me. That was a subtle fear of being around it would drop my energy. That subtle fear attracted more of the perceived negative energies. All the years I was attracting the negative energies because they had a two-folded lesson. One to support the awakening of human consciousness.

The other to strengthen the inner confidence where I would get to a high enough vibration to not fear the negative energies and thereby give my power to it. The fear of it and giving my power to it only sucked me into that vibration to wake me up to greater self-love and self-confidence. I started to feel my heart more where I was better able to experience higher loving emotions and a deeper connection to Universal Love.

September 2, 2016, I saw Sirius on the top left side of the stars in a shape of a flag. It felt like I was going to experience some closure around a lesson in my life. I headed to Beaverton Oregon. When I first arrived on Friday, it felt nurturing. As the weekend progressed, I experienced all sorts of energies that seemed heavy. I heard crows all over the place which symbolized change. I felt this energy around non-acceptance of my purpose on Earth. I started to cry and said, "I choose acceptance and I accept who I am." I went swimming on Sunday on my wake back to Bend. I was able to reconnect to Universal Love and the dense energy left my heart. Sunday night I had a dream where I was talking to this guy. I asked him, "how do you know you can trust someone?" I was cutting up an avocado and eating some of it. He replied, "when you like yourself, others see that and treat you well." I looked up what eating an avocado means when you have a dream about it. I read, "your love life will improve."

September 5, 2016, at 5:13 AM I saw Sirius at the top left of a flag shape of stars. I experienced a spiritual vision about my purpose as an Angelic on Earth. There was much transitioning going on this year. I was curious to know what my new purpose as an Angelic was. I knew through the surrendering of figuring it out, I would be able to experience the purpose of my role being more active.

September 6, 2016, I woke up at a little after 2 AM, where I saw an unfamiliar ship from the opposite side of the window I was looking out. It was quickly moving toward me. It was bright and as it went up above the house I felt guided to lay back down. I started to feel something pricking on my head and then the feet. I then saw these loving pure souls. I recognized them as being part of the Syrian family. I fell asleep and woke up at 5 AM where I saw the stars in a shape of a flag without Sirius in them.

September 7, 2016, at around 2 AM, I saw stars in a form of a smile. I felt inner joy inside as I laid back down to rest.

September 8, 2016, I got up at 11:09 PM and saw the unfamiliar ship appear again. It approached me from the opposite side. I started to feel this energy around limitation leaving the body. I saw spiritual visions explaining why I was attracting experiences that triggered money limitations and them being resolved with getting discounts and free items. This was all ancestral energies of the other expression that got played out to get resolved. I heard a voice say, "Choice of perception. You chose to see now from a loving and joyful place." I fell asleep quickly. I woke up at 5:09 AM and saw Sirius as part of the stars in the form of a square shape. I took a walk at 1:30 PM and saw all these yellow crickets jumping up around me. There were about 4 of them. I looked up the spiritual meaning of Crickets. I read that they take you on a journey to explore the many ways to raise your vibration, such as chanting, meditation, singing, and high vibration music.

September 9, 2016, I again saw stars in a shape of a flag. I started to experience being out of the body and above it. I saw all this abusive energy leaving the body. I wanted to raise the body's frequency to where I was, yet I was not able to raise it. I started to feel abusive energy dying and leaving. I heard a voice say, "goodbye." I didn't know who said it. I questioned whether it was the other expression yet for some reason I was not clear. As I took a walk again at 1:30 PM, I saw more yellow crickets around me. I also saw them on September 10. I continued to focus my energy on Universal Love and prosperity as I enjoyed the scenery.

September 11, 2016, I woke up sometime after 2 AM and saw the stars in a shape of a flag. I felt my heart really feeling vulnerable and open. It started to feel sad. I focused my energy on Universal Love and the sadness instantly turned into a feeling of joy. I became aware that the sadness was residual energy from the abusive energy that was dying off.

September 12, 2016, I saw Sirius and another ship opposite the stars in a shape of an arrow pointing south. I knew south had a spiritual meaning around growth. I had a class in that direction that morning. I experienced lots of nurturing as I was doing the meditation class. It felt different and nice. I went swimming, I felt this surge of energy around taking care of myself. I felt the Angels telling me I am doing a great job around taking care of myself. I use to put other people's needs ahead of my own. I no longer was doing this. It felt freeing to experience this.

September 13, 2016, I again saw stars in a shape of an arrow pointing south. I was having lots of insights around how the human mind operates. The human mind can pick up habits through programs based on the type of environment. Those raised in an environment filled with negative influences will have the human mind expressing from that energy level. I observed others using that energy in their thoughts with experiences where we focus more on the worst case scenarios or judge the condition. I became aware of this with the Universal Pure Loving Being's support through transforming the energy to a higher love frequency. Transforming to the higher frequencies is what shifted from participating in the negative story to that of positive thinking.

The thoughts moved from negativity, victim consciousness, limitations, and fear to that of love, abundance, and empowerment. Going through this lesson surprised me and I knew it was for a greater understanding. I saw how the human expression moved into greater self-acceptance, self-love, self-care, self-awareness, compassion, and forgiveness. For many years the human ego was controlling through its self-defeating beliefs. Moving the human ego control out-of-the-way, made it easier to express organic pure love. The human expression was evolving to a higher love based frequency and simultaneously the human ego control was moving into a more complacent place.

Love is the highest vibration and the human expression did not experience much of that on an intimate level. Rather than getting it from other humans, I received it from Universal Love.

The latter part of this year I experienced more emotional nurturing intimacy by activating more of the feminine side. Lots of visions came through the latter part of September. I saw how the other expression birthed into an abusive, dysfunctional family. Then she lived in a foster home from 10-17 years of age that helped her build her confidence and experience love. She moved to Colorado where she had lessons to learn around the ancestral family. The foster parents attempted to get her to move back. She chose to stay to grow up. She became too attached to the them. She knew she had to learn how to live on her own and become emotionally stronger. Her self-confidence was negatively affected during the years in Colorado making her feel more devalued. When I dropped in I started rebuilding self-confidence and self-love. Releasing the residual energies and simultaneously experiencing expansion helped rebuild self-empowerment. Abundance and faithfulness in love was the "key" to unlocking the chains that kept me stuck in vibrations that were dense and detrimental. I knew it was necessary to raise the energy frequency appreciate the Universal Pure Loving Beings that supported me in this process.

The higher the frequency of love, the easier it was to stand emotionally stronger in the truth of Universal Love. When we meditate, go into nature or other activities that keep us feeling connected to Universal Love, our Inner Spirit is more active. When we go into places that have lots of stimuli, the human senses start to become more active. These human senses, hearing, feeling, touching, seeing, tasting, and the 6th sense is intuition can have positive or non-positive sensations. Some people have a stronger connection to some of these senses more than others. They get triggered in a positive or non-positive way depending upon how they perceive the situation that is triggering that sense. For example, if hearing is one of your strongest senses when processing information, then soothing, calming, and uplifting sounds will relax you and create inner love. If you are hearing lots of beeping horns, babies crying, fingernails scratching a blackboard, dogs barking, or people yelling, you may have more of an overwhelming experience, resulting in unpleasant feelings and reactions. The more stimuli you experience, the greater emotional turmoil you may experience. You can set healthy boundaries based on how much stimuli you can take before it affects you detrimentally.

If we become overwhelmed by the stimulus, the human ego becomes active in a protective, flight, or fight mode. This moves us away from the higher frequency of love because there is a subtle fear energy running through the senses. Running energies of love throughout the day and especially when in places that have lots of stimuli helps to calm the human ego and prevent it from becoming overly active. The overly active stimuli overwhelm the mental realm with chattering thoughts, including judgments when we give our power to the stimuli. It can also be demonstrated through the emotional realm through fears and negativity. This is what creates the feelings of separation from Universal Love.

September 28, 2016, at 8:15 PM, I saw a UFO ship heading toward me from the opposite side. I saw bright red lights circling around the ship. I turned a flashlight on and then off as I pointed it toward the UFO ship. The UFO ship immediately turned off the bright red lights. I became amazed on how it could pick up on my energy and my awareness of the UFO ship.

September 29, 2016, at 1 AM, I saw a UFO ship with bright red lights again on the opposite side. It started to head southeast and then toward me. I didn't feel any major energy coming from it. I did feel it watching over me to see how I was doing. I had a dream two nights in a row with people from UFO ships. The first night, I met this guy who resided in the UFO ship with the bright red lights. I shared how I felt overwhelmed and asked him to help me. The second night I met another guy, and he started to scan my energy. He said that I was in the middle of a huge transition and to stay positive by focusing on gratitude.

October 1, 2016, I had a vision around how the human ego wants instant gratification and how it searches outside with this craving. I became aware how searching outside for something brings a different vibration frequency than getting it directly inside Universal Love. By feeling Universal Love fully inside me, I lost all desires to search outside. I noticed how this awareness brought the human expression into a different perspective with love. It was self-contained and fulfilling.

October 6, 2016, I had a huge revelation. I started seeing movie clip visions while reviewing chapter 7 of this book. The visions showed me how the human ego controlling mechanisms is what made me feel sad and longed for love outside. All the experiences where I noticed others' human ego control was reflecting the human ego controlling my life in the relationship area of my life. Through awareness of the human ego's energy, I was able to shift from human ego control to my Angelic expression. I was able to strengthen my connection to feeling Universal's Love frequency, which made life more enjoyable.

October 8, 2016, at 8 AM after swimming, I laid down feeling really tired. I fell into a deep sleep that lasted until 9:30 AM. I dreamt I was taking a walk, and I saw this couple with white hair. I recognized them as Syrians. They have a girl around 6 years old, a pet baby deer, and what looked like a human with 4 legs. The baby deer came up to me and let me hug her or him. I became excited since I always wanted to hug a deer and finally got to. I went over to the couple to say hi. The guy said that he didn't like living on planet Earth and that he wanted to go to his home planet. I instinctively knew to tell him that I am an Angelic walk-in. I gave him a personal card I designed with a phone number. He put it on this box. As he showed me the box, I noticed the personal card with a different phone number. The number on it was, 971-289-6589. I held the box to write my correct number on it and I felt the box shake. There was a living thing in that closed box. They live in this apartment building that has 2 floors. It was really nice looking. He had to go to work and stood next to me to get ready to leave waiting for me. I gathered my things taking longer than he was able to wait. He ended up leaving and his wife went upstairs. I said goodbye as I left. When I woke up, I dialed the number out of curiosity and it was not in service.

October 9, 2016, I experienced a message that shot into my heart saying how important it was to stay in the present moment in my daily life. When energies that no longer serve the Inner Spirit get transmuted, there is this energy void that feels like nothingness.

The Angels told me to stay in the present moment with this void and to embrace it with higher loving frequencies. To stay focused on love, prosperity, and gratitude. They said this will fill up the void, activating the Angelic expression to the higher frequencies of love and abundance. When experiencing a void, make sure the human ego doesn't go into a control mode with regard to purpose, timing, wanting it now, clarity, direction, and desired outcomes. Clarity comes at a higher level of wisdom, when the Inner Spirit gets activated, resulting in feelings of inner peace. In our daily life, as we live in the mystery of the unknown, we experience opportunities where we choose either fear or love. It feels great when there is an answer, bringing clarity, and direction from Universal Love. If there is no answer, it is best to continue to focus on love and prosperity. To allow the mystery of life to unfold, accept and to stay patient with it all. The Universe can create in an instant when the timing is right. With patience, we become less frustrated with regard to instant gratification. Life becomes more enjoyable as we listen to Universal Love for timing and clarity vs. telling the Universe what to do.

October 11, 2016, I woke up in the morning feeling the human mind instantly shift into gratitude. It just knew to do this. The human mind created a oneness connection to more love, compassion, and acceptance

October 13, 2016, I took a walk and experienced a flock of about 15 red robins to my left. Then they were on my right and left side as they flew in front of me. I looked up the spiritual meaning of a red robin. I read that a red robin signifies stimulation of new growth and renewal in many areas of one's life. To choose to joy in our life experiences. Red robins teach us how to live life with more passion and to become self-reliant and persevere through transitions in life. As I observed all these red robins, I was feeling this expansive nurturing energy. I called in their energy asking for it in all areas of my life. As I stood still and closed my eyes, I felt a surge of energy start to enter inside me and heard done. I felt like I was home with the Angels. I was experiencing so much energy it felt organic and natural in the body. I started to feel my Angelic expression as if it was in front of the human expression. I started to feel a shift from connecting WITH Universal Love to that of being IN Universal Love. I felt like I was living inside the "house" of Universal Love in place of visiting or connecting from outside the "house." Having a direction connection to Universal Love became solid. In the days that followed, I noticed how much easier it was for me to stay loving, compassionate, peaceful, and playful in the midst of others behaving negatively. I stayed neutral vs. experiencing the human expression becoming protective. I didn't feel any personalizing, fear, or insecurity.

October 18, 2016, I called a credit card company to put a return in dispute so I didn't have to pay for it since I was awaiting credit. She was extremely detail oriented wanting colors, names, descriptions, times of return, and more, which was taking lots of time to answer. I was getting impatient at first with all the questions. Then I laughed and said to her, "you are doing a great job. Were you once a lawyer being so detailed?" She laughed and shared how she wanted enough evidence to have if she needed it to back me up. I again laughed and told her how she would have been a great lawyer. Her energy became lighter, and she started to behave more loving and playful. We both expressed love and laughter. She thanked and blessed me saying she had a hard day and I made her day. I thanked her for the opportunity to see how I chose to respond in compassion, love, and joy with this experience.

October 21, 2016, at 9:37 AM I saw the UFO ship with the bright lights heading southeast. About 10 minutes later I felt ringing in my ear and loving energy in the body. I saw a vision of the inner child feeling nurtured.

October 22, 2016, at 5:55 PM I saw around 10 red robins while taking a walk. They were flying above me, to the left and right of me. I knew they were gifting me with loving to support me with the continual unfolding of my new life. I stayed in gratitude and admiration for their connection.

October 23, 2016, at 3:33 I saw a flock of swift birds flying above and in front of the house, flying like an ocean wave. They represent speed and agility, responding to opportunities as they arise. I felt the inner child and became aware how she would go into protectiveness around negative energies out of fear of getting abused. This fear ran my life as I gave my power to the negative energies all these years. It was holding me back from fully living life in a playful, loving way with others.

October 25, 2016, I awakened from sleep feeling this ancient energy from other lifetimes. I saw a vision of how this ancient energy was continuously sabotaging the Inner Spirit's frequency. It played out in the role of a social worker, teaching, through negative expressions of others, and with some in the collective consciousness where I gave it power. The Pure Universal Love Beings purified this energy, replacing it with loving energy, The energy expanded beyond the aura creating and energy field of pure love where nothing was able to hook on to it.

October 26, 2016, I took a walk, and I saw a flock of swallows coming toward me flying above my head and in all directions. Swallows mean protection and warmth for the home. They then started to head south. As I continued to walk, I experienced a flock of red robins to the right of me facing south. Later that morning, I drove to go food shopping and saw a billboard sign that said, "you deserve to be happy." I smiled saying, "of course I am choosing more and more of this."

October 27, 2016, at 8:30 PM I saw the UFO ship at a distance. For the first time that night I saw the stars shift their formation from a check mark to a semi-circle and then a flag within a few hours apart. I was experiencing so much energy I could not figure out what was going on. I went to sleep. The following morning I was experiencing lots of heavy energy inside. It felt like a deep movement of something at the core of some beliefs. I was not aware what it was all about. I was feeling so much inner turmoil.

October 29, 2016, I felt the inner child's current vibration dying. I saw how the inner child was running my life in my relationships with others. There were fear and judgment energies playing out around emotional abuse and going into protective mode when I experienced negative energies. I became aware how these last few days was leading me to this transition. This revelation on how the inner child being in fear and judgment was holding me back from experiencing the relationships at a higher loving frequency. I felt this longing to trust people on an intimate level.

October 30, 2016, I woke up feeling the abusive energy around inner child was gone. I felt a deeper connection as an Angelic expression to Universal Love. I felt lighter and free. For the first time, I was able to move all the energy in the body, mind, and heart to a higher vibration of love. This split between the inner child vibration around fear and judgment and my Angelic expression was creating this conflict. I was not able to lift the human form to a higher vibration up until now due to this split. I noticed how much easier it was for the human mind to focus fully on Universal Love and become more aligned to positive thinking, love, and prosperity at this higher vibration.

November 10, 2016, I felt myself going really deep during a meditation. I experienced being a beacon of loving light. As I dived deeper into the human expression, I felt all the remaining ancestral energies that were dormant in the physical body get released. I was witnessing the energies falling down an energy wormhole. I felt my Angelic energy in the body feeling free as the body started to lift to a higher vibration frequency. I experienced the body energetically rising beyond the human expression's current vibration. Releasing this dormant energy was necessary to raise the body's energy. I saw a huge loving energy in the form of an Angel. I never saw an Angel in such a large size while being in the human expression. I felt enormous amounts of love. I started to feel the body more in the energy realm of Universal Love.

November 12, 2016, I woke up a little after 4 AM and saw the red light flicking from the UFO ship as it was heading north. I fell back to sleep and woke up at 6:16 AM seeing a new UFO ship in the form of a star coming toward me from the east. I started to feel Mother Mary's love in such a profound way.

November 13, 2016, I woke up feeling like I was living inside Universal Love. This time I felt a *knowing* of being connected to Universal Love vs. experiencing it. I again felt Mother Mary. I heard her words of pro-peace and pro-love and felt it penetrate deeply inside. When we know the truth of being in oneness in our connection to Universal Love, we experience profound love deeply inside. We become a direct channel of Universal Love with greater ease and empowerment. We are like this beautiful instrument where Universal Love gets expressed through us.

November 18, 2016, at 5:56 PM I saw the UFO ship. It was going from the west to east direction and then east to west. I took this picture. I had a radio interview with a guy who asked lots of questions around ego control. These questions kept digging deeper into how the human ego control works and how to get out of it into a connection to oneness. The interviewer expressed so much intensity that at some point I felt guided to shift the conversation to more of Inner Spirit activation from human ego control. This completed the interview. I hung up the phone and felt lots of heavy energy. I knew there was a gift in this experience I was having. I just stayed with the experience embracing it with love to the best of my ability. I knew I had to let it go. I envisioned and felt me inside Universal Love.

TRANSFORMATION ANGEL WALK-IN'S PATH

The next day I went into a deep meditation I saw and experienced Angels and the Universal Pure Loving Beings taking me down a path different from the current life path I had been on. They took my hand, and we walked down this beautiful road filled with lots of higher frequencies of love. I felt a lot of negative energy being released that I had experienced yesterday. The beloved mate approached me. I started to cry asking what took him so long to find me. He had so much love and compassion. He held me with deep love saying everything is going to be ok now. There was a deep sense of freedom from the other expression's life to that of more nurturing love. When I completed the meditation, I felt a deep sense of love and peace. I felt a new life and new beginnings. Experiencing emotional abuse, brought about so much protection, feeling unsafe, mistrust, fears, and judgments. Healing the inner child freed me from her running my life. All these loving energy downloads and support helped me move the human expression into a oneness connection to Universal Love. I started to feel safer inside because of Universal Love's energy deep inside. The loving relationship I have toward Universal Love strengthened my truth of what Universal Love represented. Universal Love is so omnipotent and omnipresent. No matter where I was, who I was with, and where I was going, I chose Universal Love as my truth which negates duality living's illusion.

November 21, 2016, at 4:55 PM I saw the UFO ship with the red lights was heading north for a short distance and then southeast. I felt this enormous amount of a nurturing love.

November 22, 2016, at 6:20 AM, I saw the UFO ship with the red lights heading southwest and again at 1:30 PM heading north. I felt this pertinent message to channel Universal Love more often. There are fewer times I experienced taking in others' energies that felt heavy. When I did, I would imagine a stage where I'd put that energy on the stage and walk away or surrender it to Universal Love. This was helping me surrender denser energy easier and feel Universal Love more fully. The more I embodied Universal Love first, the easier it was to hold on to the vibration and then channeled it. This fullness of Universal Love was overtaking any potential depletion from others' negative behaviors.

November 24, 2016, I was listening to this interview on Angels. I felt a higher frequency as he was channeling Lord Melchizedek who brings higher wisdom. I read on a Google search, that Lord Melchizedek is an ascended master, that helps wake up humanity by bringing in higher vibrations. I felt him energetically cut away some energy cords which allowed me to ascend to a higher loving vibration. Ascending was important for me to serve my purpose better. I felt more connected to the Angelic Realm.

November 26, 2016, I listened to a radio interview who spoke an encrypted language other than from this planet. I felt the body grounding energetically and realized I never forgave planet Earth around the abusive energy I experienced. I started to forgive and send Earth love, feeling a deep inner peace that I never felt before around my discomfort with being on Earth. The language shifted to Fairy Angel energy. I experienced a re-birthing feeling peace and nurturing love. I felt more comfortable being on Earth.

November 27, 2016, at 4:58 AM I saw the UFO beaming read lights. It was real close in a square shape of stars. I felt so much love for planet Earth like I never felt before.

November 28, 2016, I felt Angelic energies inside shifting my perception as an Angelic expression having a human experience with greater levels of love and joy. I felt me moving between the Angelic Realm and the human expression. I received a channeled message from the Angels to continue to focus more on the heart with love and to bring that energy to the mind. Doing this will help have positive thinking. The Angels told me to continue to focus inwardly filling up with love and to BE that love with others without feeling I have to say anything. The higher the frequency vibrations, the greater the level of prosperity. I kept hearing to stay open to allowing and trust the process. To be open and receptive. I felt my new life opening more with a greater sense of freedom, what they called the 3rd leg of this lifetime.

December 1, 2016, at 6:34 AM I saw a UFO in the form of what looked like a 5 pointed star on the south end in between the east and west direction. On the opposite side of this 5 pointed UFO was stars formed in a shape of a smile. I felt a huge Angelic presence and saw my Guardian Angel. This amazing energy of love was pouring inside and my heart opened more. I committed to opening the heart daily.

December 2, 2016, as I woke up from sleep, I felt the Guardian Angel. She put a Halo over my head and told me it was for higher conscious thinking. I knew the Guardian Angel was shifting the energy of feeling alone on the planet to a more solid energy of love. I felt it was important to continue to hold this higher vibration of love and allow life to unfold organically. I felt more playful inside with a stronger conviction of enjoying life. When I returned to the house at 6:21 PM from an Art walk, I saw 2 UFO ships with red flickering lights like eyes. One above and on the north side of the house and another on the opposite side of the house heading south. Then at 6:51 PM, I saw the 5 pointed UFO going back and forth from north to south and south to north. I never saw so many UFOs at one time. I laid down and all of a sudden I felt the floor shaking and heard a loud sound. I felt lots of energy and fell into a deep sleep. I woke up in the middle of the night feeling the Guardian Angel and high vibrations of love.

December 3, 2016, upon awakening I felt the Guardian Angel and the higher vibrations of love. I also felt some denser energies leaving the body and the mental realm. I was feeling more ascension inside the body. It was becoming lighter, and I saw more ethereal vibration energies in the physical realm.

December 4, 2016, at 5:25 AM, I saw the UFO ship with the red flickering lights heading south. I also saw and felt Sirius. I experienced a huge surge of energy and saw a vision on how far they had traveled from their realm. It is light years away, being really far. I felt so much love and appreciation for their dedication to coming to this planet to bring these high vibrations of love. Embodying these higher frequencies of love felt empowering.

When the human expression was more active, choices got made more from that vibration. When the human ego controls, it operates at a lower frequency wanting instant gratification. There is more self-focus with emotional needs getting met, especially around love. Lots of looking outside for it due to all the emotional abuse. The focus was primarily on evolving the self-defeating beliefs to a higher frequency of love and become more empowered with self-worth. The bridge to higher love provided the freedom to allow my Angelic expression to become more active in the human form. With higher frequencies of love, I experienced seeing and feeling more of my Angelic family, the Ascended Pure Love Beings, Ascended Masters, and my Guardian Angel. The ascension was bringing about a feeling of bliss that was beyond what the human expression would experience if it was in control mode. The human filters or beliefs became less of a distraction which would have caused potential conflicts with what I was to do in that moment.

December 5, 2016, at 3:52 AM I saw a shooting star. It was really low and went all the way up to the sky. I started to feel my energy moving above fears, doubts, and insecurity about completing the second leg of my life. I did a thank you letter via email around the new chapter of my life and felt the energy shift to that of excitement. The experience I had with the two different energy vibration levels brought things to a clearer perspective. I became so aware how it is necessary to see and stand firm in the truth of the unseen. Truth includes living life with unconditional love, prosperity consciousness, inner peace, inner joy, and positive focus even if it is hard to do with what is going on in the outer world. Love replaces judging which like glue kept me stuck in the dense energies. Dense energies are a lie in Universal Love's presence and love transmutes lower vibrations. Embracing, self-focused love, or blessing people and situations, put my focus on the truth. My power was given to Universal Love. At the end of this experience, I felt the Angels' Love nurturing me.

December 8 and 9, 2016, I saw 5 doves on the deck sitting in the snow, playing with each other, eating the bird food I had put out the night before. It was amazing to see so many on the deck in the snow. To me, they symbolize love. I felt this in them as I admired their presence and playfulness.

December 14, 2016, I had a magical vision of Christ and felt so much love inside me. The doves and experiencing Christ reminded me of this vision I had when I incarnated where I saw lots of doves. I received a message from Christ then that what I wanted to experience on Earth will happen on Universal timing not my time and it will be well worth the wait.

December 15, 2016, I saw a dove that had golden red colors in it. It sat by the window on the deck staring at me. I felt so much love coming from this dove.

December 20, 2016, at 3:52 AM I saw a shooting star by the house right in front of me going up and then heading north. I felt a deep connection to the energy of the star and became energized as I tuned into it.

December 21, 2016, at 6:21 AM I saw the UFO ship with the flickering lights heading above the house and felt lots of love.

December 22, 2016, at 4:55 I saw the Star UFO ship. I awakened having this feeling of deep awareness knowing to BE love, joy, peace with compassion that seemed different. There were no mental opinions. I felt and experienced this oneness of pure love in a joyful and peaceful way.

December 25, 2016, I saw the stars in a "w" shape opposite of Sirius. I did a Google search on the meaning of "w." It said its *symbolic that relationships are getting better and that wealth is flowing into one's life now.* I saw Christ's full body. He was smiling at me with love. I wished him a happy birthday and sent him love. I stayed in silence all day feeling these emotions of Christ and love.

December 26, 2016, I saw a "w" shape with the stars and Sirius at the opposite end. I started to feel more confident with being in the human form. I became aware that as the human ego was losing more control. I was able to feel more lightness in the body.

December 27, 2016, at 9:15 PM I saw the red flickering UFO light heading southeast and another heading northwest and then east. I experienced visions with how I am having compassion with challenging situations and people knowing they are doing the best they can. There's no personalization or victimization, when we express compassion. There is more unconditional love. This unconditional love is a form of oneness. The oneness connection I have with Universal Love was becoming more profound. I obtained this connection easily by quieting the mind, calming the emotions, and relaxing the breath. Then opening the heart to Universal Love and from that place prosperity is available.

December 29, 2016, I saw a "w" shape with the stars and Sirius on the opposite end. I felt more expansion occurring around love. Instead of moving between two worlds, ethereal and physical realm, like I initially felt when I first incarnated, I felt oneness. This oneness had a frequency vibration of me seeing the ethereal realm in the physical realm. I was able to see Christ, Mother Mary, my Guardian Angel, Angels, Mother Magdalene, and the Universal Pure Love Beings so vividly.

December 30, 2016, I saw a flag shape with the stars I heard a voice from the Angels saying to focus on that which makes me happy. They said to keep focusing on the connection I have with Universal Love vs. attempting to get clarity on the new life. The Latter is human ego controlling.

December 31, 2016, I first saw a flag shape with the stars and then it changed to a "w" shape. As I fully released the old life and the human ego control, I felt my Angelic presence become more solid inside the human form and become activated. I felt amazing loving energy. I heard the Angels tell me I'm ascending the human expression in the loving frequency vibration because I have chosen to let go of the energy of fear. They said to continue to keep the heart open as if it is a new life with a new beginning.

They said yesterday is gone. Therefore, it is not necessary to focus there. Each day is a new beginning with new messages and instructions to follow. All the experiences that seemed negative and limiting were part of the fear-driven life I was evolving. This new life is full of joy, love, peace, vitality, health and prosperity.

In the month of December, I felt and saw the Angels, Christ, my Guardian Angel, Mother Mary, Some of the Arc Angels, Avatars, and Sirius so clearly. This is because I have embodied this higher loving energy in the human expression. It supported the heightened vibrations. I also experienced doves everywhere. One being a golden red dove sitting on the deck and staring at me. I felt so much love from them. They were my confirmation around embodying higher loving frequencies and the new beginnings of a new chapter in my life filled with heightened nurturing love. I kept hearing Mother Mary saying, pro-peace and pro-love throughout the month of December. I enjoyed expressing that in all situations and with all people. The truth around pro-peace and pro-love was dominating since I chose to live life this way.

As the year closed out, my experiences with situations and people shifted. I immediately expressed compassion and more of a deep understanding that everyone was doing the best they could and learning from where their consciousness was at. Personalizing, victimization, or identifying didn't exist within. Judging was not something I chose to continue as part of my life. When you are in fear or insecurity, you are giving your power to the self-defeating beliefs and to the outer world conditions. There is more of a "me" focus out of survival mentality. When you are *expressing* love and a prosperity consciousness, you are bringing the vastness of the inner world and sharing it from a "we" mentality with others. The stronger the inner connection to Universal Love the more heightened the love and prosperity will be.

You start to experience this by relaxing the breath, quieting the mind, and opening the heart to Universal Love. Let go of all human ego desires and the instant gratification the human expression wants to experience. This helps to relax the human ego from going into a control mode. It is from this place within that you can experience your Inner Spirit of pure love. It is from within that you are able to recognize the oneness to Universal Love and share that with others. As you experience this connection within to Universal Love, your vibration to love increases and the infinite blessings of Universal Prosperity become available to you.

January 1, 2017, 2 Huge Red UFO Ships From southeast. They were going up and down. I was able to take these pictures of one of them and a video of them.

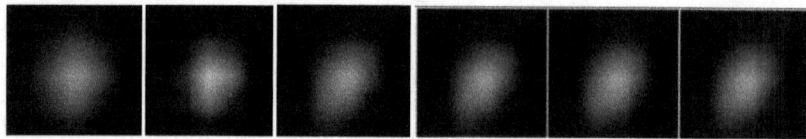

As the month unfolded, I felt me moving energetically above outer world conditions. I kept feeling and experiencing me bringing love to all situations. Doing this prevented me from experiencing any dense or negative energies. I continued feeling inner joy, love, and peace and expressed that no matter where I was, who I was with, and where I was going. Living life with self-value and self-confidence started to create many new positive possibilities. I had greater self-love and self-belief and I felt empowered with my connection to Universal Love. I was rapidly moving through mastering how I chose to feel in the outer world conditions vs. letting the conditions tell me how I am to feel. Rising above with my energy on conditions that seemed unfavorable and choosing happiness was greater than the condition running my life.

My inner awareness of love, joy, peace, and prosperity was stronger than my attention on the outer world distractions. By being aware of what I was feeling inside, I was able to choose deeper inner love and enjoy life more. Keeping my connection to Universal Love and my attention more on love and prosperity amplified living life with greater joy, peace, love, and prosperity. The connection to Universal Love is the key to heightened levels of love and prosperity. Doing it alone through the human mind doesn't work because it uses self-belief systems which can a distraction to the heighten frequency levels. I became more receptive to heighten levels of love, joy, peace, and prosperity in place of feeling I had to make it happen. I became aware how I was open to allowing the Universe to bring to me magical fun experiences in ways I could not do alone.

Imagine a life filled with unconditional love, inner joy, inner peace, prosperity, and vitality. Choose an area in your life you would like to improve. The current conditions will either propel you move forward on the bridge of life or keep you stuck in the familiar patterns of your life. With the familiar comes excuses on why you cannot move forward into the heighten levels, such as not enough money, education, time, and confidence. These excuses come from a fear and insecurity based syndrome. The more you feed the excuses the more you stay stuck in the familiar patterns. The way across the bridge is to let go of the duality and connect more to Universal Love, a oneness connection. The more you unravel the self-defeating beliefs full of limitations, negativity, insecurity, and fear, the greater the frequency of love and prosperity you experience. Some of these beliefs you are consciously aware of and others you are unconsciously aware of. While in the familiar patterns, questions can arise, wanting to fix, correct, blame, change, play teacher, or judge the condition.

Some may ask questions about *how to get rid of the condition*. That only keeps you stuck in what you don't want because your attention and focus are on the condition and judging it. The way to move into heightened levels across the bridge in life is through focusing more on the *prosperity levels of possibilities* that the new life can bring. Self-confidence, self-value, and self-belief transition you from fear based living to that of love based living. Transforming the energy frequencies of the denser vibrations is how I was able to become connected to these higher vibrations of love and prosperity. Having a positive support system helps. For me, the Ascended Masters, Angelic Realm, Ascended Loving Beings, my Guardian Angel, and Universal Love is my major support system. As an Angelic walk-In, this was necessary for me to stay connected to my purpose of channeling and assisting with awakening human consciousness. They helped me through awareness, energy downloads, and messages directly from them or through other means such as people, billboards, songs, and dreams. They helped me develop greater self-love, self-value, self-confidence, and prosperity consciousness. This brought about greater levels of opportunities and healthier relationships.

January 5, 2017, I received a message from the Universal Pure Love Beings. They said, "when we love and embrace any dense energies, while simultaneously keeping our attention on Universal Love, the dense energies diminish. These dense energies can come in the form of negative behaviors, limitations, insecurities, or fears. Attempting to change the condition, keeps us stuck in the condition. As we focus on the expansiveness of positivity vs. what we don't want and the limitations, our energy rises in frequency. This moves us into an opportunity-based mentality in place of allowing the problems, circumstances, and situations control us and complaining about them. The contrast we experience is also part of Universal Love at a different vibration. Perceiving the contrast from a loving perspective vs. a fear or insecurity based mentality gives us the opportunity to experience these contrasts as opportunities for greater growth in a more joyful way. As we embrace and focus more on what the contrast is teaching us instead of judging or resisting the contrast, we develop wisdom with greater ease. When we are "asleep" in self-defeating beliefs, we behave from that consciousness. Sometimes to a point of closing our hearts to love, prosperity, joy, peace, health, vitality, and positivity. As we wake up to love, our vibrations become higher where we are more receptive to the vastness of what Universal Love provides." What I call the truth.

When we realize we are not the emotions, thoughts, and body, we release any ownership and identification to the belief programs of the human expression. The benefit of this is we don't react, judge or attach to any thoughts, emotions, or sensations. We get to fully enjoy it without getting hooked or depleted by any beliefs that get transformed to higher frequencies. From this place, we live in the world without allowing our self to get affected by outer conditions and people's behaviors. We see it from a different perspective. We have compassion with our self and with others knowing they are doing the best they can with their level of consciousness. You are doing the best you can with your learning curve.

The conditions are what they are. By not identifying with the thoughts, emotions, and body as who you are rather what you are experiencing, you are able to detach quicker from what the lesson is teaching you. You know you are "having" an experience instead of "being" the experience. "Being" the experience is the ownership of those thoughts, feelings, and sensations. "Having," is the awareness of the experience. With every experience and person you meet, you have the choice to "BE" love or be in fear. Choose Love. To accept and embrace or give opinions and judge. Choose to Accept and Embrace. To express positivity or negativity. Choose Positivity. To enjoy and be happy or be miserable. Choose Happiness. To focus on prosperity consciousness or limitations. Choose Prosperity Consciousness. To have trust and faith, believing Universal Love has your back or to worry. Choose to Believe in Universal Love. Feeling empowered with self-value, self-confidence, and self-belief or feeding insecurity. Choose to Feel Empowered. Whatever you focus and give your attention to you become and experience in your life. Choose Love, Peace, Prosperity, Positivity, and Joy.

January 10, 2017, I saw huge amounts of red robins heading north. I felt and saw the energy of Christ and the Universal Pure Loving Beings vividly as if they were in human form.

January 13, 2017, at 12:36 AM I heard a high pitch sound. I had this deep awareness that I'm now living in expansive time. I no longer felt a connection to linear time. As I drove in the snow to go swimming, I felt and saw the Syrians and Angels like they were in human form. They were cheering me on as I focused my energy on being self-confident with my discomfort of driving in the snow. While swimming I envisioned the multi-dimensional time. I vividly felt and saw the Syrians and Angels. I started moving into that timeline. It felt so expansive with such pure love. It felt like I was in the Angelic Realm. I got jolted out of this experience when a guy tapped me on the shoulder and asked if he could share the lane with me. It was a one person lane, and he knew that. I focused on enjoying my time swimming. As I continued to swim, I envisioned the timeline again. I was not able to experience the timeline. I trusted there was a reason this happened. I continued swimming with acceptance.

January 17, 2017, I woke up with this huge awareness about Earth. Earth is a hologram filled with collective duality thoughts and emotions. For some reason, I was still experiencing lots of dense energy with people and conditions and doing what I could to adapt to them. What I experienced the summer of 2014 when I first moved to Bend was so magical with such high frequencies of love, joy, peace, prosperity, and so much positivity. I remember meeting this wonderful woman in downtown Bend when I went to the bank recently after I moved to Bend. She said to me that it takes time acclimatizing to bend and to stay patient. She hugged me and left. I will always cherish my connection with her.

Bend's energy frequency and the people I meet all changed. I became baffled by this and questioned what made it change. I kept calling the higher frequency energy back. I had passersby, experiencing these higher frequencies with others in human form these last 2.5 years when I was able to embody feelings of high vibrations of love. The family that felt like aliens with such high frequencies of loving energy. Plus the UPS guy that I saw, a guy staring at me in the parking lot at a country club, this little girl, and a guy with his son I met in downtown Bend, all had this amazing loving frequency. Except for the guy that drove the Porsche car, I was unable to talk to these people for some reason. I didn't understand until now. The experience I had with this guy tapping me on the shoulder during swimming while embodying the higher frequency energies in this multidimensional timeline, made me realize there was something more going on. Today I knew there was energy inside me that was conflicting with the 3rd leg of my new life.

I decided to play with this multidimensional timeline while meditating. I rose my energy and was easily able to take the body with me above the current timeline I was in. I noticed all these beliefs in the form of energies that had duality energies. I was awestruck with a deep realization. I became aware that the body was still attempting to adapt to these new frequencies with old energies that were dormant. These old energies from the other expression would get triggered in the memory like ghost energies creating conflicts when fed. The body was holding the higher loving frequencies from all the energy downloads from the Universal Pure Love Beings. For me to continue to ascend with the body to the next level, the old life memory cells from the other expression had to be completely be purified. That was the reason I was unable to shift the passersby to more of permanent relationships. I decided to move into a new timeline leaving all these old energies the other expression's life incurred. I created new energies filled with lots of pure love, joy, peace, prosperity, positivity, health, and vitality.

I immediately felt lighter energetically. In the meditative state, I saw the Universal Pure Loving Beings in a human form. As I approached them, I felt their loving presence. I realized my energy was moving to a new vibratory place vs. physically moving to experience the 3rd leg of my life. I incorporated these new energies into the mental and emotional realm from the invisible to the visible where it becomes form. I embodied the higher frequency thought forms and feelings in the physical realm more fully, eventually becoming new beliefs. When I came out of the meditative state, my energy felt different. I felt like I already moved and am I was living a new life. Even though the house was still the same house, I felt different in it. It was like the house was foreign to me and I was reborn into a new life. I looked inside and felt a pure loving energy. I didn't feel the conflicting energy as I scanned the body. I felt like I incarnated into a new human form with brand new energies that would create new beliefs as I moved along in life. I kept focusing on these new energies to solidify higher frequencies of positivity, joy, love, peace, prosperity, and vitality on the physical realm.

In each moment of our life, in each experience and with each person we meet, we get to choose to give our power to fear or express love. To amplify an abundant consciousness or feed a limited consciousness. My connection to Universal Love brought these heightened levels of love, prosperity, joy, peace and vitality. When I was having feelings of separation due to the old beliefs conflicting, I felt more fear and insecurity. Now I felt myself living in the "house" of Universal Love more fully as a whole Angelic expression. It felt like I incarnated again and this time in a new body full of lightness. This is what I wanted to experience when I first incarnated. As much as I wanted this from incarnation the first time, there was completion that took precedence. I had to complete where the other expression left off getting the energy high enough for me be fully in the body. As I came more fully into the body, I had experienced these conflicting energies. I thought that meant I had to keep transforming and elevating the frequency until I reached the current plateau. The human expression ascended as far as it could go and reached a plateau where the old beliefs memory cells from the other expression required purification.

I took an Epsom salt bath and closed my eyes and felt all this light energy throughout the body. If I focused on it, I became light-headed. So I felt it. It was full of pure love. I then saw the Universal Pure Loving Being moving throughout the body and solidifying the energy to make it more conformed inside the body signature. I then energetically saw the woman I met in the summer of 2014. She smiled at me and I heard her tell me that now my life is about to begin way beyond what I had experienced. She said I would be guided. I became excited to see how this would play out in the days that followed. As the day progressed, I noticed that people I interacted with, no longer triggered any reactions. It was like I was in this energy of love. With two of the people, I saw dense energy come into my energy field and immediately dissipated. I just watched with love. There were no fears or insecurity buttons getting pushed. The mind didn't register anything around their behaviors. All I experienced was a knowing of Universal Love and my Angelic connection to this pure love.

I felt inner peace and inner joy. My heart was open and receptive to love and the nurturing I was experiencing. I felt and could see the woman I met at the bank in the summer of 2014. I could see her through what seemed like an energy veil. I sensed she was going to play an important role in my new life. I became excited about potentially meeting her again. In the latter part of January, I started experiencing heightened energies around positivity, self-confidence, and self-love. This brought an even stronger connection inside Universal Love and the prosperity that comes along with that. All my focus and attention was on this and I became even more receptive to the energies around love. I started to close doors to organizations, people, and situations that didn't resonate with this frequency. I celebrated in this positive energy without sharing my experience with others. I did this to solidify what I was experiencing. I knew I was strengthening this positive energy more inside and I was optimistic

January 20, 2017, I saw spiritual movie clips about how the ancient energies were running my life. These ancient energies related to me playing social worker, teacher, and healer when I incarnated and for 18 years following my incarnation. I envisioned a contract and tore it up. As the day went on, I felt lots of energies being released. My body felt tired, and I slept for hours. When I woke up, I felt rested and peaceful.

January 21, 2017, at around 4 AM I saw stars in the shape of a flag. I was feeling all these ancient energies coming up. I still felt tired and slept for hours. Everything came to a head with regard to the negative influences. I saw vision of all the work, people, groups I belonged to, situations all behaving from the ancient energies dissolving. The mind initially started to question what was going on and then within a minute or two, the mind went into a silence. I slept on and off for hours. Emotionally I was feeling energies of Universal Love and prosperity.

January 22, 2017, In meditation I noticed how my Angelic energy resided more fully in the human form. I noticed that the human ego control was not active at all. I felt the human expression being more receptive and open to experiencing these heightened levels of love, joy, peace, and prosperity in a deeper way. I felt greater self-confidence and empowered. This replaced the insecurities and fear allowing for healthier choices and experiences to come into my life. I felted guided to purify more energy in the 3rd chakra which is the source of self-esteem and willpower. I would focus on white and pink light running through the 3rd chakra. White symbolizes purification and pink is love. I put a serpentine crystal there which helps with kundalini energy, love, and prosperity. I love the energy I feel with crystals. This crystal is very powerful. I use it to energize other crystal that I may use often. I like to meditate with the crystal as well.

January 25, 2017, I woke up feeling lots of energy and a burning sensation in the 3rd chakra. While swimming I felt Universal Love's energy flowing with ease throughout the body, mind, and emotions. I saw and felt pure loving energy within the human form that I have not felt at this heightened level. The thoughts weren't active. The 3rd chakra was pure white light, and I felt lots of empowerment and love.

January 26, 2017, Throughout the day, I noticed how easy it was to raise the frequency of any thoughts. The thoughts immediately became quiet. I felt the heart chakra opening up more.

January 27, 2017, I saw the "w" shape in the stars and had this experience of the thoughts moving into energy which is formless. At that moment, there was no thinking, and I felt nurturing love. Throughout the week, I noticed as I moved thoughts to energy, I felt this surge of loving energy inside the heart and the body. The thoughts immediately became meaningless and love took over.

February 5, 2017, I saw a "w" in the shape of stars. I experienced true emotional freedom in a deeper way. while meditating, I felt enormous levels of loving energy as the body energetically ascended in frequency. I saw the Angels and my Guardian Angel. I became aware as the body ascends, any dense energy gets transmuted, including memories and discomforting emotions. If I gave the thoughts or emotions any attention, I immediately became caught up in them. I became confused and insecure. I remembered how I was experiencing this confusion and insecurity yesterday as I was giving my attention to memories and emotions. I left the house and took a walk, focusing on love and appreciating the birds and trees along the way. I sat down and relaxed enjoying the sunshine. At that moment, I knew by taking a walk, I was able to shift the thoughts into silence and feel the pleasures of nature and the birds. I was able to move my energy and focus on love easier which raised my energy back up. This reminded me of Superman and kryptonite when he is too close it affects his power.

For many years I allowed myself to become overwhelmed with lots of heavy energy, where it affected my vibration. It felt like I left the "house" of Universal Love by becoming the emotional discomforts where mental judgments can occur. Through attentive awareness, I was able to see how my energy got depleted. The awareness showed me how I had fear centered around the negative frequencies making me feel inadequate. As I "numbed" the mind from any form of thinking, I was able to shift from identifying with the thoughts and becoming attached. It became easier to give my attention to love and raise my energy to higher vibrations of love which transmuted any fear. Now, Instead of attempting to change the environment, I shifted my energy into a higher frequency of love. As I channel Universal Love with greater strength, others in that environment are positively affected. My focus was on Universal Love not the environment.

While I was shopping at the grocery store, I was aware of how some clerks were literally living in their mind. They made sad faces and I could feel the denseness of their energy. I also was aware of how others made contact with me, were very present, and in their heart. They had a happy smile and their energy felt light and peaceful. Living more from the heart and less from the mental chatter is the first step to emotional and mental freedom. Each day, we get to *choose* our thoughts and feelings in place of allowing the human mind and emotions to run our life. On a daily basis, I focused on relaxing the mind through this "numb" approach where the thoughts became silent. I did this by focusing on gaps of silence. I took deep breaths to relax the body and felt vibrations of love. I envisioned becoming an energy of love inside the heart and then turned it into the form of the heart. This amplified the energy frequencies. From that place, I felt my connection inside Universal Love. I felt these high frequencies of love and prosperity. As I felt a confident connection, I was able to become a channel of Universal Love to remind others of their own divinity. Some smiled at me remembering their truth while others were busy on the cell phone and tablets and allowing their chattered thoughts get in the way.

February 6, 2017, at around 4:30 AM, I saw the "w" in the star formation. I felt the words of Mother Mary, "pro-peace and pro-love." During a meditation class I gave, I felt the Syrians loving energy really strong. One woman mentioned that she felt a higher frequency of love and was enjoying it. Yesterday and today, I noticed how I was not overwhelmed by others' negative energies when I was around them. I was happily amazed on how the compassion and choice for inner peace replaced any judgment or fear. I was hearing people make comments on how we are getting along. The same people I had issues in the past with. I exuded this energy of peace and love which relaxed others. It is easy to get others who have controlling negative behaviors upset if we give our power to them and react. By staying calm, choosing peace, amplifying self-love, and compassion, I became more of a channel of Universal Love. Responding in love and compassion instead of reacting in judgment and fear.

February 10, 2017, I woke up a little after 4 AM and saw a "v" shape with the stars. When I went food shopping this morning, One of the female employees who has a negative and an angry vibe came by the register bagging area. In the past, I would avoid her having huge discomforts. This was because the other expression's energy was getting released so my energy could come in more fully. I had more contrasting energy going on inside the human expression. As she approached me while I was talking to the cashier, I felt her channeling some angry energy. This time with my Angelic energy more fully in the human form, I looked at her with love and said I do not need any help from you. She immediately ran to the other side, and I saw how she was in fear. I became aware that my Angelic presence was so strong that the light of love made her unable to stay near me. This made me feel peaceful and grateful. I left and saw about 20 crows on the snow. I have never seen that many crows where I leave. Crows represent change. I understood this to mean a huge change. At 8:35 PM I saw a UFO ship at a distant. I felt lots of energy moving inside me. The next day I felt the body ascending in energy.

February 12, 2017, I woke up feeling a huge surge of loving energy. I knew something huge was coming forth by the way I was feeling. Some form of transformation that would be a major step in my new life. I started to feel the body ascending energetically. The new few days I was feeling lots of shifts in the heart. I had dreams and visions around the old life and the other expression around her emotional needs being ignored and how she played a "servant" role with her ancestral and foster family. She would cancel plans with friends to drive the foster mom around town, babysit and other things instead of playing.

February 14, 2017, I saw a "v" shape with the stars. I felt the energy of Arc Angel Michael, Christ and Mother Mary. I started feeling energy around going deeper in trust with the bond I have with Universal Love and being open and allowing what the Universe feels is best for my life. I established a loving bond in my connection with the Universal Pure Love Beings and Universal Love where I was consistently getting fed with loving energy. Emotionally, I felt more confident, nurtured, and stronger inside. I am so grateful to feel wholeness with self-love.

In the second half of February, I noticed that when I felt other people's energy, if it was not coming from a higher frequency of love or if it felt dense, it would immediately get transmuted before it entered deeply into my energy field. My connection to Universal Love and self-empowerment was at a high enough vibration that it transmuted the denser energies. As a result, I became more effective in channeling the higher love frequencies in my daily life. In the 3rd leg of my life, I became more aware of allowing the Universe to deliver experiences that aligned with prosperity and love. Human ego control attempting to take charge out of a desire for instant gratification was no longer effective. I was learning to live moment to moment with the unknown and felt delighted to live more fully in. The old life, symbolized as the 2nd leg, was falling away, which the other expression represented. I was intently focused on not giving my power to it and instead chose to focus on that which I would enjoy.

When energies that are in the form of self-defeating beliefs get released, the ego will attempt to pull you in through control protective mechanisms. The human ego is use to and familiar with the habitual pattern. It becomes attached to the belief systems it is familiar with and protects it when it feels something new or different. It does that through a fight, flight, protect mode. Giving your attention to that will keep you stuck, feeling the limitations around what you are letting go of creating fear, negativity, and insecurity. Giving attention on what you are releasing gives it power, where you begin to feel that is your continued truth instead of it being a lie that doesn't serve your overall well-being. What is important is to let go of any attachment with your focus and attention on what you are releasing and focus more on enjoying life. Focus more on what you would enjoy and on the energy of love, joy, peace, prosperity, health, and vitality. Celebrate in that. Relax in the timing of the process that is unfolding and stay patient compassionately with being impatient on having it now.

Allowing and being receptive to the Universe means to not be in charge by telling the Universe what to do or controlling the desired outcome. To impose our human will and force the instant gratification we would like to have, only creates more of a limitation around the desired outcome. We become out of sync with the flow of the energy behind the desire creating blockages. Any energy that contrasts trust, allowing, joy, peace, love, prosperity, vitality and health only creates a limitation. This creates more discomfort and struggles. I was driving from Bed,

Bath, and Beyond when I approached a red light. I started to imagine the red light changing to green. I heard a voice say, "let go and let Universal Love change the light." I was awestruck that even that was taking charge. How relaxing it felt to sit back and allow the Universe to change the light. It took longer than I would like and laughed at how the human expression wants instant gratification. The Universe knew that I had to relax into trusting the timing and when I did, the light changed. It is best to relax and be in the flow with trust. To continually tap into Universal Love's omnipotence to enhance self-love, self-worth, and prosperity consciousness. To share this love and prosperity from a "we" mentality, which includes the highest good for all. To know that the Universe delivers what is best, and it is far better than the human expression can ever imagine.

February 23, 2017, at 12:09 PM I saw 2 UFOs. One with red flickering lights heading east and the other going the opposite direction. I heard to continue to relax into the unknown and allow Universal Love to deliver what is best for me. I heard to continue to keep the love frequency high.

February 26, 2017, at 8:40 PM I saw stars in the shape of a smile and the UFO with the red flickering lights. I started to feel loving energy in my heart feeling greater self-love and self-worth.

As I look back on this journey I have been on in the last 19 years, my heartfelt message is to remember to always come from Love. Forgive those you have been hurt by. They are where they are in their consciousness. Connect to Universal Love for heightened levels of love, joy, peace, health, vitality, and prosperity. Feel the connection in your heart with joy and be open to receive this heightened potent level of love. This will nurture you emotionally enhancing self-empowerment. Feel it in the mind which will shift the thoughts to optimism over negativity. You are then able to connect with others and handle outer world conditions, with greater compassion, confidence, positivity, and love. As you share Universal Love with conviction, joy, and peace, you become an amazing role model to help others remember the truth of love over fear, joy over sadness, and peace over hate. Giving your power to Universal Love over the outer world conditions, keeps you connected to the truth vs. the false illusions played out as fear, limitations, negativity, judgments, and insecurity. Life is more enjoyable as you let go of the self-defeating beliefs that would otherwise keep you "chained" if you give your power to them.

The human expression has imperfections and the Inner Spirit is perfect. Lessons you are learning are temporary to awaken more of the human expression to the Inner Spirit's perfection of love, joy, peace, health, vitality, and prosperity. The human expression is a temporary vehicle to live on Earth and the Inner Spirit continues on. Lessons are part of being on Earth to become smarter and struggle is optional. Let go of the attachments you may have to the stories and discomforts and enjoy and love everything. Be in your heart vs. over thinking and living in the past. This allows you to make choices more aligned with NOW vs. yesterday's outdated ways of living.

When you are confident, and experience heightened levels of love you make smarter choices that resonate with the life you would love to live. We are living in a vibrational planet. The Universe delivers a match with what we are putting out into the world. Fear and insecurity will only attract more of what we do not like or want. It keeps you stuck in old paradigms and prevents you from expanding into greatness. If we put our attention on what we are grateful for and appreciate as well as what we would enjoy, we have a greater opportunity of attracting that into our life. Choosing love and being happy requires awareness with the thoughts and emotions. To be aware the words we speak, our actions, thoughts, and feelings making sure they come from a higher frequency vibration. Choose positive thoughts and focus on what makes us feel happy. This will solidify the vibration where it become more natural to stay in that vibration. Always live life with the vibrations of love intact. May your Inner Spirit shine forth with the power of love in the human form.

Chapter 10

Living the Angelic purpose

Reprogramming the human mind and emotions from what it was born into was both challenging and rewarding. Through enhanced self-love and empowerment, I have emotional and spiritual freedom. Activating the human expression to a point of me feeling more comfortable being in the physical form was a difficult journey. I feel spiritually free for the first time in the 19 years of living on Earth because I am complete with the other expression's belief system. I experienced a feeling of being reborn into this amazing energy of pure love. . The body adapting to these higher frequencies required time and patience. I feel happier in the human expression instead of dealing with the conflicting energies I had to transform. I feel so full of joy, peace, vitality, and love inside the human expression. It is so freeing I get to enjoy life more fully as my Angelic expression and no longer have to focus on evolving the belief system of the other expression. We incur pain and struggles from our attention on them and continuously feeding them. To let go of the pain and struggles, we have to be committed to let go of the focus and attention on them. That includes the words we speak, our actions and the way we feel. If we focus on being happy, feeling appreciation, staying in gratitude, and doing activities that enhance joy, love, and peace, we will live a happier life.

The downloads from the Universal Pure Love Beings raised the frequency vibration where I was able to transition from duality thinking to a oneness connection with Universal Love. Now I am living in the "house" of Universal Love where I feel this amazing omnipotent love pouring inside the human form continuously. I am receptive to its unlimited vastness of pure unconditional love and the unlimited prosperity. I am so grateful that the Universal Pure Love Beings are in my life. I continue to channel the frequency of Universal Love to remind others of the truth of Universal Love. While swimming on March 15, 2017, I experienced this high frequency of love really deep in the heart way beyond anything I ever felt The love was so pure. I felt so receptive to receiving this heightened frequency of love. As I looked inside my heart, I noticed there was no fear from getting hurt or insecurity. I felt empowered. I became aware that this deep love inside my heart replaced the protection and insecurity I had once felt there and no longer do, I realized I can share this love with empowerment in denser environments This deep connection I now feel with love and self empowerment will prevent me from going back into fear, protection and insecurity.

My purpose as an Angelic walk-in continues to unfold. Each day is an amazing new day with new instructions. Being a channel of Universal Love's frequency reaches beyond the city and state I am living. It touches those all over the world because of the connection to the collective consciousness. It is a huge spiritual responsibility and an honor to be a conduit of Universal Love. I am excited when I hear people talk about love at this higher frequency and when I read about it. I wake up each day hoping that everyone on Earth will wake up to this frequency of love so we can all live in peace and get along. So we can all enjoy and accept each other. The first step is to let go of the fears and insecurities. The second step is to be open and receptive to allowing Universal Love inside your heart. The rest will come together as planned by the Universe.

As I continue to ascend the human expression, I find myself more connected to the ethereal realm on Earth. I use to have to close my eyes to experience the Universal Pure Love Beings. Now I see them with my eyes wide open. I am able to see, feel, and hear the Universal Pure Love Beings as if they are in human form. I can have these conversations and see them smile, hear them talk to me, and feel their love hugging me. I feel their love, their joyful spirit, and their playfulness. It is so comforting for me to have the higher frequencies in the human form. Rather than having to go out of the body to the ethereal realm to experience this, I have it inside the human expression. I am so blessed and grateful to have the Universal Pure Love Beings' support. Their dedication and commitment to being there for me throughout this journey was beyond anything I have experienced with human relationships.

While human relationships came and went throughout these 19 years, they stayed in my life. They are my friends when I need comfort. My cheerleader when I need a boost or to cheer me on. My confident when I need to talk to them and get their loving support. A family I didn't have incarnating on Earth. I get to have the best of both worlds. Their presence is always with me and will never die like a physical body.

When I talk about them with others that are sensitive to energies, they feel their presence. I see how it opens their heart even more. They have greater levels of joy and peace during our interaction even though they don't see or hear them like I do. My wish is for the veil to be lifted so we all can experience them. These two women I met at an event felt the Universal Pure Love Beings as I was talking about them. I told them how I wish the veil would drop so we all can experience them. I believe we would have so much love, joy and peace on the planet. She shared how some are not ready. Some fear the higher vibrations of love because their human expression is comfortable with denser vibrations. I understood what she meant because for some it would be so foreign. Their human ego would become protective. I know in my heart that many would eventually be ready for this heightened level of love.

My purpose is being a conduit of this loving energy to get people ready for the great awakening. Even though some are not ready and would react or become fearful, they still benefit. They still receive the energy. Eventually, their human expression will acclimate to the frequency and become receptive to it. I am optimistic that we are already adapting to these higher vibrations which is why so much of the contrast is coming up to get transformed. Earth is also experiencing this through climate change. People are reacting through activism and committing to their spiritual evolution. Some are leaving Earth because their human expression isn't able to hold on to the frequency and they are not ready for it. While others are committing to this amazing journey. Once you feel this pure loving energy, you won't want to go back into the fear and insecurity. You become hooked into this amazing vibration. You then start your ascending journey into greater levels of love, prosperity, peace, joy, health, and vitality. When the human expression accepts the truth around pure love, joy, and peace, it adapts with greater ease and receptivity.

When enough people wake up to these omnipotent levels of love, we will experience peace beyond what the Earth has ever experienced. It is imperative to focus our thoughts and emotions on what Universal Love represents and refuse to give our power away to the illusions, such as insecurity, fears, limitations, and negativity. To do this with love, not judgment. Judgment keeps us in the loop of the denser energies where we fall "asleep" in them experiencing feelings of stuckness. That only prolongs duality living, a problem-focused life filled with struggles.

Love is empowering and frees us from the hold these dense energies have on us. Speaking the truth of Universal Love amplifies the energy and creates a rippling effect for all involved. As we focus our attention and energy on love with confidence and not on fear of the dense energy hurting us, we become free. Empowerment and self-love are the key stepping stone in the process of greater awakening.

May the power of love be with you and joy and peace enfold within you. Please share this truth with excitement where ever you go, whoever you are with, and whatever you are doing.

www.ingramcontent.com/pod-product-compliance
Lightning Source LLC
Chambersburg PA
CBHW070549160426
43199CB00014B/2435